Secrets of the Bible

AUTHOR
Rabbi Yanki Tauber

INSTRUCTOR ADVISORY BOARD
Rabbi Menachem Feldman
Rabbi Dovid Labkowski
Rabbi Yossi Mendelson
Rabbi Benjy Silverman

COORDINATOR
Mrs. Rivki Mockin

ADMINISTRATOR
Mrs. Chana Dechter

Printed in the United States of America

by **THE ROHR JEWISH LEARNING INSTITUTE**
822 Eastern Parkway, Brooklyn, NY 11213

Cover Art: *The Tower of Babel* (detail), Bruegel the Elder, oil on wood, 1563. (Kunsthistorisches Museum Wien, Vienna)

(888) YOUR-JLI/718-221-6900
WWW.MYJLI.COM

Secrets of the Bible

ICONIC STORIES,
MYSTICAL MEANINGS,
AND THEIR LESSONS
FOR LIFE

JLI
Jewish Learning Institute

STUDENT TEXTBOOK

The Rohr Jewish Learning Institute
gratefully acknowledges the pioneering
and ongoing support of

George and Pamela Rohr

Since its inception, the Rohr JLI has been a beneficiary of the vision, generosity, care, and concern of the Rohr family.

In the merit of the tens of thousands of hours of Torah study by JLI students worldwide, may they be blessed with health, *Yiddishe nachas* from all their loved ones, and extraordinary success in all their endeavors.

LOCAL COURSE SPONSORSHIPS

Mr. and Mrs. David Beesemer
AMSTERDAM, NL

In honor of Mitchell and Matthew August
BLOOMFIELD HILLS, MI

Mr. and Mrs. Jim and Renee Hon
BOISE, ID

Dr. Yura Stoly
BROOKLYN, NY

Mr. Louis Berkowitz
FAIRFIELD, CT

Dr. and Mrs. Gary and Marlene Price
FORT MYERS, FL

Eugene and Marjorie Lipsky Jewish Learning Academy
LEAWOOD, KS

In memory of Rivka Sara bat Efraim Fishel Gejerman
LOS ANGELES, CA

In memory of Mr. Isidor Blumenthal
MADISON, NJ

Mr. and Mrs. Y. K. Cohen
MILWAUKEE, WI

Norman and Sally Raicek
MONTREAL, QC

In memory of Shmuel Leib ben Avraham Dovber
NEWTON, MA

In honor of Mrs. Maxine Finkel
NORTHEAST PORTLAND, OR

Kensington Capital Corporation
NYACK, NY

Shark Demolition
NYACK, NY

In memory of Meyer Goldberg
ORINDA, CA

Mr. Robert Sacks
S. FE, NM

In memory of those who came before us
SOUTH LAKE TAHOE, CA

The Hellman Memorial Chapels
SPRING VALLEY, NY

The Jewish Federation of Sarasota-Manatee
VENICE, FL

www.HelixReports.com
VENTNOR, NJ

In memory of Dr. Arthur Conn
VIENNA, VA

In memory of Rabbi Levi Deitsch
VIENNA, VA

Jackson, Chasen and Ilan
WESTMINSTER, CO

Kosins Family Foundation
WEST BLOOMFIELD, MI

DEDICATED IN LOVING MEMORY OF

David Samuel Rock

דוד שמואל ע"ה בן יבלחט"א זלמן גרשון

May the study of this JLI course
by thousands of students worldwide
be a source of merit to his soul.

And in tribute to

Neil and Sarah Rock

May they go from strength to strength
and enjoy good health, happiness,
nachas, and success in all their endeavors
לאורך ימים ושנים טובות.

Foreword

Adam and Eve in the Garden of Eden. Noah's Ark. Jacob and Esau. Joseph and his brothers . . . We've all heard these stories; some of us grew up on them. But what do these stories really mean? How should they be understood?

Many of us heard these stories for the first time as children. So, obviously, we understood them with a child's mind. And that is, more or less, how they remained with us. But the Torah is certainly much more than a collection of children's stories—or even stories for adults.

How, then, are we to understand the stories of the Torah?

In this course, we will be guided by two great principles established by the sages. The first principle is that the Torah has both a *body* and a *soul*. The "body" of the Torah are the stories it tells and the laws it legislates. The "soul" of the Torah is the mystical meanings contained within these stories and laws. In the same way that our own body and soul are interdependent—the soul gives life to the body and the body serves as a tool of the soul—so, too, the "body" and "soul" of the Torah are dependent on each other, as one actualizes and illuminates the other.

A second principle taught by the sages is that the Torah is eternal, meaning that everything in it—down to every last detail of its stories—is relevant to each and every one of us, in every place and in every generation.

At first glance, it may seem that these two goals—the quest to uncover the mystical "soul" of the Torah and the search for contemporary relevance—are very different, if not contradictory, endeavors. In seeking out the mystical meaning of a Torah story, we seem to be moving further away from the story's relevance to our lives, rather than closer to it.

In truth, however, the very opposite is the case. When the stories recounted in the Torah are viewed only as historical events, they are of limited relevance to us. They may yield some useful insights and lessons, but at the end of the day, these are things that happened to other people who lived thousands of years ago. But when we understand these stories in terms of their mystical "soul," then—as we will see in the case of the stories we will explore in this course—they reveal to us universal truths and processes that underlie every aspect of our existence.

In the final analysis, it is the esoteric version of the story that is most readily applicable to our lives.

THE ROHR JEWISH LEARNING INSTITUTE (JLI)

Endorsements

"*Secrets of the Bible* presents wonderful ancient biblical stories in fresh and modern ways that deal with universal human dilemmas. The wisdom it shares should not remain a secret."

DR. ERICA BROWN

Director of the Mayberg Center for Jewish Education and Leadership, George Washington University; and Author, *The Book of Esther: Power, Fate and Fragility in Exile*

"*Secrets of the Bible* is unafraid to ask challenging questions and offers fascinating insights based on Jewish mystical and Hasidic teachings."

RABBI DR. ZVI GRUMET

Senior Staff, The Lookstein Center for Jewish Education, Editor, Jewish Educational Leadership; and Author, *Genesis: From Creation to Covenant*

"The Torah, the primary source of all Jewish literature, speaks to every generation anew. So, too, it is understood differently by each person at different stages in our lives. Here is a wonderful opportunity for adults to revisit childhood biblical stories in a new light and with mature understanding. Do not miss the opportunity to experience this new Rohr JLI course bringing together biblical stories with a completely new twenty-first-century approach."

CAROLYN STARMAN HESSEL

Director Emerita, Sami Rohr Prize for Jewish Literature; and Director Emerita, Jewish Book Council

"*Secrets of the Bible* brings to an intelligent lay readership . . . texts so formative to so many cultures worldwide that they cannot be ignored even by cultures looking on from without. By addressing these tales as 'stories for adults,' the JLI recognizes how the Hebrew Bible speaks in mischievous and consequential ways that enable us to understand its plea for literacy—the underpinnings of that commonwealth-in-time we call humanity. By embracing post-biblical Jewish tradition, the course recognizes an interpretative process that begins with the Bible itself (interpreting its own past) and goes on to awaken the interpretive impulse in later readers exploring the experience of their own era."

DR. JOEL ROSENBERG

Lee S. McCollester Professor of Biblical Literature, Director of Program in Judaic Studies, and Faculty, Department of International Literary and Cultural Studies, Tufts University

"The sterling reputation of the Rohr Jewish Learning Institute is even further enhanced by their latest course, *Secrets of the Bible*. The six episodes explored in each unit allow the student to immerse in some of the most formative moments recounted in the Bible, feel the transcendent effect of its words and develop a personal sense of Nahmanides's conviction that 'The Deeds of the Fathers are a signpost for their descendants.'"

PROFESSOR JEFFREY WOOLF

Talmud Department, Bar-Ilan University

Contents

Lesson 1

THE TREE OF KNOWLEDGE

Adam en Eva (detail), Johann Sadeler (printmaker), after Crispijn van den Broeck, engraving, Antwerp, 1575. (Rijksmuseum, Amsterdam)

Unraveling the mystery of the "Tree of the Knowledge of Good and Bad" from which Adam and Eve ate illuminates many of the questions we grapple with in our own lives. Why do we desire things that we know are bad for ourselves and for others? Why does everything we achieve require hardship and struggle? How much should we care: Is it better to be objective and true or subjective and engaged?

[2]

TEXT 1a

GENESIS 2:8–3:7

THE GARDEN OF EDEN AND THE TREE OF KNOWLEDGE (2:8–9)

G-d* Almighty planted a garden in Eden, in the east;
and He placed there the man that He had created.
And G-d Almighty made grow from the soil
every tree that is desirable to the sight and good for eating;
and the tree of life in the middle of the garden
and the tree of the knowledge of good and bad. . . .

MANKIND'S MISSION (2:15)

G-d Almighty took the man
and He put him in the Garden of Eden
to work it and to keep it.

THE COMMANDMENT (2:16–17)

And G-d Almighty commanded the man, to say:
"Of all the trees of the garden, eat you shall eat.
And of the tree of the knowledge of good and bad
do not eat of it;
because on the day you eat of it, die you shall die. . . ."

---

* Throughout this book, "G-d" and "L-rd" are written with a hyphen instead of an "o" (both in our own translations and when quoting others). This is one way we accord reverence to the sacred divine name. This also reminds us that, even as we seek G-d, He transcends any human effort to describe His reality.

NO SHAME (2:25)

They were both naked, the man and his wife;
and they were not ashamed.

THE SERPENT'S DECEPTION (3:1–5)

The serpent was the most shrewd of all animals. . . .
And the serpent said to the woman:
"No, die you will not die.
For G-d knows that on the day you eat from it
your eyes will be opened;
and you will be as G-d, knowers of good and bad."

THE TRANSGRESSION (3:6)

The woman saw that the tree is good for eating
and that it is lusty to the eyes
and the tree is desirable to make wise
and she took of its fruit and she ate;
and she gave also to her husband with her, and he ate.

THE FIRST CLOTHING (3:7)

And the eyes of the both of them were opened
and they knew that they were naked;
and they sewed the leaves of a fig tree
and they made themselves girdles.

Does Judaism Believe in Original Sin? A panel discussion ***Rabbis Yitzchak Breitowitz, Simon Jacobson,*** *and* ***Ari Sollish:***

MYJLI.COM/BIBLE

TEXT 1b

GENESIS 3:16–24

THE FALLOUT: PAIN OF CHILDBIRTH, THE STRUGGLE TO EARN A LIVING, AND DEATH (3:16–19)

To the woman He said:
"Multiply I will multiply your pain and your pregnancy
in pain you will give birth to children;
and to your husband will be your desire
and he will rule over you."
And to the man He said:
". . . Cursed is the soil on your account
painfully you shall eat of it, all the days of your life. . . .
By the sweat of your brow you shall eat bread
until you return to the soil, as from it you were taken;
for dust you are, and to dust you shall return. . . ."

ADAM AND EVE BANISHED FROM THE GARDEN (3:21–24)

G-d Almighty made coats of skin
for Adam and his wife
and He clothed them.
And G-d Almighty said:
"Here the human has become like one of us
to know good and bad;
and now, perhaps he will send forth his hand
and he will take also from the tree of life
and he will eat and live forever."

Handling Our Mistakes Without Hiding
Rabbi Aryeh Weinstein:

MYJLI.COM/BIBLE

And G-d Almighty sent him out
from the Garden of Eden;
to work the soil wherefrom he was taken. . . .

TEXT 2

NACHMANIDES, *COMMENTARY ON THE TORAH*, GENESIS 3:22

אִם הָיָה הָעֵץ טוֹב לָאָדָם לְמַאֲכָל וְנֶחְמָד אֵלָיו לְהַשְׂכִּיל, לָמָּה מְנָעוֹ מִמֶּנּוּ? וְהָאֱלוֹקִים הוּא הַטּוֹב וְהַמֵּטִיב, לֹא יִמְנַע טוֹב לַהוֹלְכִים בְּתָמִים.

If the tree was so good to eat, and so attractive as a source of wisdom, why did G-d withhold it from man? For G-d is good and beneficent and does not withhold goodness from those who live wholesomely!

RABBI MOSHE BEN NACHMAN (NACHMANIDES, RAMBAN) 1194–1270

Scholar, philosopher, author, and physician. Nachmanides was born in Spain and served as leader of Iberian Jewry. In 1263, he was summoned by King James of Aragon to a public disputation with Pablo Cristiani, a Jewish apostate. Though Nachmanides was the clear victor of the debate, he had to flee Spain because of the resulting persecution. He moved to Israel and helped reestablish communal life in Jerusalem. He authored a classic commentary on the Pentateuch and a commentary on the Talmud.

TEXT 3

MAIMONIDES, *GUIDE FOR THE PERPLEXED* 1:2

הִקְשָׁה לִי אִישׁ חָכָם זֶה לוֹ שָׁנִים קוּשְׁיָה גְדוֹלָה . . . יֵרָאֶה מִפְּשׁוּטוֹ שֶׁל כָּתוּב כִּי הַכַּוָּנָה הָרִאשׁוֹנָה בָּאָדָם שֶׁיִּהְיֶה כִּשְׁאָר בַּעֲלֵי חַיִּים אֵין שֵׂכֶל לוֹ בְּמַחֲשָׁבָה, וְלֹא יַבְדִּיל בֵּין הַטּוֹב וּבֵין הָרַע; וְכַאֲשֶׁר הִמְרָה הֵבִיא לוֹ מֶרְיוֹ זֶה הַשְּׁלֵמוּת הַגָּדוֹל הַמְיוּחָד בָּאָדָם . . . וְזֶה הַפֶּלֶא שֶׁיִּהְיֶה עָנְשׁוֹ עַל מֶרְיוֹ תֵּת לוֹ שְׁלֵמוּת שֶׁלֹּא הָיָה לוֹ . . . וְאֵין זֶה אֶלָּא כִּדְבַר מִי שֶׁאָמַר כִּי אִישׁ מִן הָאֲנָשִׁים מָרָה וְהִפְלִיג בְּעָוֶל וּלְפִיכָךְ שָׁנוּ בְּרִיָּתוֹ לְטוֹב וְהוּשַּׂם כּוֹכָב בַּשָּׁמַיִם!

Some years ago, a learned man asked me a great question. . . . It would appear, from a basic reading of the Torah's words, that the human being was originally intended to be like the rest of the animal creation, without intelligence in his mind, and without the ability to distinguish between good and bad; and that Adam's disobedience is what procured him that great perfection that is the uniqueness of the human being. . . . It thus appears strange that the punishment for his disobedience should be the elevation of man to a pinnacle of perfection that he did not previously have. . . . This is like saying that a certain person was disobedient and extremely wicked, wherefore his nature was changed for the better, and he was placed as a star in the heavens!

RABBI MOSHE BEN MAIMON (MAIMONIDES, RAMBAM) 1135–1204

Halachist, philosopher, author, and physician. Maimonides was born in Córdoba, Spain. After the conquest of Córdoba by the Almohads, he fled Spain and eventually settled in Cairo, Egypt. There, he became the leader of the Jewish community and served as court physician to the vizier of Egypt. He is most noted for authoring the *Mishneh Torah,* an encyclopedic arrangement of Jewish law; and for his philosophical work, *Guide for the Perplexed.* His rulings on Jewish law are integral to the formation of halachic consensus.

Figure 1.1

The Locked Box Parable

Figure 1.2

The Serpent's Words: Deception or Truth?

GENESIS 3:4–5	GENESIS 3:22
The serpent said to the woman: "No, die you will not die. "For G-d knows that on the day you eat from it, your eyes will be opened; and you will be as G-d, knowers of good and bad."	G-d Almighty said: "Here the human has become like one of us, to know good and bad; and now, perhaps he will send forth his hand, and he will take also from the tree of life, and he will eat and live forever."

Torah Has
Body (stories)
and soul (meaning)

Figure 1.3

Seven Questions on the Tree of Knowledge Story

1 How did eating the fruit of a certain tree impart "knowledge of good and bad"?

2 Why was the Tree forbidden? Doesn't G-d want us to enjoy the gifts of life?

3 Isn't knowledge a good thing? Why would it be a sin or the result of sin?

4 Did Adam and Eve have Free Choice before they ate from the Tree?

5 Everything the serpent said was true. So where is the deception?

6 Why did eating from the Tree cause human mortality, the pain of childbirth, and the struggle to earn a living?

7 What is the role of nakedness, clothing, and shame in the Tree of Knowledge story?

Figure 1.4

The Ten Faculties

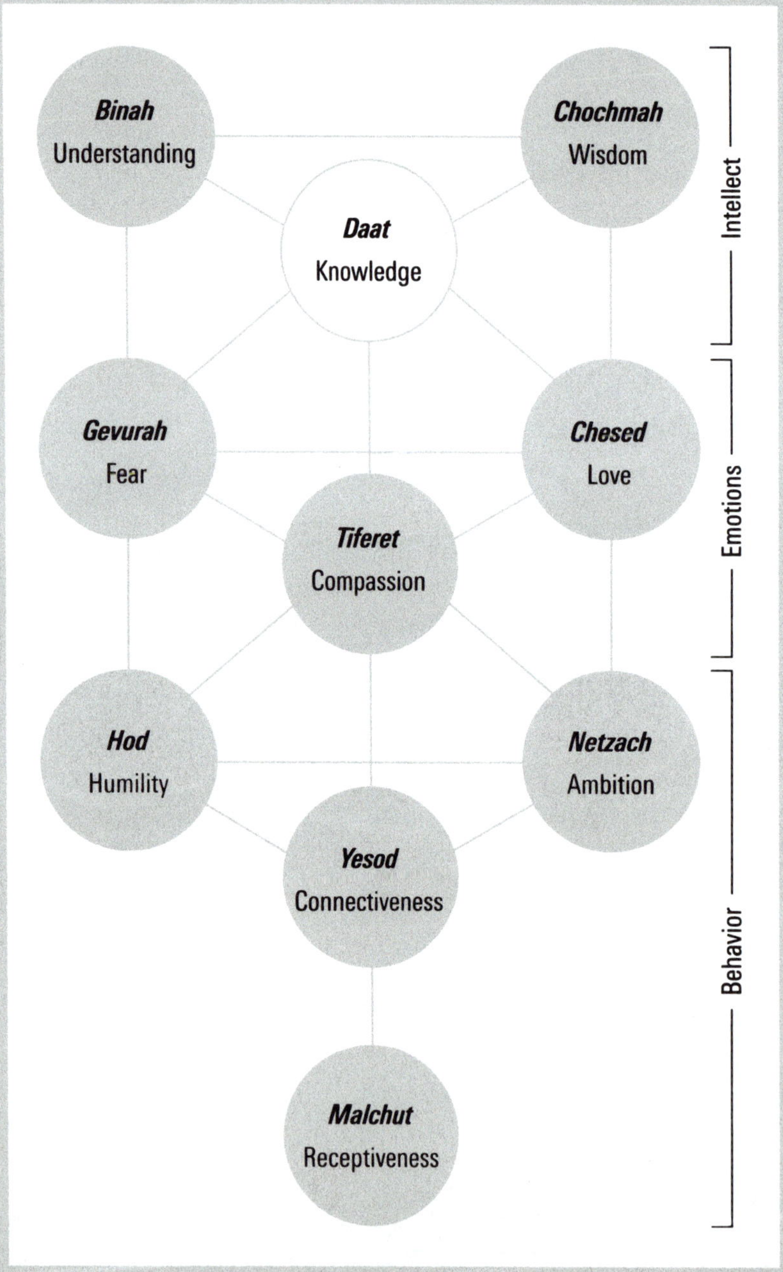

Daat is interconnect between intellect & emotion.

~~Daat~~ Daat may bring subjectivity

TEXT 4

YANKI TAUBER, *ONCE UPON A CHASSID*
(BROOKLYN: KEHOT PUBLICATION SOCIETY, 1994), P. 53

An official-looking letter, adorned with stamps and seals, arrived at a small wayside inn somewhere in the backwoods of Russia. The illiterate innkeeper ran to find the local schoolteacher in order to enlist his assistance.

As the teacher read the letter aloud, the innkeeper turned white, uttered a small cry, and fainted. For the letter contained shocking and tragic news for this simple, good-hearted man: his beloved father had passed away.

RABBI YANKI TAUBER
1965–

Chasidic scholar and author. A native of Brooklyn, N.Y., Rabbi Tauber is an internationally renowned author who specializes in adapting the teachings of the Lubavitcher Rebbe. He is a member of the JLI curriculum development team and has written numerous articles and books, including *Once Upon a Chassid* and *Beyond the Letter of the Law.*

Girl Reading a Letter by an Open Window, Johannes Vermeer, oil on canvas, c. 1659. (Dresden State Art Museum, Germany)

QUESTION FOR DISCUSSION

Does our faculty of *daat* **help** us or **hinder** us in making important life decisions?

Examples:

1 Who can better diagnose and treat an illness—an objective professional, or a doctor who is a close friend and deeply cares about the patient?

2 Who will do a better job at running a business—a hired genius with a PhD in business administration, or a family member who is personally and emotionally invested in the family business?

3 Which would be a better judge in a criminal case—a computer that is fed all the relevant facts and algorithms, or a human judge with feelings of sympathy for the victim and outrage toward the criminal?

TEXT 5

RABBI SHNE'UR ZALMAN OF LIADI, *TORAH OR*, BEREISHIT 5C–D

וְזֶהוּ שֶׁכָּתוּב הֵן הָאָדָם הָיָה כְּאַחַד מִמֶּנּוּ . . . פֵּירוּשׁ כְּמוֹ שֶׁבִּבְחִינַת אַחְדוּת, דְהַיְינוּ לְמַעְלָה, יָדוּעַ הַטּוֹב וָרַע, כֵּן הָיָה גַם הוּא עַל יְדֵי שֶׁטָּעַם מֵעֵץ הַדַּעַת הַמְעוּרָב טוֹב וָרַע. אֲבָל לוֹ הַדָּבָר מַזִּיק . . .

לֹא כְּמוֹ שֶׁהוּא לְמַעְלָה, שֶׁאַף עַל פִּי שֶׁיּוֹדְעִים גַּם אֶת הָרַע מִכָּל מָקוֹם מוּבְדָּל הוּא וּמְרוּחָק מִן הַטּוֹב . . . אֲבָל הָאָדָם, שֶׁהוּא מִבְּחִינַת פְּנִימִי, כְּשֶׁיֵּדַע גַּם הוּא מִן הָרַע אֲזַי יִתְעָרֵב הוּא גַם הוּא מַמָּשׁ עִם הָרַע . . . וְאָז הוּא קָשֶׁה מְאֹד לְהַפְרִיד אֶת הָרַע. אֶלָּא מִלְחָמָה עֲצוּמָה הִיא, "וּלְאֹם מִלְאֹם יֶאֱמָץ", פְּעָמִים זֶה גּוֹבֵר וּפְעָמִים שֶׁכְּנֶגְדּוֹ גּוֹבֵר . . .

וְלָכֵן לֹא רָצָה הַקָּדוֹשׁ בָּרוּךְ הוּא שֶׁיִּטְעַם הָאָדָם מֵעֵץ הַדַּעַת . . . וְהָיָה רוֹצֶה שֶׁלֹּא יֵדַע מִמְּצִיאַת הָרַע כְּלָל וְיִהְיֶה כּוּלּוֹ קָדוֹשׁ וְלֹא רָצָה לְהַכְנִיסוֹ בְּמִלְחָמָה עֲצוּמָה הַזֹּאת.

This is the meaning of what [G-d] says [after Adam and Eve ate from the Tree:] "Here, the human has become like one of us . . ." (GENESIS 3:22). Meaning that in the same way that in the Supernal Oneness there is knowledge of good and bad, so, too, has man [gained this knowledge] as a result of his tasting of the Tree of Knowledge in which good and bad are commingled. But for man, this is damaging. . . .

The way that it is Above is that although the bad is also known, it remains separate and distant from the good. . . . The human being, however, is a *penimi* ("internalizer"): when the human being knows the bad, he becomes mixed up with it . . . and then it is extremely

RABBI SHNE'UR ZALMAN OF LIADI (ALTER REBBE) 1745–1812

Chasidic rebbe, halachic authority, and founder of the Chabad movement. The Alter Rebbe was born in Liozna, Belarus, and was among the principal students of the Magid of Mezeritch. His numerous works include the *Tanya*, an early classic containing the fundamentals of Chabad Chasidism; and *Shulchan Aruch HaRav*, an expanded and reworked code of Jewish law.

A Kabbalistic View of the Tree of Knowledge
Rabbi Laibl Wolf:

MYJLI.COM/BIBLE

difficult to separate from the bad. Rather, it is a great battle, in which "kingdom overpowers kingdom"—at times one side overpowers, and at times the other side overpowers. . . .

This is why G-d did not want that man should taste from the Tree of Knowledge. . . . G-d wanted that man should not have any knowledge at all of the bad, and that man should remain exclusively holy; as G-d did not desire to cast man into this great battle.

The Temptation in the Garden of Eden, Jan Bruegel the Elder, oil on oak panel, Antwerp, c. 1600. (Victoria and Albert Museum, London)

TEXT 6

MAIMONIDES, *GUIDE FOR THE PERPLEXED* 1:2

שֶׁהַשֵּׂכֶל אֲשֶׁר הִשְׁפִּיעַ ה' עַל הָאָדָם, שֶׁהוּא שְׁלֵמוּתוֹ הַסּוֹפִית, הוּא אֲשֶׁר נִיתַּן לָאָדָם קוֹדֶם מְרוּתוֹ; וְעָלָיו נֶאֱמַר בּוֹ שֶׁהוּא בְּצֶלֶם אֱלוֹקִים וּבִדְמוּתוֹ, וּבִגְלָלוֹ דִיבֵּר אִתּוֹ וְצִוָּוה אוֹתוֹ . . . כִּי לֹא תִּהְיֶה הַצִּיוּוּי לִבְהֵמוֹת וְלֹא לְמִי שֶׁאֵין לוֹ שֵׂכֶל. וּבְשֵׂכֶל יַבְדִּיל הָאָדָם בֵּין הָאֱמֶת וְהַשֶּׁקֶר; וְזֶה הָיָה נִמְצָא בּוֹ עַל שְׁלֵמוּתוֹ וְתַמּוּתוֹ.

אֲבָל הַ"טּוֹב וְהָרַע" הוּא בַּמְפוּרְסָמוֹת, לֹא בְּמוּשְׂכָּלוֹת . . . וְכֵן בִּלְשׁוֹנֵנוּ יֹאמַר עַל הַנָּכוֹן וְהַשָּׁוְוא "אֱמֶת וְשֶׁקֶר", וְעַל הַנָּאֶה וְהַמְגוּנָּה "טוֹב וָרַע" . . . וְכַאֲשֶׁר מָרָה וְנָטָה אֶל תַּאֲווֹתָיו הַדִּמְיוֹנִיּוֹת וְתַעֲנוּגוֹת חוּשָׁיו הַגּוּפְנִיִּים–כְּמוֹ שֶׁאָמַר: "כִּי טוֹב הָעֵץ לְמַאֲכָל וְכִי תַאֲוָה הוּא לָעֵינַיִם"– נֶעֱנַשׁ שֶׁנִּשְׁלְלָה מִמֶּנּוּ אוֹתָהּ הַהַשָּׂגָה הַשִּׂכְלִית . . . וְנִקְנֵית לוֹ הַשָּׂגַת הַמְפוּרְסָמוֹת וְשָׁקַע בְּהַבְחָנַת הָרַע וְהַטּוֹב . . . וְלָזֶה נֶאֱמַר . . . "יוֹדְעֵי טוֹב וָרָע", וְלֹא אָמַר, "יוֹדְעֵי שֶׁקֶר וֶאֱמֶת" אוֹ "מַשִּׂיגֵי שֶׁקֶר וֶאֱמֶת".

A Text-Based Study of the Sin of the Tree of Knowledge
Rabbi Avrohom Bergstein:

MYJLI.COM/BIBLE

The intelligence that G-d imparted to man, which is man's ultimate perfection, was given to him before his disobedience. Indeed, it is because of this intelligence that it is said that man was made in the divine image and likeness, and it is due to this intelligence that G-d spoke to man and instructed him . . . as one does not commission animals or those without intelligence. With this intelligence, man was able to differentiate between truth and falsehood. This ability man possessed in fullness and perfection.

"Good" and "bad," on the other hand, are subjective conventions, not objective truths . . . When speaking of the correct and incorrect, we use the terminology "true" and "false"; regarding what is attractive or repulsive, we use the terms "good" and "bad." . . . When man rebelled and followed his imagined desires and the pleasure of his physical instincts—as it is written, "[The woman saw] that the tree is good for eating and that it is lusty to the eyes"—his punishment was to be deprived of that objective understanding. . . . He was inundated by the subjectivity of worldly conventions, and he sank to the level of discerning in terms of "good" and "bad." . . . Thus, it says that [Adam and Eve became] "knowers of good and bad," rather than "knowers of falsehood and truth" or "comprehenders of falsehood and truth."

TEXT 7

RABBI ELIYAHU DESSLER, *MICHTAV MI'ELIYAHU*, VOL. 2, PP. 138–139

עַכְשָׁיו, בְּמַצָּב שֶׁלְּאַחַר הַחֵטְא, נִשְׁמָעִים לָנוּ דִּבְרֵי הַיֵּצֶר הָרַע בְּגוּף רִאשׁוֹן: "אֲנִי" רוֹצֶה, "אֲנִי" מִתְאַוֶּה . . . אֲבָל לֹא כֵן אֵצֶל אָדָם הָרִאשׁוֹן, כִּי "הָאֱלוֹקִים עָשָׂה אֶת הָאָדָם יָשָׁר", וְהָיָה עוֹשֶׂה מִטִּבְעוֹ מַה שֶּׁרָאוּי לַעֲשׂוֹת . . . אֲשֶׁר עַל כֵּן הָיָה צָרִיךְ הַנָּחָשׁ לָבוֹא "מִבַּחוּץ" לְפַתּוֹתוֹ . . . בִּלְשׁוֹן "אַתָּה", קוֹל הַבָּא אֵלָיו מִבַּחוּץ, וְלֹא מִתּוֹךְ הָ"אֲנִי" שֶׁהָיָה מוּשְׁרָשׁ בַּטּוֹב.

Today, in the post-transgression reality, the evil inclination is an internal voice that speaks in the first person: "I want," "I desire." . . . This was not the original state of the human being. For "G-d created man straight" (ECCLESIASTES 7:29), as one who would naturally do the right thing. . . . Which is why the serpent had to come from the outside to entice man . . . with a "you" voice coming from without, rather than with man's "I" voice, which was rooted in good.

RABBI ELIYAHU DESSLER
1892–1953

Talmudic scholar and philosopher. Rabbi Dessler is best known for being the spiritual counselor of the Ponevezh Yeshiva in Israel. His pupils edited his writings and correspondence and published them in a 6-volume series titled *Michtav Mi'Eliyahu.*

TEXT 8

ZOHAR 1:27A

> וַיִּקַח ה' אֱלֹקִים אֶת הָאָדָם וַיַּנִּיחֵהוּ בְגַן עֵדֶן וְגוֹמֵר... לְעָבְדָהּ - בְּפִקּוּדִין
> דְעֲשֵׂה, וּלְשָׁמְרָהּ - בְּפִקּוּדִין דְלֹא תַעֲשֶׂה.

"G-d Almighty took the man, and He put him in the Garden of Eden, to work it and to keep it" (GENESIS 2:15). "To work it"—these are the positive commandments of the Torah; "and to keep it"—these are the prohibitions.

ZOHAR

The seminal work of kabbalah, Jewish mysticism. The *Zohar* is a mystical commentary on the Torah, written in Aramaic and Hebrew. According to the Arizal, the *Zohar* contains the teachings of Rabbi Shimon bar Yocha'i, who lived in the Land of Israel during the 2nd century. The *Zohar* has become one of the indispensable texts of traditional Judaism, alongside and nearly equal in stature to the Mishnah and Talmud.

QUESTION FOR DISCUSSION

Which path would you choose for your child?

TEXT 9

RABBI CHAIM VITAL, *SHAAREI KEDUSHAH* 1:1

וְדַע כִּי אַחַר שֶׁחָטָא אָדָם הָרִאשׁוֹן וְאָכַל מֵעֵץ הַדַּעַת טוֹב וָרָע, חוּבְּרוּ נַפְשׁוֹ וְגוּפוֹ גַּם הֵם כָּל אֶחָד מִטּוֹב וָרָע... וְזֶהוּ שֶׁכָּתוּב (בְּרֵאשִׁית ב׳ י״ז) כִּי בְּיוֹם אֲכָלְךָ מִמֶּנּוּ מוֹת תָּמוּת, מִיתַת הַנֶּפֶשׁ וּמִיתַת הַגּוּף... הִנֵּה כַּאֲשֶׁר חָטָא בְּעֵץ הַדַּעַת טוֹב וָרָע, גָּרַם תַּעֲרוֹבֶת הַזֶּה בְּכָל הָעוֹלָמוֹת וְאֵין לְךָ דָּבָר שֶׁאֵינוֹ כָּלוּל מִטּוֹב וָרָע.

Know that after Adam sinned and ate from the Tree of Knowledge of Good and Bad, both his soul and his body became integrated with both good and bad. . . . This is the significance of that which is written (GENESIS 2:17), "Because on the day that you eat from it, die you will die"—both the death of the soul and the death of the body. . . . [And] when he sinned with the Tree of Knowledge of Good and Bad, man caused this intermixing in all the worlds, so that there is nothing that does not include within itself both good and bad.

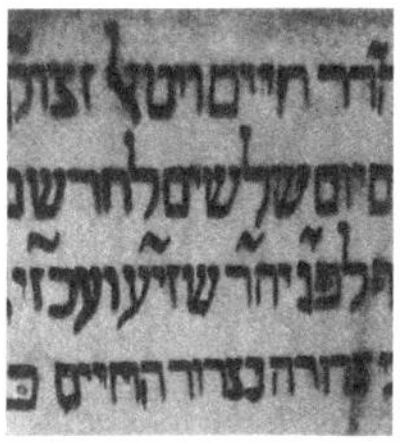

RABBI CHAIM VITAL
C. 1542–1620

Lurianic kabbalist. Rabbi Vital was born in Israel, lived in Safed and Jerusalem, and later lived in Damascus. He was authorized by his teacher, Rabbi Yitschak Luria, the Arizal, to record his teachings. Acting on this mandate, Vital began arranging his master's teachings in written form, and his many works constitute the foundation of the Lurianic school of Jewish mysticism. His most famous work is *Ets Chaim.*

Original Sin Revisited—
What Really Happened?
Rabbi Mendel Kaplan:

MYJLI.COM/BIBLE

TEXT **10**

THE REBBE, RABBI MENACHEM MENDEL SCHNEERSON,
SEFER HAMAAMARIM 5725, P. 344 👥

דְּעַל יְדֵי חֵטְא עֵץ הַדַּעַת נַעֲשֶׂה תַּעֲרוּבוֹת טוֹב וָרָע. דִּמְצִיאוּת הָרַע הָיָה
גַּם קוֹדֶם הַחֵטְא, אֶלָּא שֶׁאָז הָיָה הָרַע מוּבְדָּל מֵהַטּוֹב. וְכַיָּדוּעַ, שֶׁבִּתְחִלַּת
הַבְּרִיאָה הָיָה מָדוֹר הַקְּלִיפּוֹת לְמַטָּה מֵהָעוֹלָמוֹת דִּקְדוּשָׁה, וְעַל יְדֵי חֵטְא
עֵץ הַדַּעַת נַעֲשֶׂה תַּעֲרוּבוֹת טוֹב וָרָע בְּכָל הָעוֹלָם: שֶׁהָרַע מְעוֹרָב בְּהַטּוֹב
וְהַטּוֹב בְּהָרַע, וְעַד אֲשֶׁר אֵין טוֹב בְּלֹא רַע וְאֵין רַע בְּלֹא טוֹב.

As a result of the sin of the Tree of Knowledge, there was
a blending of good and bad. Evil existed before the sin,
but then it was separated from the good. As is known,
in the beginning of Creation, the domain of *kelipah* [the
"husks" that conceal G-dliness] was beneath the realms
of holiness. But through the sin of the Tree of Knowledge,
the entire world became a mixture of good and bad: the
bad is mixed into the good, and the good is mixed into
the bad, to the extent that there is no good without some
bad in it, and no bad without some good in it.

**RABBI MENACHEM MENDEL SCHNEERSON
1902–1994**

The towering Jewish leader of
the 20th century, known as "the
Lubavitcher Rebbe," or simply as "the
Rebbe." Born in southern Ukraine,
the Rebbe escaped Nazi-occupied
Europe, arriving in the U.S. in June
1941. The Rebbe inspired and guided
the revival of traditional Judaism
after the European devastation,
impacting virtually every Jewish
community the world over. The
Rebbe often emphasized that the
performance of just one additional
good deed could usher in the era
of Mashiach. The Rebbe's scholarly
talks and writings have been printed
in more than 200 volumes.

*The Secret of the Snake
and the Garden of Eden*
Rabbi DovBer Pinson:

MYJLI.COM/BIBLE

QUESTION FOR DISCUSSION

Are we better off or worse off as a result of Adam and Eve's deed?

QUESTION FOR DISCUSSION

What life lessons can we take from the story of the Tree of Knowledge?

The Secret of the Pomegranate, Shternie Zaltzman, paint, beads and clasps on wood, Brooklyn, N.Y., 2017.

KEY POINTS

1 The plain meaning of the Torah's text and its inner mystical "soul" are interrelated. The many questions, mysteries, and dilemmas posed by the stories of the Torah are resolved when we understand the stories' mystical significance. The mystical meanings also show us how these stories are applicable to our own lives in the here and now.

2 The Torah's account of the "Tree of Knowledge" presents us with many perplexing questions. How did eating the fruit of a certain tree impart "knowledge of good and bad"? Why was the Tree forbidden? Isn't knowledge a good thing? Did Adam and Eve have Free Choice before they ate from the Tree? If everything the serpent said was true, where was the deception? How did eating from the Tree cause human mortality, the pain of childbirth, and the struggle to earn a living? What is the role of nakedness, clothing, and shame in the Tree of Knowledge story?

3 The faculty of *daat* ("knowledge") is that part of our psyche that causes us to become personally invested in what we know and experience. While our *daat* is a reflection of G-d's *daat*, there is an important distinction between the two. G-d is fully invested in His Creation, yet remains unchanged by it. In contrast, everything that we know and experience becomes part of who and what we are.

4 Before partaking of the Tree, Adam and Eve had a perfect objective understanding of right and wrong, which fully equipped them to fulfill their mission of cultivating G-dliness in the world and rejecting evil. As a result of their transgression, their divine intellect was degraded to a subjective "*daat* of good and bad," where personal prejudice and shortsighted cravings cloud a person's judgment. This is why G-d forbade them to partake of the Tree of Knowledge: G-d desired to spare them the struggle and anguish that the entanglement of *daat* would bring.

5 The human being is a microcosm of the whole of Creation. By absorbing the "*daat* of good and bad" into themselves, Adam and Eve caused all of Creation to become a mishmash of good and bad, to the extent that "there is no good without some bad in it, and no bad without some good in it."

6 The story of the Tree of Knowledge teaches us to appreciate the positive elements that exist in the "other" with whom we disagree and in the paradigms that we reject. It encourages us to embrace the "messiness" of life as an opportunity for deeper and more meaningful engagement. It also teaches us to acknowledge our blunders, while discovering how a past negative can be transformed into a future positive.

Appendix

TEXT 11

ZOHAR, 3:152A

רַבִּי שִׁמְעוֹן אָמַר, וַוי לְהַהוּא בַּר נַשׁ דְּאָמַר דְּהָא אוֹרַיְיתָא אָתָא לְאַחְזָאָה סִפּוּרִין בְּעָלְמָא וּמִלִּין דְּהֶדְיוֹטֵי, דְּאִי הָכִי אֲפִילּוּ בְּזִמְנָא דָא אֲנָן יָכְלִין לְמֶעְבַּד אוֹרַיְיתָא בְּמִלִּין דְּהֶדְיוֹטֵי וּבִשְׁבָחָא יַתִּיר מִכֻּלְּהוּ . . . אֶלָּא כָּל מִלִּין דְּאוֹרַיְיתָא מִלִּין עִלָּאִין אִינּוּן וְרָזִין עִלָּאִין . . .

תָּא חֲזִי, אִית לְבוּשָׁא דְּאִתְחֲזֵי לְכֹלָּא, וְאִינּוּן טִפְּשִׁין כַּד חֲמָאן לְבַר נַשׁ בִּלְבוּשָׁא דְּאִתְחֲזֵי לוֹן שַׁפִּירָא, לָא מִסְתַּכְּלִין יַתִּיר, חֲשִׁיבוּ דְּהַהוּא לְבוּשָׁא גּוּפָא, חֲשִׁיבוּתָא דְּגוּפָא נִשְׁמָתָא. כְּהַאי גַּוְונָא אוֹרַיְיתָא. אִית לָהּ גּוּפָא, וְאִינּוּן פִּקּוּדֵי אוֹרַיְיתָא . . . הַאי גּוּפָא מִתְלַבְּשָׁא בִּלְבוּשִׁין דְּאִינּוּן סִפּוּרִין דְּהַאי עָלְמָא. טִפְּשִׁין דְּעָלְמָא לָא מִסְתַּכְּלֵי אֶלָּא בְּהַהוּא לְבוּשָׁא, דְּאִיהוּ סִפּוּר דְּאוֹרַיְיתָא, וְלָא יָדְעֵי יַתִּיר . . . אִינּוּן דְּיָדְעִין יַתִּיר, לָא מִסְתַּכְּלָן בִּלְבוּשָׁא אֶלָּא בְּגוּפָא דְּאִיהוּ תְּחוֹת הַהוּא לְבוּשָׁא. חַכִּימִין עַבְדֵי דְּמַלְכָּא עִלָּאָה, אִינּוּן דְּקָיְימוּ בְּטוּרָא דְּסִינַי, לָא מִסְתַּכְּלֵי אֶלָּא בְּנִשְׁמָתָא, דְּאִיהִי עִקָּרָא דְּכֹלָּא אוֹרַיְיתָא מַמָּשׁ (וּלְעָלְמָא) וּלְזִמְנָא דְּאָתֵי, זַמִּינִין לְאִסְתַּכְּלָא בְּנִשְׁמָתָא דְּנִשְׁמָתָא דְּאוֹרַיְיתָא . . .

חַמְרָא לָא יָתִיב אֶלָּא בְּקַנְקַן, כָּךְ אוֹרַיְיתָא לָא יָתִיב אֶלָּא בִּלְבוּשָׁא דָא, וְעַל דָּא לָא בָּעֵי לְאִסְתַּכְּלָא אֶלָּא בְּמַה דְּאִית תְּחוֹת לְבוּשָׁא, וְעַל דָּא כָּל אִינּוּן מִלִּין וְכָל אִינּוּן סִפּוּרִין, לְבוּשִׁין אִינּוּן.

Rabbi Shimon [bar Yocha'i] said:

Woe to the person who says that the Torah presents mere stories and ordinary words. If this were the case, we could compose a Torah right now with ordinary words, and better than any of them. . . . Rather, all the words of the Torah are sublime words and sublime secrets. . . .

Come and see: There is a garment that is visible to all. When the fools of the world see someone in a handsome garment, they look no further. Yet the significance of the garment is the body; and the significance of the body is the soul. So it is with the Torah. It has a body: the commandments of the Torah. . . . This body is clothed in garments—stories of this world. Fools look only at that garment, the story of the Torah; they know nothing more. . . . Those who know better look at the body within the garment. The truly wise—servants of the Supernal King, those who stood at Mount Sinai—look at the soul, the root of all, the real Torah. In the World to Come, they are destined to gaze at the soul of the soul of the Torah. . . .

As wine must be contained in a jug, so the Torah must be contained in these garments. But look to what is within the garments. All those words, all those stories, are garments.

TEXT 12

NACHMANIDES, *COMMENTARY ON THE TORAH*, GENESIS 3:22

וְדַע וְהַאֲמֵן כִּי גַן עֵדֶן בָּאָרֶץ וּבוֹ עֵץ הַחַיִּים וְעֵץ הַדַּעַת וּמִשָּׁם יֵצֵא הַנָּהָר וְיִפָּרֵד לְאַרְבָּעָה רָאשִׁים . . . אֲבָל כַּאֲשֶׁר הֵם בָּאָרֶץ כֵּן יֵשׁ בַּשָּׁמַיִם דְּבָרִים יִקָּרְאוּ כֵן וְהֵם לְאֵלֶּה יְסוֹד . . .

וְהָאָדָם חָטָא בִּפְרִי עֵץ הַדַּעַת תַּחְתּוֹן וְעֶלְיוֹן, בְּמַעֲשֶׂה וּבְמַחְשָׁבָה . . . כָּל אֵלֶּה הַדְּבָרִים כְּפוּלִים, הַגָּלוּי וְהֶחָתוּם בָּהֶם אֱמֶת.

Know and believe that the Garden of Eden is a place here on earth, in which there is the Tree of Life and the Tree of Knowledge, and from which flows the river that separates into four streams. . . . But just as these exist on earth, so are there realities in the heavens that are also called by these names, and that serve as their foundation and source. . . .

Man sinned with the fruit of the Tree of Knowledge below and above, in deed as well as in concept. . . . All the events recounted here are two-dimensional: the revealed meaning and the hidden meaning are both true.

TEXT 13

ZOHAR 1:35B

> וְהַנָּחָשׁ, רַבִּי יִצְחָק אָמַר: דָּא יֵצֶר הָרַע. רַבִּי יְהוּדָה אָמַר: נָחָשׁ מַמָּשׁ. אָתוּ לְקַמֵּיהּ דְּרַבִּי שִׁמְעוֹן, אָמַר לוֹן: וַדַּאי כֻּלָּא חַד, וְסַמָּאֵ"ל הֲוָה וְאִתְחֲזֵי עַל נָחָשׁ.

"And the serpent [was most cunning]" (GENESIS 3:1).

Rabbi Isaac said, "It was the evil inclination."

Rabbi Judah said, "It was an actual snake."

They came before Rabbi Shimon [bar Yocha'i], who said to them, "It was both as one; it was Samael [Satan] who appeared as a snake."

Black Snake, Pseudechis porphyriacus, Helena Scott, ink on paper, 1869. (Museums Victoria, Carlton, Australia)

TEXT 14

THE REBBE, RABBI MENACHEM MENDEL SCHNEERSON, *LIKUTEI SICHOT* 21 (HEBREW VERSION), PP. 40–41

שֶׁכָּל חֶלְקֵי הַתּוֹרָה מַרְכִּיבִים בְּיַחַד קוֹמָה שְׁלֵימָה אַחַת, כְּשֵׁם שֶׁכָּל אֵבָרֵי הָאָדָם הֵן אֵבָרֵי גוּפוֹ וְהֵן אֵבָרֵי נַפְשׁוֹ מַרְכִּיבִים יַחְדָיו אֶת הָאָדָם כּוּלוֹ . . .

גַם לְגַבֵּי פְּנִימִיּוּת הַתּוֹרָה, נִשְׁמְתָא דְאוֹרַיְיתָא . . . שֶׁהִיא מְאוּחֶדֶת עִם הַנִּגְלֶה שֶׁבַּתּוֹרָה, גוּפָא דְאוֹרַיְיתָא. עַד כְּדֵי כַּךְ, שֶׁרוֹאִים בְּמִסְפַּר מְקוֹמוֹת . . . [שֶׁ]הַנִּגְלֶה שֶׁבַּתּוֹרָה עַצְמוֹ מְחַיֵּיב פֵּירוּשׁ שֶׁל נִשְׁמְתָא דְאוֹרַיְיתָא . . . וְכֵן מִצַּד שֵׁנִי . . . כְּפִי שֶׁמּוֹצְאִים בְּרַבִּים מִכִּתְבֵי הָאֲרִ״י זִכְרוֹנוֹ לִבְרָכָה פֵּירוּשִׁים וְעִנְיָנִים בְּדֶרֶךְ הַפְּשַׁט.

All parts of the Torah comprise one integral structure, in the same way that all of a person's components—the organs and limbs of their body as well as the organs and limbs of their soul—together constitute the whole person.

In the same way, the inner part—or "soul"—of the Torah is one with the revealed part of the Torah. Indeed, we find in several places that the revealed part of Torah can only be explained by the soul of the Torah. The reverse is also the case . . . as we find in the [kabbalistic] writings of the Ari explanations of the plain meaning of the text.

TEXT 15

THE REBBE, RABBI MENACHEM MENDEL SCHNEERSON,
LIKUTEI SICHOT 2 (HEBREW VERSION), P. 38

לַמְרוֹת שֶׁהַתּוֹרָה הִיא חָכְמָה–כַּכָּתוּב: "כִּי הִיא חָכְמַתְכֶם וּבִינַתְכֶם לְעֵינֵי הָעַמִּים"–אֵין הִיא נִקְרֵאת בְּשֵׁם "חָכְמָה," כִּי אִם בְּשֵׁם "תּוֹרָה" מִלָּשׁוֹן "הוֹרָאָה". וּמַשְׁמָעוּת הַדָּבָר, שֶׁכָּל עִנְיָן הַמְסוּפָּר בַּתּוֹרָה מְשַׁמֵּשׁ הוֹרָאָה לְתָמִיד וּלְכָל מָקוֹם בְּחַיֵּי יוֹם יוֹם.

The Torah is our "wisdom and understanding in the eyes of the nations" (DEUTERONOMY 4:6). Nevertheless, the word *torah* doesn't mean "wisdom"; rather, it means "instruction." This tells us that every single thing that the Torah relates serves as an instruction in a person's daily life, for all times and in every place.

TEXT 16

RABBI SHNE'UR ZALMAN OF LIADI, *TORAH OR*, BEREISHIT 5C

יֵשׁ לְהָבִין . . . מַה שֶּׁאָמַר ה' אֱלֹקִים "וְעַתָּה פֶּן יִשְׁלַח יָדוֹ וְלָקַח גַּם מֵעֵץ הַחַיִּים וְאָכַל וָחַי לְעוֹלָם." וּמַה אִיכְפַּת לוֹ בָּזֶה? הֲרֵי מַה שֶּׁצִּוָּה אוֹתוֹ שֶׁלֹּא לֶאֱכוֹל הוּא גַּם כֵּן כְּדֵי שֶׁלֹּא יָמוּת.

It needs to be understood: Why does G-d say, "And now, perhaps he will send forth his hand, and he will also take from the tree of life, and he will eat and live forever"? Why is G-d concerned over this, when the reason why He commanded Adam not to eat [from the Tree of Knowledge] in the first place was so that he should not die?

TEXT 17

RABBI SHNE'UR ZALMAN OF LIADI, *TORAH OR*, BEREISHIT 5D

אַחַר שֶׁכְּבָר טָעַם מֵעֵץ הַדַּעַת וְנִתְעָרֵב בְּרַע, אָז אָמַר "פֶּן יִשְׁלַח יָדוֹ וְלָקַח גַּם מֵעֵץ הַחַיִּים וְאָכַל וָחַי לְעוֹלָם." פֵּירוּשׁ שֶׁחָשַׁשׁ . . . וְלָקַח גַּם מֵעֵץ הַחַיִּים שֶׁשָּׁרְשׁוֹ מִבְּחִינָה שֶׁלְּמַעֲלָה מֵהַשְּׁבִירָה שֶׁמִּשָּׁם הוּא שֶׁהָיָה הַתְחָלַת הַמִּיתָה וְהִתְהַוּוּת עֵץ הַדַּעַת טוֹב וָרַע . . . כִּי הֲרֵי בֶּאֱמֶת בִּבְחִינָה זוּ נֶאֱמַר "אִם צָדַקְתָּ מַה תִּתֶּן לוֹ", "וְרַבּוּ פְשָׁעֶיךָ מַה תַּעֲשֶׂה לוֹ" (אִיּוֹב לה). וְאִם כֵּן אַף שֶׁמְּעוֹרָב בָּרַע . . . יָכוֹל לִהְיוֹת וָחַי לְעוֹלָם, וְאָז גַּם הָרַע שֶׁבּוֹ יִהְיֶה לוֹ קִיּוּם לְעוֹלָם . . .

וְזֶהוּ הֵיפֶךְ הַכַּוָּונָה שֶׁהֲרֵי צָרִיךְ לִהְיוֹת . . . שֶׁיִּהְיֶה וּבִעַרְתָּ הָרָע . . . שֶׁזֶּה יִהְיֶה לִימוֹת הַמָּשִׁיחַ. כִּי בְּכָל מֶשֶׁךְ הַגָּלוּת הוּא עֵת הַבֵּירוּרִים וְהַפְרָדַת הָרַע . . . וְלָכֵן מִיַּד "וַיְשַׁלְּחֵהוּ מִגַּן עֵדֶן לַעֲבֹד אֶת הָאֲדָמָה אֲשֶׁר לֻקַּח מִשָּׁם"–דְהַיְינוּ עֲבוֹדַת הַבֵּירוּרִים.

After man had already tasted of the Tree of Knowledge and became mixed up with the bad, G-d said, "Perhaps he will send forth his hand and also take from the tree of life, and eat and live forever." G-d feared that man would . . . partake also of the Tree of Life, which is rooted higher than the "shattering of the vessels" from which death originates and which generated the Tree of Knowledge of Good and Bad. . . . For regarding this level, it is said, "If your sins are multiplied, what do you do to Him?" and "If you are righteous, what do you give Him?" (JOB 35:6–7). So [if man will partake of the Tree of Life] . . . he could still live forever even though he has bad mixed in within him, and then the bad within him will also exist forever. . . .

This is against that which G-d intended, for G-d desires that ultimately the bad should be exterminated . . . as will come to pass in the times of Mashiach. [Until then,] throughout the period of exile is the time of the "work of refinement" of separating the bad [from the good]. . . . That is why immediately after [man ate from the Tree], "G-d Almighty sent him out from the Garden of Eden, to work the soil wherefrom he was taken" (GENESIS 3:23)—i.e., the work of refinement.

Additional Readings

"THE HUMAN BEING HAS BECOME LIKE ONE OF US"

EXCERPT FROM *TORAH OR* BY RABBI SHNE'UR ZALMAN OF LIADI
TRANSLATION BY RABBI SHMUEL KLATZKIN

[It is written,] "G-d said, 'Here the human being has become like one of us, to know good and bad; and now, perhaps he will send forth his hand . . .'" (Genesis 3:22).

One needs to understand:

1. How is it that through the Tree of Knowledge their eyes were opened to be like G-d, knowing good and bad?
2. Also, what G-d says, ". . . and now, perhaps he will send forth his hand, and he will take also from the Tree of Life, and he will eat and live forever"—why should this bother G-d? After all, His command to Adam not to eat [from the Tree] was also in order that he should not die!
3. Moreover, and this is essential: From where did the serpent know that "On the day you eat from it, your eyes will be opened" (Genesis 3:5)? For in truth, this was correct. Adam, who heard the command from G-d, did not know this; only the simple sense of what G-d told him, "For on the day you eat from it, die you will die" (Genesis 2:17). Nor is it mentioned at all that the serpent heard when Adam was commanded. So how did the serpent have such an extraordinary understanding, that he could infer more than Adam himself? Must we say that he was on a higher level than Adam? This is all very mysterious.

We will begin by explaining the statement that "the human has become like one of us, to know good and bad." This was G-d's statement to the angels, and it implies that on high, they know both good and evil. Nonetheless, the two are not blended together, for it is clearly known that this is good and this is evil. The evil is separate from the good, although good and evil are both known there. That is not the case with the Tree of Knowledge of Good and Bad, where the good and evil are blended together, the evil nursing from the good and the good from the evil, so that they are integrated.

We need to understand this. The phrase, "the Tree of Knowledge of Good and Bad" employs the term "knowledge" (*daat*). Why does knowledge of good and evil result in their being blended together? Good and evil are known on high as well [without that result].

The difference lies in the distinction between the "encompassing" (*makif*) and "permeating" (*penimi*) modes. The knowledge of good and evil on high is solely in the encompassing mode. Therefore, there can be a distinction between good and evil, with one knowing the evil and not exchanging it for the good, G-d forbid.

This is like the concept, "The spider clings [to the wall] with its hands, and it is in a king's palace" (Proverbs 30:28). Although it is in the royal palace, we know and recognize that it is a spider. The good and evil are differentiated, as we say [in the Havdalah blessing], "He who differentiates between the holy and the mundane." Because G-d knows good and evil in an "encompassing" manner, they are not blended together.

RABBI SHNE'UR ZALMAN OF LIADI (ALTER REBBE), 1745–1812

Chasidic rebbe, halachic authority, and founder of the Chabad movement. The Alter Rebbe was born in Liozna, Belarus, and was among the principal students of the Magid of Mezeritch. His numerous works include the *Tanya*, an early classic containing the fundamentals of Chabad Chasidism; and *Shulchan Aruch HaRav*, an expanded and reworked code of Jewish law.

This is like the pure frankincense, one of the eleven spices in the *ketoret*, ten of which are sparks of holiness swallowed by the forces of impurity (*kelipot*), and the eleventh, the frankincense, encompasses them and is not invested within them. The frankincense is also their source of vitality, but because this life force vivifies them only in an encompassing manner, it does not mix with them at all and remains entirely good.

This encompassing force also repels the external forces of evil, as is apparent from the illustration of the "Tree" [of the *seder hishtalshelut*] in the [kabbalistic work] *Pardes*, which depicts the encompassing and permeating forces, and where the position of the evil forces is that their back is to the encompassing force.

That is not the case with the Tree of Knowledge of Good and Bad, which is an internal and permeating force, and as a consequence, the good is fully blended with the evil.

That, then, is the meaning of the text, "Here the human being has become like one of us. . . ." Meaning that just as in the Oneness above, good and evil are known, so, too, has the human being [acquired this knowledge] by having tasted from the Tree of Knowledge of Good and Bad in which good and evil were blended. But for the human, this was injurious, for he is of the internal "permeating" mode, and immediately upon knowing of evil, he becomes mixed in with it.

This is not the way it is above, where, although evil, too, is known, it is nonetheless separate and distinct from the good, and it has no closeness to it, since it is in the encompassing mode. But when the human being, who is of the permeating mode, comes to know evil, then he will truly be blended into the evil. For it is impossible for anything in the permeating mode to be so separated from evil, as we explained above.

Consequently, it is very difficult [for the human being] to separate the evil [from himself]. Rather, it is an intense battle, [as it is written,] "kingdom will overpower kingdom" (Genesis 25:23)—at times one side will be the stronger, and at times the opposite force will be the stronger.

Indeed, we find this to be the case with the souls of Israel from their earliest generations until now—that there were different times and eras. In one generation, there were souls on a high level who triumphed over evil, while in another generation, there were greatly wicked people, and evil very much had the upper hand. All of these souls came from Adam, the first man, within whom there were also these changes—sometimes he had the upper hand, and sometimes the evil overpowered him.

All this is because the human being is of the permeating mode, so that immediately upon knowing evil, it is blended into him. As a result, it requires a very great and difficult battle to separate it, with the battle sometimes going this way, sometimes the other way, as we said.

We also see this from the simple sense of the text (Genesis 2:25 and 3:7–11). At first, Adam and Eve were naked, and they engaged in intercourse to bring forth children, but they were not embarrassed, just as if they were eating or drinking, for this was a command of G-d. They had no knowledge of any lust being involved. But after they ate from the Tree of Knowledge and they knew there was lust for this, then it became difficult to resist it.

That is why G-d did not want that the human being should eat from the Tree of Knowledge—it would harm him, as we have explained. G-d wanted that the human being should not know of the reality of evil at all, and that he should be entirely holy, as G-d did not want to put him into this intense battle.

But after man had already tasted from the Tree of Knowledge and had become mixed up with evil, then G-d said, ". . . and now, perhaps he will send forth his hand, and he will take also from the Tree of Life, and he will eat and live forever." The meaning of this is that G-d was concerned that since now man was already mixed up with evil, he might take from the Tree of Life, which is rooted in a level higher than where the Shattering of the Vessels took place, which is the place where death began and the Tree of Knowledge of Good and Bad came into being. Higher than the place of the Shattering is the Tree of Life, and if man were to eat of it, he would live forever.

The explanation of this is as follows. In truth, it is said of this level [of the Tree of Life], "If you have been righteous, what did you give Him? And if your sins were many, what did you do to Him?" (Job 35:6–7). That being the case, even one who is mixed up with evil—even one who is in a state of "if your sins were many"—could still live forever, and then the evil in that person would also have a permanent existence. Becuase the human being is of the "permeated" mode, and the evil was blended into him, he cannot separate it from himself. If so, were the human being to live forever, the evil in him would exist forever as well.

This would be the opposite of the Divine intention that "Death shall be destroyed forever" (Isaiah 25:8) and "You shall eradicate the evil from your midst" (Deuteronomy 17:7)—and as we say, "And all wickedness will go up in smoke" (High Holiday prayers)—all of which will come to pass in the days of Mashiach.

For the entire duration of the exile is a time for refinement and for separating the evil from the good by means of [the *sefirah* of] *chochmah* (wisdom)—as in the saying, "For through *chochmah*, they are refined" (*Zohar*). For this reason, *chochmah* is referred to as *din* (strict judgment)—not as the early kabbalists imagined, that *chochmah* is composed entirely of *chesed* (kindness), being that it is the root of *chesed*. The Chayat [the kabbalist R. Yehudah Chayat, c. 1500] proposed that the quality of *din* is also present in *chochmah*, for which the Arizal, of blessed memory, praised him; as it is thus explained in the *Zohar*, in the *Idra*, that it is like wine that is left still and remains over the dregs that drop off from it. This is because [the role of *chochmah*] is refinement, to separate the evil, and this is accomplished by means of severity. As it says, "Fortunate is the man whom G-d (*Yah*) afflicts" (Psalms 94:12)—meaning that also the afflictions that are for the purpose of removing evil are from the level of the divine name *Yah* [which is associated with the *sefirah* of *chesed*].

For as it is known, suffering is for the purpose of removing evil. For the forces of evil are compared to the leech, which dies immediately when it sucks out blood, as the verse says, "The leech has two daughters" (Proverbs 30:15). This is also the idea of the scapegoat (Leviticus 17), and similarly of "Jacob sent . . . an offering to Esau, his brother: two hundred goats. . . ."—by giving [the forces of evil] their portion, one separates it [from the good]. With this, he gave to him his portion, separating him.

That is how it has to be after Adam tasted from the Tree of Knowledge and became mixed up with evil. From that point, a refining process is needed, until [the evil] is separated by extracting all the sparks of holiness that are in it. All this is achieved by means of *chochmah*—"for through *chochmah* they are refined"—since *chochmah* also has severity in it, so that G-d may correct through suffering; as it is written (Deuteronomy 8:5), "As a man chastises his child. . . ."

This, however, would not be possible on the level of *keter* [the level of the Tree of Life]. *Keter* is higher than *chochmah*, and is the quality of absolute compassion, where "darkness and light are the same" (Psalms 139:12).

Therefore, [G-d says,] "Perhaps he will send forth his hand, and he will take also from the Tree of Life, and he will eat and live forever." Because [then the human being would be on the level of which it is said,] "If you have been righteous, what did you give Him?" And since the human being is of the permeating mode, and therefore the evil is bound and fastened to him, it too will endure—something that is against the Divine intent, as discussed above. As it is written in the *Zohar* regarding Rabbi Acha from Kfar Tarsha, who atoned with incense for a place where there had been a plague. They said to him, however, that he was ineffective, since the people there were still guilty, not having repented.

Therefore, immediately after Adam and Eve ate from the Tree, "G-d sent him out from the Garden of Eden, to work the earth wherefrom he was taken" (Genesis 3:23). This refers to the work of refining, which is accomplished through sowing, plowing, and harvesting, and then, when one eats from this crop [and uses the energy] to say [the verses of the *Shema*], "G-d is One" and "You shall love . . .", one refines it and elevates it. Consequently, the human being had to literally go to "the earth wherefrom he was taken"—there he should eat, and there he should carry out the refining process.

Still, we need to understand: What was the original divine intent, when man did not know of good and bad at all? Since there exists evil in the world, how would the refinement be achieved, as this is something that must be accomplished by the human being?

The explanation of the matter is that then it would have been achieved in a different manner entirely: not as a battle, but rather in the mode suggested by the verse, "[G-d] placed him in the Garden of Eden to work it" (Genesis 2:15), which refers to the 248 positive commandments, which draw down the light of the Infinite into the Garden of Eden. Through that profuse revelation of light, the sparks of holiness that fell and became mixed in with evil would automatically be elevated and subsumed within the supernal radiance that the human being would draw down.

This process is like a small flame placed before a torch. Even if the torch is small, if the flame is placed near it, it will be subsumed within it; but if it is distanced from it just a bit, it will not be subsumed, since the torch is small. But if the torch is large, then even if the flame is set at a distance, it will still be subsumed within it.

This is similar to the way it was when the Holy Temple was standing. For the sages said that "Israel was exiled only in order that converts should be added to them" (Talmud, Pesachim 87b)—that is to say, to elevate sparks. But if that is the case, what would have happened had they not sinned and been exiled? We must say, therefore, that the sparks then would have been spontaneously subsumed, like a small flame before a torch, as in the case of Naamah the Ammonite, and all the peoples who came to hear the wisdom of King Solomon, as in the case of the Queen of Sheba. This is because then [the people of Israel were], metaphorically, like a great torch, which automatically subsumed all the sparks. Had the Holy Temple stood longer, all the sparks would have been refined in this way. As it is written regarding the World to Come, "Then I will turn to the peoples in a clear tongue" (Zephaniah 3:9), and "Nations will walk in your light" (Isaiah 60:3).

That is the way it would have been if man had not sinned. The human being was entirely holy, for even the human body had been taken from the place where the Altar would stand, and from that earth all its 248 organs were made, blended with oil. The human being would have remained in the Garden of Eden and increased the divine radiance. The *kelipot* would have automatically *been* dissolved when the sparks of holiness were extracted from them. All this would have been achieved not in a way of battle.

That changed after man sinned. Since then, the refinement process has required labor and battle—"the time of prayer is a time of battle"—as stated earlier. One must descend to the place of the *kelipot* and refine them there. That is the meaning of the verse, "The earth wherefrom he was taken."

We can now understand how the serpent knew all this. Adam and Eve were entirely holy, higher than the Tree of Knowledge of Good and Bad, and they did not know the reality of evil at all, as stated earlier. But the serpent was himself derived from the level of the Tree of Knowledge of Good and Bad, and knew of this. He knew that G-d had commanded not to eat from the Tree so that mankind should not have a knowledge of evil at all, so that they should not at all have to enter into a battle against him.

It very much angered the serpent that the human being was so guarded against him, to the point that they would not know of him and thus be spared from erring through him. The serpent reached the conclusion that it would be better for him that man should engage with him and there should be a battle, for in that case, there will be times that he, too, will triumph, as it is written, "A time that a man ruled over man for his detriment" (Ecclesiastes 8:9)—rather than man should never know of evil at all, in which case the good that is mixed within the serpent would be subsumed in Adam like a flame before a torch, and the serpent would die and be completely destroyed.

So the serpent came cunningly to Eve—as it is said, "Samael came and rode on the serpent" (*Pirkei d'Rabbi Eliezer* 13)—and said, "For G-d knows that on the day you eat from it . . . you will be as G-d, knowers of good and bad." Indeed, this was true; the serpent did not actually lie, as earlier clarified. But it was a shrewdly deceitful statement. For he said, "You will be like G-d," implying that this was an advantage; whereas in truth, this was a detriment. Indeed, the human being would know good and evil as G-d does; nonetheless, on high, this knowledge is not detrimental at all, for although good and evil are known, the evil is separate from the good, because on high the knowledge is of the encompassing mode. For the human, however, it is another matter, for man is of the permeating mode. When man acquires knowledge of good and evil, this is injurious to him, as we explained.

Rabbi Shne'ur Zalman of Liadi, *Torah Or*, Bereishit 5c–6a

Lesson 2

NOAH'S ARK

De Ark van Noach (Noah's Ark) (detail), Jacques Callot, etching on paper, c. 1625 and/or 1646. (Rijksmuseum, Amsterdam)

Can G-d's plan for His world fail so catastrophically that the Creator regrets its very creation? And if it can, why can't it happen again? How does the rainbow symbolize the new world generated from Noah's Ark? Exploring the answers to these questions reveals the inner dynamics of the relationships that define our lives: the relationships between parent and child, between teacher and student, between employer and employee, and between G-d and us.

TEXT 1a

GENESIS 6:5–8:17

Have Remnants of Noah's Ark Been Found on Mount Ararat?

MYJLI.COM/BIBLE

G-D REGRETS HIS CREATION (6:5–8)

G-d saw that the evil of man
was multiplying upon the earth;
and that every impulse of the thoughts of his heart
is only evil, all day . . .
and He was pained to His heart.
And G-d said:
"I will erase the human being that I have created
from upon the face of the earth;
from man to beast, to crawling-thing, to bird of the heavens;
for I have regretted that I have made them."
But Noah found grace in the eyes of G-d.

NOAH WAS RIGHTEOUS (6:9–10)

These are the descendants of Noah:
Noah was a perfectly righteous man in his generations;
Noah walked with G-d.
Noah fathered three sons: Shem, and Ham, and Japheth.

G-D TELLS NOAH THAT THE WORLD WILL BE DESTROYED (6:12–13)

G-d saw the earth, and behold: it was corrupted
as all flesh had corrupted its way on the earth.
And G-d said to Noah:

"The end of all flesh has come before Me
as the earth is filled with violence from them;
and here I will destroy them from the earth.

NOAH IS INSTRUCTED TO MAKE AN ARK . . . (6:14–16)

"Make yourself an ark of gopher wood . . .
and coat it from within and from without with pitch.
And thus you shall make it:
three hundred cubits—the length of the ark
fifty cubits its width
and thirty cubits its height . . .
bottom, second, and third levels you shall make it.

. . . IN WHICH TO SURVIVE THE FLOOD (6:17–22)

"And I, here I will bring the flood of water
upon the earth . . .
all that is on the earth shall expire.
I will establish My covenant with you;
and you will come into the ark
you, and your sons
and your wife, and your sons' wives with you.
And from all that lives . . . two of each
bring into the ark to keep alive with you;
male and female they should be. . . ."
And Noah did as all that G-d commanded him. . . .

THE FLOOD BEGINS (7:11–12)

In the six hundredth year of Noah's life
in the second month
on the seventeenth day of the month . . .
all the wellsprings of the great deep split open
and the hatches of the heavens were opened.
And the rain was upon the earth
forty days and forty nights. . . .

THE ARK IS RAISED ABOVE THE WATERS (7:17–24)

The waters increased
and they lifted the ark
and it rose above the earth . . .
and the ark moved upon the surface of the waters. . . .
And the waters surged upon the earth
one hundred and fifty days.

A DIVINE WIND CALMS THE FLOOD (8:1–5)

And G-d remembered Noah
and all the animals . . . that were with him in the ark;
and G-d made a wind pass over the earth
and the waters subsided. . . .
In the seventh month
on the seventeenth day of the month
the ark rested upon the mountains of Ararat.

The waters went on diminishing. . . .
In the tenth month, on the first of the month
the tops of the mountains were seen. . . .

G-D COMMANDS NOAH TO EXIT THE ARK (8:13–17)

And it was in the six hundred and first year . . .
in the second month
on the twenty-seventh day of the month;
the earth was fully dried.
And G-d spoke to Noah, to say:
“Go out from the ark;
You, and your wife, and your sons, and your sons’ wives with you.
All the animals that are with you . . .
take them out with you. . . .”

Duif Keert Terug met Olijftak (Dove Returns with Olive Branch), Bernard Picart, etching and engraving—book illustration, Amsterdam, c. 1683–1733. (Rijksmuseum, Amsterdam)

TEXT 1b

GENESIS 8:20–9:17

G-D VOWS TO NEVER AGAIN BRING A FLOOD (8:20–21)

1 Noah built an altar to G-d . . .
2 and he brought up ascent-offerings on the altar.
3 G-d smelled the soothing aroma
4 and G-d said to His heart:
5 "Nevermore shall I again curse the soil on account of man
6 for the impulse of the heart of man is evil from his youth;
7 and nevermore shall I again smite all living things, as I have done. . . ."

G-D BLESSES NOAH'S FAMILY TO BE FRUITFUL (9:1–2)

8 G-d blessed Noah and his children;
9 and He said to them:
10 "Be fruitful and multiply and fill the earth.
11 And the awe and dread of you will be
12 upon all animals of the earth . . .
13 in your hands they are given. . . ."

THE COVENANT OF THE RAINBOW (9:8–17)

14 G-d said to Noah and to his children with him, to say:
15 "And I, here I am establishing My covenant with you;
16 and with your seed after you.
17 And with all living souls that are with you. . . .

My bow, I have set in the cloud;
and it shall be as a sign of a covenant between Me and the world.
And it will be, when I darken clouds upon the earth;
and the bow will appear in the cloud.
And I will remember My covenant
which is between Me and you and all living souls . . .
that the waters will not again become a flood to destroy all flesh. . . .
This is the sign of the covenant that I have established
between Me and all flesh that is upon the earth."

Noah's Sacrifice (detail), James Jacques Joseph Tissot, gouache on board, c. 1896–1902. (The Jewish Museum, New York)

Figure 2.1

The Nature of Man

GENESIS 6:5–7	GENESIS 8:21
G-d saw that . . . every impulse of the thoughts of [man's] heart is only evil, all day . . . and He was pained to His heart. And G-d said: "I will erase the human being that I have created from upon the face of the earth, from man to beast, to crawling-thing, to bird of the heavens; for I have regretted that I made them."	G-d said to His heart: "Nevermore shall I again curse the soil on account of man, for the impulse of the heart of man is evil from his youth; and nevermore shall I again smite all living things, as I have done."

TEXT 2

RABBI MEIR SIMCHAH OF DVINSK, *MESHECH CHOCHMAH*, GENESIS 8:19

הַמַּבּוּל הָיָה שׁוֹהֶה שְׁנֵים עָשָׂר חוֹדֶשׁ . . . אַף שֶׁכָּל עִנְיַן הַמַּבּוּל הָיָה
שֶׁלֹּא עַל דֶּרֶךְ הַסִּדּוּר הַטִּבְעִי, וְקִיּוּם נֹחַ וְהַבַּעֲלֵי חַיִּים הָיוּ בְּעִנְיַן הַשְׁגָּחָה
מְיוּחֶדֶת . . . וְאִם כֵּן הָיָה בִּיכוֹלֶת הַהַשְׁגָּחָה לִמְחוֹת כָּל הַיְקוּם כְּרֶגַע!

The Flood lasted a full twelve months. . . . This, despite the fact that the entire Flood was a supernatural event, and the survival of Noah and the animals in the Ark required special divine intervention. . . . Being that this was the case, why couldn't G-d simply destroy all creations in a single instant?

RABBI MEIR SIMCHAH HAKOHEN OF DVINSK
1843–1926

Served as rabbi of Dvinsk for nearly 40 years. He is renowned for 2 works: *Or Same'ach*, a commentary on Maimonides's *Mishneh Torah*, and *Meshech Chochmah*, a profound commentary on the Bible. In the latter work, Rabbi Meir Simchah demonstrates the unity between the Written and Oral Laws and presents original interpretations of biblical and Talmudic passages. In 1906, he was offered the position of rabbi of Jerusalem but bowed to the entreaties of the city folk to remain in Dvinsk.

How to Destroy?
A lesson from the Flood
Mrs. Sharon Freundel:

MYJLI.COM/BIBLE

TEXT 3

GENESIS 1:2–9

וְהָאָרֶץ הָיְתָה תֹהוּ וָבֹהוּ וְחֹשֶׁךְ עַל פְּנֵי תְהוֹם וְרוּחַ אֱלֹקִים מְרַחֶפֶת עַל פְּנֵי הַמָּיִם . . .

וַיַּעַשׂ אֱלֹקִים אֶת הָרָקִיעַ וַיַּבְדֵּל בֵּין הַמַּיִם אֲשֶׁר מִתַּחַת לָרָקִיעַ וּבֵין הַמַּיִם אֲשֶׁר מֵעַל לָרָקִיעַ וַיְהִי כֵן . . .

וַיֹּאמֶר אֱלֹקִים יִקָּווּ הַמַּיִם מִתַּחַת הַשָּׁמַיִם אֶל מָקוֹם אֶחָד וְתֵרָאֶה הַיַּבָּשָׁה וַיְהִי כֵן.

The earth was desolate and void, and darkness was on the face of the watery-depths; and a wind of G-d hovered upon the surface of the waters. . . .

G-d made the firmament; and He separated between the waters that are below the firmament and the waters that are above the firmament. . . .

And G-d said: "The waters below the heavens shall pool to one place, and the dry-land shall be seen"; and it was so.

Figure 2.2

Mankind's "Mission Statement"

G-D'S FIRST WORDS TO ADAM AND EVE (GENESIS 1:28)	**G-D'S FIRST WORDS TO NOAH AND HIS FAMILY** (GENESIS 9:1–2)
G-d blessed them, and G-d said to them:	G-d blessed Noah and his children, and He said to them:
"Be fruitful and multiply and fill the earth and conquer it.	"Be fruitful and multiply and fill the earth.
"Dominate the fish of the sea and the bird of the heavens and every animal that crawls upon the earth."	"The awe and dread of you will be upon all animals of the earth and upon all birds of the heavens, in all that crawls upon the ground, and in all the fishes of the sea—in your hands they are given."

TEXT 4

RABBI SHMUEL SCHNEERSOHN, *VEKACHA* 5637, SECTION 95

הִנֵּה בְּתֵיבַת נֹחַ הָיָה דוּגְמַת וּמֵעֵין לֶעָתִיד לָבוֹא. שֶׁהֲרֵי בְּתֵיבַת נֹחַ הָיָה כָּל הַחַיּוֹת וְכָל הַבְּהֵמוֹת יַחְדָּיו, וְעִם כָּל זֶה לֹא עָשׂוּ רָעָה זֶה לָזֶה כְּלָל וְלֹא הִשְׁחִיתוּ זֶה לָזֶה. שֶׁנִּמְצָא גַם עַכְשָׁיו "גָר זְאֵב עִם כֶּבֶשׂ . . . וְעֵגֶל וּכְפִיר . . . יַחְדָּיו" . . . הֲרֵי זֶה מֵעֵין לֶעָתִיד לָבוֹא שֶׁ"לֹא יָרֵעוּ וְלֹא יַשְׁחִיתוּ בְּכָל הַר קָדְשִׁי."

Noah's Ark was a prototype of the future era [of Mashiach]. Within the Ark, every type of animal lived together, yet they did not harm each other in any way. This presaged a reality in which "the wolf will dwell with the lamb, and a calf and a lion together" (ISAIAH 11:6). . . . This being a similitude of the future world when "they shall neither harm nor destroy in all of My holy mountain" (IBID., VERSE 9).

RABBI SHMUEL SCHNEERSOHN (REBBE MAHARASH) 1834–1882

Known by the acronym "Maharash"; fourth Chabad rebbe and leader of Russian Jewry. Born in Lubavitch, Russia, he was the youngest son of Rabbi Menachem Mendel of Lubavitch (the *Tsemach Tsedek*). Much of his leadership was devoted to combating anti-Jewish policies. His discourses have been collected and published as *Likutei Torah: Torat Shmuel.*

Figure 2.3

Parallels between the Creation and Ark Stories

	CREATION STORY	ARK STORY
1	World emerges from water	New world emerges from water
2	Created by ten divine "utterances"	Regenerated from a *tevah* ("word")
3	Blessing/command to Adam and Eve: "Be fruitful and multiply and fill the earth."	Blessing/command to Noah and his children: "Be fruitful and multiply and fill the earth."
4	Adam and Eve are placed in a utopia (the Garden of Eden) and then banished from it.	Noah and family are placed in a utopia (the Ark) and then commanded to leave it.
5	Humanity begins with Adam and Eve and their three children—Cain, Abel, and Seth.	Humanity regenerated from Noah and his wife (Naamah) and their three children—Shem, Ham, and Japheth

TEXT 5

GENESIS 9:18–19

וַיִּהְיוּ בְנֵי נֹחַ הַיֹּצְאִים מִן הַתֵּבָה, שֵׁם וְחָם וָיָפֶת . . . וּמֵאֵלֶּה נָפְצָה כָל הָאָרֶץ.

And these were the children of Noah, those going out from the ark: Shem, and Ham, and Japheth . . . and from these dispersed the whole world.

The Manner How the Whole Earth Was Peopled by Noah and His Descendants after the Flood, illustration for the *Universal Magazine*, 1749. (The British Museum, London)

Figure 2.4

Differences between the Two Worlds

	FIRST CREATION	POST-FLOOD WORLD
Utopian Model	Planted by G-d	Humanly constructed
Originality	Created after the waters receded	Regenerated from specimens of the pre-Flood world
Ancestry	Homogenous	Pluralistic

TEXT 6

THE REBBE, RABBI MENACHEM MENDEL SCHNEERSON,
LIKUTEI SICHOT 15 (HEBREW VERSION), P. 92

נִיתַּן לְהָבִין טוֹב יוֹתֵר בְּאֶמְצָעוּת הַמָּשָׁל אוֹדוֹת הַהַשְׁפָּעָה הַשִּׂכְלִית שֶׁל הָרַב לְתַלְמִידוֹ . . .

דֶּרֶךְ אַחַת הִיא, שֶׁהָרַב מַסְבִּיר לְתַלְמִידוֹ רַק אֶת הָרַעְיוֹן שֶׁהוּא מְלַמְּדוֹ, אַךְ אֵין הוּא מַדְרִיכוֹ כֵּיצַד לְהָבִין דְּבָרִים בְּכוֹחוֹת עַצְמוֹ. הַדֶּרֶךְ הַשְּׁנִיָּה הִיא: הָרַב מַקְנֶה לְתַלְמִיד כֵּלִים אֲשֶׁר בָּהֶם יוּכַל לִלְמוֹד וּלְהָבִין בְּכוֹחוֹת עַצְמוֹ.

מוּבָן, שֶׁבְּכָל אַחַת מִשְּׁתֵּי הַדְּרָכִים הַלָּלוּ יֵשׁ יִתְרוֹן אֲשֶׁר אֵינֶנּוּ בָּאַחֶרֶת. מִבְּחִינַת כּוֹשְׁרוֹ שֶׁל הַתַּלְמִיד, טוֹבָה יוֹתֵר הַדֶּרֶךְ הַשְּׁנִיָּה, כִּי רַק הִיא מְבִיאָה אוֹתוֹ לִיכוֹלֶת לִלְמוֹד וּלְהָבִין בְּכוֹחוֹת עַצְמוֹ. אַךְ לְגַבֵּי עֶצֶם הַקְנָיַת הָרַעְיוֹן, טוֹבָה יוֹתֵר הַדֶּרֶךְ הָרִאשׁוֹנָה, כִּי הֲבָנַת הַתַּלְמִיד בְּכוֹחַ עַצְמוֹ . . . הִיא פְּחוּתָה יַחֲסִית לְתוֹכֶן שֶׁהָרַב מְלַמְּדוֹ.

We can better understand [the difference] by using the example of a teacher imparting ideas to a student. . . .

One approach is that the teacher explains the idea to the student, but does not train the student to understand it on their own. The second approach is that the teacher provides the student with the tools by means of which the student can study and understand the idea on their own.

Each of these two approaches has an advantage over the other. In regard to the personal development of the student, the second approach is better, as only this approach imparts the ability to independently

RABBI MENACHEM MENDEL SCHNEERSON 1902–1994

The towering Jewish leader of the 20th century, known as "the Lubavitcher Rebbe," or simply as "the Rebbe." Born in southern Ukraine, the Rebbe escaped Nazi-occupied Europe, arriving in the U.S. in June 1941. The Rebbe inspired and guided the revival of traditional Judaism after the European devastation, impacting virtually every Jewish community the world over. The Rebbe often emphasized that the performance of just one additional good deed could usher in the era of Mashiach. The Rebbe's scholarly talks and writings have been printed in more than 200 volumes.

Water, Water Everywhere
A mystical perspective on the Flood
Rabbi Moishe New:

MYJLI.COM/BIBLE

learn and understand. But in regard to the quality of the reception of the idea itself, the first approach is better, because the way that the student understands the idea on their own . . . is inferior to how the teacher teaches it.

The Talmudists, Max Weber, oil on canvas, 1934. (The Jewish Museum, New York) © Estate of Max Weber

TEXT 7

THE REBBE, RABBI MENACHEM MENDEL SCHNEERSON,
LIKUTEI SICHOT 15 (HEBREW VERSION), P. 58

שֶׁהָעוּבְדָה שֶׁ"עוֹלָם עַל מִילוּאוֹ נִבְרָא" נָבְעָה מֵעֶצֶם אוֹפֶן בְּרִיאָתוֹ עַל יְדֵי הַבּוֹרֵא, וְלֹא מֵעַצְמוֹ. לָכֵן . . . כַּאֲשֶׁר בְּחַטָאֵי דוֹר הַמַּבּוּל נִתְקַלְקֵל הָעוֹלָם כָּל כַּךְ עַד אֲשֶׁר "וַתִּמָּלֵא הָאָרֶץ חָמָס" . . . אָז לֹא הָיָה טַעַם לְקִיּוּמוֹ . . . (כִּי עַל יְדֵי יְרִידַת הָעוֹלָם וְהִתְרַחֲקוּתוֹ מֵהַקָּדוֹשׁ בָּרוּךְ הוּא, נִסְתַּלֵּק מִמֶּנּוּ רְצוֹן הַבּוֹרֵא).

לְעוּמַת זֹאת, לְאַחַר הַמַּבּוּל נוֹצְרָה בָּעוֹלָם אֶפְשָׁרוּת שֶׁל זִיכּוּךְ וְהִתְעַלּוּת הָעוֹלָם מִצַּד עַצְמוֹ. וְגַם כַּאֲשֶׁר הוּא שָׁרוּי בְּמַצָּב יָרוּד בְּיוֹתֵר הוּא יָכוֹל לְהִתְעַלּוֹת (עַל יְדֵי עֲבוֹדַת הַתְּשׁוּבָה). וּלְפִיכָךְ נִכְרְתָה אָז הַבְּרִית שֶׁל "וְלֹא יִכָּרֵת כָּל בָּשָׂר . . . וְלֹא יִהְיֶה עוֹד מַבּוּל" בְּכָל מַצָּב שֶׁבּוֹ הָעוֹלָם שָׁרוּי.

The goodness that the world possessed [before the Flood] derived not from its own nature, but from the fact that it was so created by G-d. Therefore, . . . when the sins of the generation of the Flood corrupted the world to such an extent that "the earth was filled with violence," . . . there was no longer any purpose to its existence. . . . The world had fallen so low, and had so far distanced itself from its Creator, that the divine desire for a world was withdrawn.

On the other hand, after the Flood, the world possessed the ability to elevate and refine itself on its own. Therefore, even when it falls to a very lowly state, it can repent and lift itself up. This is why G-d made a covenant that "never shall all flesh be cut off . . . and never again will there be a flood," regardless of the world's moral state.

Figure 2.5

The Refraction of a Ray of Light

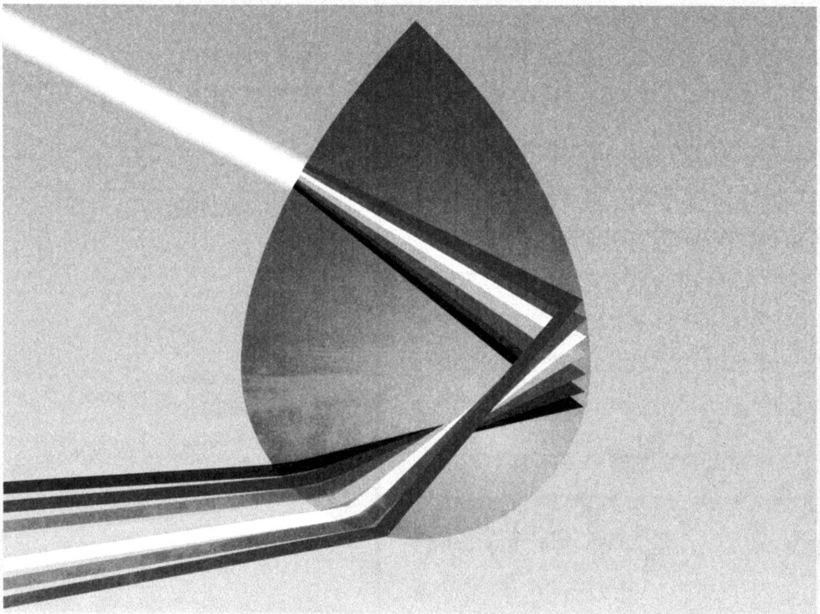

TEXT 8

THE REBBE, RABBI MENACHEM MENDEL SCHNEERSON,
LIKUTEI SICHOT 15 (HEBREW VERSION), PP. 56–57

עַל הַפָּסוּק, "אֶת קַשְׁתִּי נָתַתִּי בֶּעָנָן וְהָיְתָה לְאוֹת בְּרִית בֵּינִי וּבֵין הָאָרֶץ", שׁוֹאֲלִים הַמְפָרְשִׁים: הַקֶּשֶׁת הִיא תּוֹפָעָה טִבְעִית, הִיא נוֹצֶרֶת כַּאֲשֶׁר קַרְנֵי הַשֶּׁמֶשׁ מִשְׁתַּקְּפוֹת בְּאוֹפֶן מְסוּיָּם מִן הָעֲנָנִים. וְאִם כַּךְ, כֵּיצַד הִיא יְכוֹלָה לַהֲווֹת אוֹת בְּרִית?

וְהֵם עוֹנִים: תּוֹפָעָה טִבְעִית זוֹ, הִמָּצְאוּת קַרְנֵי הַשֶּׁמֶשׁ וְהָעֲנָנִים בְּמַצָּב מְסוּיָּם שֶׁבּוֹ הַקְּרָנַיִם נִרְאוֹת כְּקֶשֶׁת, בָּרָא הַקָּדוֹשׁ בָּרוּךְ הוּא לְאַחַר הַמַּבּוּל. לִפְנֵי הַמַּבּוּל הָיָה הָעוֹלָם גַּשְׁמִי יוֹתֵר, וְגַם הָעֲנָנִים (הַנּוֹצָרִים מִ"אֵד יַעֲלֶה מִן הָאָרֶץ") הָיוּ חוּמְרִיִּים יוֹתֵר וְלֹא יָכְלוּ לְקַבֵּל וּלְהַקְרִין אֶת אוֹר הַשֶּׁמֶשׁ, וְלָכֵן לֹא הָיְתָה מְצִיאוּת שֶׁל קֶשֶׁת. רַק לְאַחַר שֶׁהָעוֹלָם נִזְדַּכֵּךְ יוֹתֵר, נַעֲשׂוּ גַּם הָעֲנָנִים זַכִּים וַ"עֲדִינִים" יוֹתֵר, פָּחוֹת עָבִים וְגַסִּים, עַד כְּדֵי כַּךְ שֶׁהֵם יְכוֹלִים לְשַׁקֵּף וּלְהַקְרִין אֶת הַגְּוָנִים שֶׁל אוֹר הַשֶּׁמֶשׁ . . .

לְפִיכָךְ הַקֶּשֶׁת הִיא "אוֹת בְּרִית בֵּינִי וּבֵין הָאָרֶץ", כִּי בְּאֶמְצָעוּתָהּ מִתְבַּטְּאִים הַטָּהֳרָה וְהַזִּיכּוּךְ שֶׁנִּתְהַוּוּ בָּאָרֶץ . . . בִּתְחִלַּת הַבְּרִיאָה לֹא הָיְתָה שְׁלֵימוּת הָעוֹלָם בִּתְכוּנוֹתָיו וּמְצִיאוּתוֹ שֶׁל הָעוֹלָם עַצְמוֹ, אֶלָּא בְּאוֹפֶן בְּרִיאָתוֹ עַל יְדֵי הַקָּדוֹשׁ בָּרוּךְ הוּא . . . אַךְ יְכוֹלְתּוֹ שֶׁל הָעוֹלָם לְהַגִּיעַ מֵעַצְמוֹ לְזִיכּוּךְ נוֹצְרָה רַק בְּאֶמְצָעוּת הַמַּבּוּל: הַקָּדוֹשׁ בָּרוּךְ הוּא טָבַע תְּכוּנָה חֲדָשָׁה בָּעוֹלָם, שֶׁיְּהֵא בִּיכָלְתּוֹ לְהִזְדַּכֵּךְ וּלְהִתְעַלּוֹת מֵעַצְמוֹ.

וְזוֹהִי הַסִּיבָּה לְכַךְ שֶׁדַּוְקָא אָז נִתְהַוְּתָה מְצִיאוּת הַקֶּשֶׁת. אָמְנָם הַקֶּשֶׁת נוֹצֶרֶת מִקַּרְנֵי הַשֶּׁמֶשׁ וּמִן הָעֲנָנִים בְּיַחַד . . . אַךְ . . . קַרְנֵי הַשֶּׁמֶשׁ, בִּבְחִינַת "שֶׁמֶשׁ הֲוָיֶ'", שֶׁכְּשֶׁלְעַצְמָן הֵן פְּשׁוּטוֹת בְּצִבְעָן - שֶׁהֲרֵי צִבְעֵי הַקֶּשֶׁת נוֹצָרִים דַּוְקָא בְּאֶמְצָעוּת הָעֲנָנִים הַמִּתְהַוִּים מִן הָאֵדִים שֶׁעוֹלִים מִן הָאָרֶץ, וְהָאֵדִים הָעוֹלִים מִן הָאָרֶץ מְזוּכָּכִים עַד כְּדֵי הִשְׁתַּקְּפוּת אוֹר הַשֶּׁמֶשׁ בְּאֶמְצָעוּתָם. וְכֵיוָן שֶׁהַיְכוֹלֶת לְזִיכּוּךְ הָאָרֶץ מֵעַצְמָהּ נִתְחַדְּשָׁה לְאַחַר הַמַּבּוּל, לָכֵן הָיָה דַּוְקָא אָז הָעִנְיָן שֶׁל "אֶת קַשְׁתִּי נָתַתִּי בֶּעָנָן".

Hi-Tech Rainbow—
A KabbalaToon
***Tzvi Freeman** and*
***Pilar Newton**:*

MYJLI.COM/BIBLE

The Torah states: “My bow, I have set in the cloud; and it shall be as a sign of a covenant between Me and the world” (GENESIS 9:13). The commentaries ask: The rainbow is a natural phenomenon, formed when the rays of sunlight are reflected in a certain way through the mist. So how does it serve as a "sign of the covenant"?

The answer given is that this natural phenomenon itself—the fact that, under certain conditions, sunlight and clouds produce a rainbow—was created by G-d after the Flood. Before the Flood, the world was more materialistic. So also the clouds—which form when "a mist rises up from the earth" (GENESIS 2:6)—were coarser, and did not possess the ability to receive and reflect the rays of the sun. Therefore, there were no rainbows. But when the world became more refined, the clouds, too, became more refined and translucent, and they now possessed this ability to reflect and radiate the array of colors contained within the light of the sun. . . .

Therefore, the rainbow serves as "a sign of the covenant between Me and the world," as it expresses the purity and refinement that the world has attained. . . . Originally, the world's greatness was not an inherent quality that it possessed, only the product of the manner in which it was created by G-d. . . . It was only as a result of the Flood that G-d imbued a new quality into the world: the ability to elevate and refine itself on its own.

This is why the phenomenon of the rainbow came to exist only after the Flood. A rainbow is formed by the convergence of sunlight and clouds. . . . But the rays of the sun themselves, representing the divine radiance bestowed from Above, are of an abstract color. The colors of the rainbow are extracted by means of the clouds formed by the mist rising from the earth, and only when this rising mist is sufficiently refined and transparent to reflect the light of the sun. Since the world's ability for self-refinement came to be only after the Flood, it was only then that "the rainbow was set in the cloud."

Rainy Season in the Tropics, Frederic Edwin Church, oil on canvas, 1866. (M. H. de Young Museum, S. Francisco)

TEXT 9

THE REBBE, RABBI MENACHEM MENDEL SCHNEERSON,
LIKUTEI SICHOT 15 (HEBREW VERSION), P. 56

הָעוֹלָם נִבְרָא בִּשְׁבִיל הַתּוֹרָה . . . וְכַוָּונַת מַתַּן תּוֹרָה הִיא אִיחוּד בֵּין "עֶלְיוֹנִים" לְ"תַחְתּוֹנִים." לְפִיכָךְ הָיוּ צְרִיכִים לִהְיוֹת בָּעוֹלָם "עֶלְיוֹנִים" וְ"תַחְתּוֹנִים", כְּדֵי שֶׁאַחַר כָּךְ . . . יִיוָּוצֵר הָאִיחוּד שֶׁל שְׁתֵּי דַרְגוֹת אֵלּוּ . . .

וּבִשְׁתֵּי דַרְגוֹת אֵלּוּ בָּעוֹלָם חָל שִׁינּוּי בִּזְמַן הַמַּבּוּל: לִפְנֵי הַמַּבּוּל הָיָה הָעוֹלָם בִּכְלָלוּת קַיָּים בְּמַצָּב כְּפִי שֶׁהוּא מִצַּד "לְמַעֲלָה", וּלְאַחֲרָיו מִצַּד "לְמַטָּה".

The world was created for the sake of the Torah . . . and the goal of the giving of the Torah was to achieve a union of the "higher realms" and the "lower realms." Therefore, the world needed to incorporate both states—a "top-down" mode of existence, and a "bottom-up" mode—so that, subsequently, the two could be unified. . . .

This was the change achieved by the Flood. Before the Flood, the nature of the world was, generally speaking, a "top-down" existence; whereas after the Flood, it was defined by a "bottom-up" existence.

QUESTION FOR DISCUSSION

What are the pros and cons of each of these types of relationships?

Figure 2.6

Two Types of Relationships

TOP-DOWN	BOTTOM-UP
TEACHER / STUDENT	
Teacher lectures; student listens	Teacher trains student in learning skills and tools
Pros: Cons:	Pros: Cons:
EMPLOYER / EMPLOYEE	
Employer gives instructions, which the employee follows	Employer outlines the goals of the business; employee develops strategies on how to realize them
Pros: Cons:	Pros: Cons:
PHILANTHROPIST / BENEFICIARY	
Philanthropist contributes money to feed and clothe the needy	Philanthropist funds educational and employment opportunities for the needy to lift themselves out of poverty
Pros: Cons:	Pros: Cons:

TOP-DOWN	BOTTOM-UP
PARENT/CHILD	
Parent provides child with all their needs	Parent offers guidance and support, but encourages child to build their own life based on the child's abilities and aspirations
Pros:	Pros:
Cons:	Cons:
G-D/US	
G-d commands; we obey.	We use our own understanding and creativity to understand the meaning of the *mitzvot* and their relevance to our lives.
Pros:	Pros:
Cons:	Cons:

KEY POINTS

1 The story of Noah's Ark raises a number of compelling questions. If the principle of Free Choice dictated that the world could become so corrupted that the very basis of its existence was destroyed, why can't it happen again? Why a year-long Flood and an Ark that Noah labored for decades to build? Couldn't G-d have destroyed the world in an instant, and then created a new one? How does the rainbow symbolize the "new world order" generated from the Ark? If the first version of Creation was vulnerable to such catastrophic failure, why didn't the Creator go straight to Plan B?

2 The various relationships that comprise our lives come in two forms: (a) A "top-down" model, in which one party gives and the other receives. (b) A "bottom-up" model, in which the recipient is equipped with the tools to initiate the relationship on their own. Each of these two models has advantages over the other.

3 Before the Flood, the relationship between the Creator and His creation was defined by the "top-down" model. When the world ceased to become worthy of the divine gift of life, the entire basis for the relationship was undermined. After the Flood, G-d established the relationship on the "bottom-up" model. The world now inherently possesses the ability to elevate itself and interact with the Divine. So the possibility for a renewed relationship always remains.

4 A rainbow is formed when water vapor, rising from the earth, interacts with sunlight, streaming down from above, to extract from the light previously unrevealed colors and beauty. Thus, the rainbow symbolizes the new "bottom-up" model for the relationship between Creator and creation.

5 The post-Flood world was not a new creation. Rather, it was generated from the remnants of the pre-Flood world preserved in the Ark. As a result, our own existence incorporates both models, empowering us to draw on the advantages of both worlds.

6 The story of Noah's Ark teaches us to strive for the "best of both worlds" in our relationships with each other and with our Creator. On the one hand, we need to learn to be receptive to what is granted to us. On the other hand, we need to draw on our own resources to initiate new and innovative interactions with the divine gifts of life.

Appendix

Figure 2.7

Time Line of the Flood

Date	Day	Event
CHESHVAN 10	7 days before the Flood	G-d commands Noah to enter the Ark.
CHESHVAN 17 7 days later	Day 1 of the Flood	Rains begin to fall.
KISLEV 28 40 days later	Day 40 of the Flood	Rains stop, but the floodwaters continue to surge and churn.
SIVAN 1 150 days later	Day 190 of the Flood	Waters calm and begin to recede.
SIVAN 17 16 days later	Day 206 of the Flood	The Ark, still partly submerged in water, settles on the top of Mount Ararat; waters continue to recede.
AV 1 44 days later	Day 250 of the Flood	Waters have now receded to the point that the mountain peaks become visible.
ELUL 10 40 days later	Day 289 of the Flood	Noah dispatches a raven to test the state of the world outside the Ark, but the raven refuses the mission.
ELUL 17 7 days later	Day 296 of the Flood	Noah dispatches a dove, who immediately returns because there is no habitable land.
ELUL 23 7 days later	Day 302 of the Flood	The dove's second mission, from which it returns clutching an olive leaf in its beak.
TISHREI 1* 7 days later	Day 309 of the Flood	The dove's third mission, which confirms that it has found habitable land. Noah removes the cover of the Ark and discovers that the floodwaters have fully receded.
CHESHVAN 27 57 days later	Day 365 of the Flood	Land is fully dry. G-d commands Noah to leave the Ark and resettle the earth.

*Note that this day is Rosh Hashanah, the date of Adam and Eve's creation.

QUESTION FOR DISCUSSION

Has anyone experienced a flood lately? Other than a literal flood in which your basement is knee-deep in water, what would you consider a "flood" in your personal life?

TEXT 10

RABBI SHNE'UR ZALMAN OF LIADI, *TORAH OR*, NOACH 8C

"מַיִם רַבִּים לֹא יוּכְלוּ לְכַבּוֹת אֶת הָאַהֲבָה וּנְהָרוֹת לֹא יִשְׁטְפוּהָ . . ." הִנֵּה "מַיִם רַבִּים" הֵם כָּל טִרְדוֹת הַפַּרְנָסָה וְהַמַּחֲשָׁבוֹת שֶׁבְּעִנְיָנֵי עוֹלָם הַזֶּה כו'. וְעִם כָּל זֶה לֹא יוּכְלוּ לְכַבּוֹת אֶת הָאַהֲבָה שֶׁהוּא בְּחִינַת הָאַהֲבָה הַמּוּסְתֶּרֶת שֶׁיֵּשׁ בְּכָל נֶפֶשׁ מִיִּשְׂרָאֵל בְּטֶבַע . . .

שֶׁקּוֹדֶם הִתְלַבְּשׁוּתָהּ בְּגוּף הַגַּשְׁמִי הָיְתָה נֶהֱנֵית מִזִּיו הַשְּׁכִינָה, וְהָיְתָה מְיוּחֶדֶת בְּתַכְלִית הַיִּחוּד בְּאֵין סוֹף בָּרוּךְ הוּא. וּלְזֹאת, גַּם אַחַר הִתְלַבְּשׁוּתָהּ בְּגוּף הַגַּשְׁמִי לַעֲסוֹק בְּעִנְיָנִים גַּשְׁמִיִּים, שֶׁהֵן הַנִּקְרָאִים "מַיִם רַבִּים", עִם כָּל זֶה לֹא יוּכְלוּ לְכַבּוֹתָהּ מִלִּהְיוֹת תָּמִיד בִּבְחִינַת אַהֲבָה וּתְשׁוּקָה נִפְלָאָה לַעֲלוֹת וְלִיכָּלֵל לְמַעֲלָה. וְאַדְרַבָּה עַל יְדֵי הִתְלַבְּשׁוּתָהּ בְּמַיִם רַבִּים הַנִּזְכָּר לְעֵיל יְכוֹלָה לְהַגִּיעַ לְמַדְרֵגָה הַיּוֹתֵר גָּבוֹהַּ מִקּוֹדֶם שֶׁיָּרְדָה לָעוֹלָם הַזֶּה, כַּאֲשֶׁר יִתְבָּאֵר.

"Great waters cannot extinguish the love, nor can rivers wash it away. . ." (SONG OF SONGS 8:7). The "great waters" are all the worries in earning a living, all the preoccupations in worldly matters, and so on. Nevertheless, they "cannot extinguish the love"—the

RABBI SHNE'UR ZALMAN OF LIADI (ALTER REBBE) 1745–1812

Chasidic rebbe, halachic authority, and founder of the Chabad movement. The Alter Rebbe was born in Liozna, Belarus, and was among the principal students of the Magid of Mezeritch. His numerous works include the *Tanya*, an early classic containing the fundamentals of Chabad Chasidism; and *Shulchan Aruch HaRav*, an expanded and reworked code of Jewish law.

hidden love that exists within every Jewish soul by its very nature. . . .

Before the soul was placed within the body, it enjoyed the radiance of the Divine Presence and was utterly unified with the infinite light of G-d. Therefore, even after it became invested in a material body and became preoccupied in material affairs—which are called "great waters"—these do not have the power to extinguish the soul's constant and wonderous love and desire to ascend and be subsumed within [its source] above. Even more so: The soul's involvement in these "great waters" actually raise it to a higher level than it was before it came down into this world, as will be explained.

Dealing with the Flood of Life
A 5-minute insight
Chana Weisberg:

MYJLI.COM/BIBLE

TEXT 11

RABBI YISRAEL BAAL SHEM TOV, *KETER SHEM TOV*, ADDENDUM 9

אָמַר מוֹרֵנוּ הַבַּעַל שֵׁם טוֹב . . . דְ"תֵּיבָה" הֵם אוֹתִיּוֹת הַתּוֹרָה וְהַתְּפִלָּה.
וּ"בֹּא אֶל הַתֵּיבָה" הוּא הַכְּנִיסָה בְּתוֹךְ הָאוֹתִיּוֹת שֶׁל תּוֹרָה וּתְפִלָּה–לֶערְנֶען
מִיט אַ חַיּוּת אוּן דַאוְונֶען מִיט אַ חַיּוּת.

Our master the Baal Shem Tov taught . . . that *teivah* ("Ark") is the letters of the Torah and prayer. "Come into the *teivah*" means: Enter into the letters of Torah learning and prayer—that one's learning should be full of life, and one's praying should be full of life.

RABBI YISRAEL BAAL SHEM TOV (BESHT) 1698–1760

Founder of the Chasidic movement. Born in Slutsk, Belarus, the Baal Shem Tov was orphaned as a child. He served as a teacher's assistant and clay digger before founding the Chasidic movement and revolutionizing the Jewish world with his emphasis on prayer, joy, and love for every Jew, regardless of his or her level of Torah knowledge.

Noah's Ark, Edward Hicks, oil on canvas, 1846. (Philadelphia Museum of Art)

TEXT 12

RABBI SHNE'UR ZALMAN OF LIADI, *TORAH OR*, NOACH 9A

וְזֶהוּ "וַתֵּלֶךְ הַתֵּיבָה עַל פְּנֵי הַמָּיִם"... "וַתָּרָם הַתֵּיבָה כו'" שֶׁעַל יְדֵי הַמַּיִם דַּוְוקָא מִתְעַלּוֹת תֵּיבוֹת הַתְּפִלָּה וְעוֹלֶה לְמַעְלָה מַעְלָה כְּנִזְכָּר לְעֵיל.

וְזֶהוּ טָעוּת הַבַּעֲלֵי עֲסָקִים שֶׁבְּדַעְתָּם שֶׁאֵין יְכוֹלִים לְהִתְפַּלֵּל כָּל כַּךְ כְּמוֹ הַיּוֹשְׁבֵי אוֹהָלִים. כִּי אַדְרַבָּה נַהֲפוֹךְ הוּא: שֶׁהֵם יְכוֹלִים לְהִתְפַּלֵּל יוֹתֵר, כִּי יִתְרוֹן הָאוֹר הוּא מִתּוֹךְ הַחֹשֶׁךְ דַּוְוקָא כו'.

This is the meaning of the verse, "The Ark moved upon the surface of the waters" (GENESIS 7:18) . . . "[the waters increased, and they lifted the Ark,] and it rose above the earth" (IBID., VERSE 17). It is specifically the waters [of the Flood] that lift up the words of prayer and elevate them higher.

This is a common mistake made by business people: They think that their prayers are inferior to those of the "tent dwellers" [i.e., people who are engaged all day in Torah learning and spiritual pursuits]. In truth, the very opposite is the case: Their prayer is of a higher quality, as in the superiority of light that specifically emerges out of the darkness.

TEXT 13

MIDRASH, *TANCHUMA*, NOACH 8

כֵּיוָן שֶׁנָּחוּ הַמַּיִם הָיָה צָרִיךְ נֹחַ לָצֵאת מִן הַתֵּיבָה. אֶלָּא אָמַר: בִּרְשׁוּת הַקָּדוֹשׁ בָּרוּךְ הוּא נִכְנַסְתִּי, שֶׁאָמַר לִי "בֹּא אַתָּה וְכָל בֵּיתְךָ אֶל הַתֵּיבָה"; וְעַכְשָׁיו אֵינִי יוֹצֵא אֶלָּא בִּרְשׁוּתוֹ.

Why didn't Noah leave the ark as soon as the waters subsided? Because, he said: "It was on G-d's authority that I entered into the ark, when He said to me, 'Come in, you and all your household, into the ark' (GENESIS 7:1); now, too, I shall not go out without G-d's authorization."

TANCHUMA

A Midrashic work bearing the name of Rabbi Tanchuma, a 4th-century Talmudic sage quoted often in this work. "Midrash" is the designation of a particular genre of rabbinic literature usually forming a running commentary on specific books of the Bible. *Tanchuma* provides textual exegeses, expounds upon the biblical narrative, and develops and illustrates moral principles. *Tanchuma* is unique in that many of its sections commence with a halachic discussion, which subsequently leads into nonhalachic teachings.

Paradise Landscape with the Animals Entering Noah's Ark, Jan Bruegel the Elder, oil on oak, c. 1613–1615. (Museum of Fine Arts, Budapest)

TEXT 14

THE REBBE, RABBI MENACHEM MENDEL SCHNEERSON,
LIKUTEI SICHOT 25 (HEBREW VERSION), PP. 33–35

בְּתֵיבַת נֹחַ שָׂרַר מַצָּב שֶׁל שָׁלוֹם, מֵעֵין זֶה שֶׁיִּהְיֶה לֶעָתִיד לָבֹא–"וְגָר זְאֵב עִם כֶּבֶשׂ", "לֹא יָרֵעוּ וְלֹא יַשְׁחִיתוּ". הֲרֵי בְּתֵיבַת נֹחַ חָיוּ בְּיַחַד כָּל סוּגֵי הַבְּהֵמוֹת וְהַחַיּוֹת, כּוֹלֵל חַיּוֹת טוֹרְפוֹת וְדוֹרְסוֹת, וְלַמְרוֹת זֹאת לֹא עָשׂוּ רָעָה זֶה לָזֶה כְּלַל וְלֹא הִשְׁחִיתוּ זֶה לָזֶה . . .

זֶהוּ הַטַּעַם לְכָךְ מַדּוּעַ לְאַחַר שֶׁיָּבְשָׁה הָאָרֶץ הָיָה צוֹרֶךְ בְּצִיּוּוּי "צֵא מִן הַתֵּיבָה". מִשּׁוּם שֶׁנֹּחַ לֹא רָצָה לָצֵאת מֵהַתֵּיבָה–הוּא הָיָה בְּמָקוֹם בּוֹ שָׂרַר מַצָּב שֶׁל לֶעָתִיד לָבֹא . . . וְעַל אַחַת כַּמָּה וְכַמָּה בְּיַחַס לְחַיּוֹת . . . שֶׁמִּצַּד עַצְמָם לֹא רָצוּ לָצֵאת מֵהַתֵּיבָה, וּבְכָךְ לָשׁוּב וְלִהְיוֹת חַיּוֹת טוֹרְפוֹת וּמַזִּיקוֹת.

Within Noah's Ark there prevailed a state of harmony, similar to what will be in the future era of Mashiach, when "the wolf will dwell with the lamb" and "neither shall they do evil nor destroy" (ISAIAH 11:6 AND 9). Indeed, all sorts of beasts and animals, including dangerous predators, lived together in the Ark, yet they did not harm one another. . . .

This is the reason why even after "the land was fully dried," it was still necessary that G-d should command, "Go out from the Ark." For Noah did not want to leave the Ark—he was in a place where the future messianic state of perfection prevailed. . . . And the animals certainly did not want to leave and go back to being killers and predators.

TEXT 15

THE REBBE, RABBI MENACHEM MENDEL SCHNEERSON,
LIKUTEI SICHOT 25 (HEBREW VERSION), P. 37

הַהוֹרָאָה מִכַּךְ בַּעֲבוֹדַת הַשֵּׁם:

יֶשְׁנָם כָּאֵלוּ הַסְּבוּרִים שֶׁנִּיתָּן לְהִסְתַּגֵּר בְּאַרְבַּע אַמּוֹת שֶׁלָּהֶם וְלַעֲסוֹק כָּל הַיּוֹם בַּתּוֹרָה, וּכְלָל לֹא נוֹגֵעַ לָהֶם מַה נַּעֲשֶׂה בָּעוֹלָם מִסְּבִיבָם . . . שֶׁהֲרֵי אָז יִדְמֶה מַצָּבוֹ הָאִישִׁי לָזֶה שֶׁל יְמוֹת הַמָּשִׁיחַ, כִּפְסַק הָרַמְבַּ"ם . . . "וּבְאוֹתוֹ הַזְּמַן . . . לֹא יִהְיֶה עֵסֶק כָּל הָעוֹלָם אֶלָּא לָדַעַת אֶת ה' בִּלְבָד" . . .

עַל כַּךְ הִיא הַהוֹרָאָה: "צֵא מִן הַתֵּיבָה". צָרִיךְ לָצֵאת מֵהַתֵּיבָה וְלִפְעוֹל בָּעוֹלָם שֶׁמִּסָּבִיב. אָכֵן יֵשׁ לִפְעָמִים סֵדֶר שֶׁל "בֹּא אֶל הַתֵּיבָה". כַּאֲשֶׁר בַּחוּץ יוֹרֵד מַבּוּל, וְקַיָּים חַשָּׁשׁ פֶּן יִיטָּבַע בְּ"מַיִם הַזֵּידוֹנִים" שֶׁל מֵי הַמַּבּוּל, אוֹ אָז יֵשׁ לְהִתְגּוֹנֵן מִכַּךְ בְּאֶמְצָעוּת "בֹּא אֶל הַתֵּיבָה" . . . אַךְ צָרִיךְ לָדַעַת, אֲשֶׁר סוֹף סוֹף חַיָּיב לְהַגִּיעַ זְמַן שֶׁל "צֵא מִן הַתֵּיבָה". מִשּׁוּם שֶׁהַמַּטָּרָה וְהַתַּכְלִית הִיא לִפְעוֹל בָּעוֹלָם שֶׁמִּחוּץ לַתֵּיבָה שֶׁלְּךָ.

This is the lesson for us in our personal service of G-d:

There are those who believe that they can seclude themselves in their own private space and study Torah all day long, without concerning themselves in any way with what is happening in the world around them. . . . They will then achieve, on the personal level, a messianic-like existence, as Maimonides writes . . . "In those times . . . the entire world will be solely occupied with knowing G-d." . . .

The Torah therefore instructs us, "Go out from the Ark!" You must leave your Ark and become active in the outside world. True, there are times when an approach of "Come into the Ark" is called for. When a "flood" rages without, and there exists the danger that one might drown in the "waters of wickedness," we must protect ourselves by entering into the Ark. . . . But we must know that, ultimately, there must come a time for "Go out of the Ark." Because the purpose and goal is to transform the world outside your Ark.

QUESTION FOR DISCUSSION

Which do you think is the more worthy goal—to live a righteous life, or to change the world for the better?

Additional Readings

THE THIRD MILLENNIUM

BASED ON THE TEACHINGS OF THE LUBAVITCHER REBBE; ADAPTED BY RABBI YANKI TAUBER

When did the "two thousand years of Torah" begin?... When "[Abraham and Sarah] made souls in Charan" (Genesis 12:5). We deduce that Abraham was fifty-two years old at that time. (Talmud, Avodah Zarah 9a)

The Torah is divided into fifty-four sections or *parashiot* (singular: *parashah*), each of which is studied and publicly read in the synagogue in the course of one week of the year. In this way, we "live with the times,"[1] finding guidance and inspiration in the Torah section that pertains to the specific segment of time that we occupy.

On the face of it, the *parashiot* seem a rather arbitrary division of Torah. They vary greatly in length (from as few as 30 to as many as 176 verses), and do not conform to the Torah's logical division into "chapters" (which is actually of non-Jewish origin). Many of them seem to include a number of unconnected events and laws, or seem to begin or end in mid-narrative. But a deeper examination always reveals the *parashah* to be an integral unit of Torah, with a distinct theme and context of its own.

A case in point concerns the first three *parashiot* of the Torah—*Bereishith* (Genesis 1:1–6:8), *Noach* (Genesis 6:9–11:32), and *Lech Lecha* (Genesis 12:1–17:27). At first glance, the divisions between these *parashiot* seem inconsistent with their storylines. But once we understand the deeper significance of the events that they chronicle, the underlying theme of each *parashah* emerges.

Living with the Times

The sixth Lubavitcher Rebbe, Rabbi Yosef Yitzchak Schneersohn (1880–1950), related an exchange he had when he was ten years old with his father, Rabbi Shalom DovBer:

> *When I entered my father's room in the early morning of Shabbat Lech Lecha of 5651 [1890], I found him sitting at his table, reviewing the Torah section of the week. Father was in very high spirits, yet tears were streaming from his eyes. I was very confused, for I was unable to understand this combination of elation and tears; but I did not dare to ask him about it.*
>
> *That evening, father noticed that I very much wanted to say something and encouraged me to speak my mind. So I asked him about what I had seen that morning.*
>
> *Father explained: "Those were tears of joy."*
>
> *"Once, in the early years of his leadership," he continued, "our ancestor, Rabbi Schneur Zalman of Liadi, told his disciples: 'One must live with the times.' The younger* chassidim *asked their elders*

RABBI MENACHEM MENDEL SCHNEERSON, 1902–1994

The towering Jewish leader of the 20th century, known as "the Lubavitcher Rebbe," or simply as "the Rebbe." Born in southern Ukraine, the Rebbe escaped Nazi-occupied Europe, arriving in the U.S. in June 1941. The Rebbe inspired and guided the revival of traditional Judaism after the European devastation, impacting virtually every Jewish community the world over. The Rebbe often emphasized that the performance of just one additional good deed could usher in the era of Mashiach. The Rebbe's scholarly talks and writings have been printed in more than 200 volumes.

RABBI YANKI TAUBER, 1965–

Chasidic scholar and author. A native of Brooklyn, N.Y., Rabbi Tauber is an internationally renowned author who specializes in adapting the teachings of the Lubavitcher Rebbe. He is a member of the JLI curriculum development team and has written numerous articles and books, including *Once Upon a Chassid* and *Beyond the Letter of the Law.*

> *to explain the Rebbe's statement, but they, too, had failed to grasp its significance. Finally, Rabbi Schneur Zalman's brother, our [great-great-great] uncle Rabbi Yehudah Leib, explained what the Rebbe had meant: One should 'live with' and experience, each day of one's life, the Torah section of the week, and the specific portion of the week's section which belongs to that day. . . .*[2]
>
> *"The section of* Bereishith*," continued my father, "is a happy section: G-d is creating worlds and creatures and is satisfied that 'it is good.'*[3] *But its ending [which describes the corruption of humanity and G-d's 'regret' of man's creation] is not so pleasant. . . . In the section of* Noach *comes the Flood. It is a depressing week, but with a happy ending—our father Abraham is born.*
>
> *"But the truly joyous week," father concluded, explaining his mood that morning, "is Lech Lecha. Every day of the week we live with our father Abraham. Together with Abraham, the first to sacrifice himself to bring G-dliness to the world. Together with Abraham, who bequeathed his self-sacrifice for Torah and* mitzvot *as an inheritance to each and every Jew."*[4]

Rabbi Shalom DovBer's description of the Torah's first three sections raises the obvious question of why, indeed, are they structured this way? Why mar the "happy section" of *Bereishith* with its "not so pleasant ending," describing the corruption of humanity and G-d's regret of His creation—especially since these last few verses (Genesis 6:1–8) actually begin the story of the Flood, the central theme of the section of *Noach*? A similar thing occurs at the end of *Noach*: After a detailed description of the events of the Flood and the Tower of Babel, the section closes with a brief account of the birth and early life of Abraham, whose life is to fill, with rich detail, the next three sections (*Lech Lecha*, *Vayeira*, and *Chayei Sarah*). Surely, a far more natural division would have been for *Noach* to begin with the last eight verses of *Bereishith*, and for *Lech Lecha* to open with Abraham's birth, a mere seven verses before the end of *Noach*!

Seven Days of History

"A thousand years, in Your eyes," proclaims the Psalmist, "is like yesterday's day."[5] The sages expound that the seven days of creation are replayed, on the macro-historical level, in the seven-millennia course of human history, which likewise consists of six "workdays" followed by a seventh millennium "that is wholly Shabbat and rest, for life everlasting"[6]—the age of Moshiach.[7]

The seven days of creation embody the seven divine attributes (*sefirot*) through which G-d defines His relationship with His creation.[8] The first *sefirah* is *chesed*, the attribute of love; thus the first day of creation saw the creation of light, which represents the "giving" and "bestowing" elements of the created reality. On the second day, G-d created the "firmament" which "divided between the waters that are above the heavens, and the waters that are beneath the heavens"[9] (i.e., between the spiritual and the physical realms); this was the day of *gevurah*, the attribute of rigor, restraint, judgment, and delimitation. The third attribute, *tiferet* ("harmony"), is a synthesis of *chesed* and *gevurah*, reflected in the fact that G-d's work on the third day also included the setting of boundaries (of land and sea), but also the spawning of plant life on the face of earth.

The same is true of the corresponding millennia of history. The first millennium was the millennium of *chesed*—an era of divine generosity and benevolence. In the second thousand years of history, G-d's relationship with His world was characterized by the rigor and judgment of *gevurah*. These were followed by the millennium of *tiferet*—the age of synthesis and harmony.[10]

The first three millennia of biblical history correlate with the first three *parashiot* of the Torah. When we calculate the years given in the Torah for the events of these three *parashiot*, we discover that the section of *Bereishith* corresponds with the first millennium of history.[11] We further calculate that the section of *Noach* chronicles the major events of its second millennium—the Flood (in the year 1656 from creation), the breakup of mankind into nations in the aftermath of the Tower of Babel (1996 from creation), and the birth of Abraham (in 1948 from creation) and his early years. Finally, we find that the event with which the section of *Lech Lecha* opens—i.e., G-d's call to Abraham to "Go you, from your land, and from your birthplace, and from your father's house, to the land which I shall show you"—occurs in Abraham's seventy-fifth year,[12] meaning that this event took place in the year 2023 from creation.[13]

Lech Lecha thus begins the story of the third millennium—a story that continues through the remaining fifty-two *parashiot* of the Torah: the lives of Abraham, Isaac, and Jacob, founding fathers of the Jewish people; the descent into Egypt and the Exodus; and the highlight of the millennium, the revelation at Sinai and G-d's communication of His Torah to man.

We can now begin to understand the delineation of these three sections. All the events of *Bereishith*, including its "uncharacteristic" ending, belong to the age of *chesed* or divine benevolence. All of *Noach*, including its account of the early years of Abraham, belongs to the age of *gevurah*, characterized by divine justice. And the events of *Lech Lecha* describe the first generation of the age of *tiferet* and harmony.

The Three Mentors

Chassidic teaching defines the differences between these three phases of human history by employing the model of the relationship between a teacher and his pupil.

A great master wishes to impart wisdom to a vastly inferior pupil. One approach is to go ahead and communicate his ideas to the pupil: If the teacher is wise enough, patient enough, and resourceful enough, he will find the words and analogies with which to convey the loftiest of concepts even to a mediocre mind.

A second approach is for the teacher to compel the pupil to conceive, analyze, and comprehend the ideas on his own. The teacher will withhold the knowledge from the pupil, and provide him only with the pertinent rules and the methodology. The teacher will then stand by as the pupil struggles on his own, intervening only to rebuke his blunders and prod his achievements. By this method, the pupil will learn to use his own faculties to arrive at his own insights.

Each of these two approaches has its advantages and its shortcomings. In the case of the "benevolent master," the pupil benefits from a level of understanding that is vastly superior to anything he is capable of attaining on his own. But such intellectual charity does little to develop the mind of the pupil. The pupil has gained only the specific ideas that have been imparted to him; on his own, he cannot repeat the process by which they were conceived, nor can he expand on them or apply them to other areas and dimensions of knowledge.

The "withholding master" has a more meaningful effect on his pupil. His restraint and ungenerosity pay off: by refusing to reveal anything that lies beyond the student's intellectual range, the teacher unearths his student's true abilities, bringing to light potential powers which would never have been realized under the tutelage of a more "generous" master. On the other hand, whatever understanding the student can attain on his own will always be greatly inferior to what the teacher could confer upon him as a gift.

There is, however, a third approach that combines the virtues of the first two. A truly great teacher will integrate both these methods in his teaching, stimulating the pupil's mind to overreach itself by feeding it with thoughts and insights that lie just beyond its capacity, yet never revealing enough to allow the pupil to become a passive recipient. The teacher then repeats the process with successively more profound ideas, which, when digested by the pupil's mind, nourish it and expand it from within. Ultimately, the teacher's blend of benevolence and restraint will elevate the pupil's mind to the level on which it not only comprehends the most sublime thoughts the teacher has to offer, but also assimilates them into his or her own thought process and intellectual self.

From Creation to Sinai

For the first thousand years of history, G-d was a benevolent teacher who indulges the shortcomings of his pupil. Life *was* a free lunch. Righteous and wicked alike enjoyed long and prosperous lives. In a sense, this era was an extension of G-d's original act of creation. In its initial state of nonexistence, the world obviously did not "deserve" to be created; its creation was an act of pure charity on the part of G-d, who granted it existence, purpose, and the potential for deservingness. Likewise, in the first millennium G-d gave indiscriminately, in order to provide humanity with the basis upon which to build and develop the world in accordance with His plan.

Thus, the corrupt world described in the last verses of *Bereishith* represents not the beginning of the age of rigor, but the closing years of the age of benevolence. They describe a morally immature world, in which all blessing, material or spiritual, is taken for granted. Indeed, it is the natural end of an era in which responsibility is neither assumed nor exacted, for humanity is yet to be weaned from an infantile dependence upon its Creator.

After a thousand years of unilateral bestowal, the era of *chesed* came to a close. In the second thousand years of creation, G-d challenged humanity to make it on its own. On the surface, the second millennium was a harsh, even tragic era, for everything, including life itself, was earned solely by merit. At one point, there were only eight deserving human beings, and the rest of humanity perished in the Flood. At another point, the misguided building of the Tower of Babel resulted in the dispersion of the human race and its disintegration into nations separated by walls of incommunicativeness and xenophobia. But this exacting justice on the part of G-d is what allowed the world to develop from within—to become a vital, productive world whose deeds have consequence and significance, instead of a world that is the passive recipient of divine charity.

The last generation of the second millennium yielded Abraham, the ultimate spiritually self-made man. The son of a Mesopotamian idol-maker, Abraham came to recognize the truth of a One G-d with nothing but the majesty of the universe and his own inquisitive mind to guide him. Single-handedly, he battled the entrenched paganism of his native land and won over a large following to the monotheistic faith and ethos he espoused. So the Abraham (or rather the Abram, as he was then called) of his first 75 years is very much a part of the *Noach* era; indeed, he represents its culminating and finest expression.[14] If there is one theme that characterizes Abraham's early years it is that yes, man *can* make it on his own.

Then, upon the onset of the third millennium, Abraham heard the voice of G-d. "Go you," was the divine call, "from your land, from your birthplace, and from your father's house, to the land which I will show you." Now that you have obtained the utmost of your own inborn potentials ("your land, your birthplace, your father's house"), you must reach beyond yourself, for the land that *I* will show you.

Thus began the journey into the millennium of *tiferet*, the millennium which saw the synthesis of the divinely bestowed and the humanly earned. This millennium reached its climax at Mount Sinai, where G-d communicated to us His wisdom and will enclothed in the garments of human reason and human endeavor. The Torah breached the barrier between the G-dly and the terrestrial, allowing a divine gift to become a human achievement, and human effort to touch the divine.[15]

Endnotes

1 See narrative by Rabbi Yosef Yitzchak of Lubavitch, cited in this essay.
2 Each Torah section is divided into seven readings, for the seven individuals called to read from the Torah on Shabbat. An old chassidic custom is to study one of these readings, together with Rashi's commentary, on each of the seven days of the week.
3 Genesis 1:4, 1:10, et al.
4 *Sefer HaSichot* 5702, pp. 29–30.
5 Psalms 90:4.
6 Shabbat addendum for *Grace after Meals*.
7 Talmud, *Avodah Zarah* 9a; *Zohar* 1:116b; Nachmanides and Bechayei on Genesis 2:3; et al.
8 *Zohar* 1:247a.
9 Genesis 1:7.
10 See sources in footnote 7 above for the characteristics, and corresponding events, of the remaining four millennia.
11 The chronologies presented in Genesis 5:1–32 and 11:10–26, which enumerate the lifespans of the twenty generations from Adam to Abraham, enable us to calculate the year (counting from the creation of Adam) that Noah was born, the year of the Flood, the year of Abraham's birth, and so on.
12 Genesis 12:4.
13 More specifically, the Talmud sees the beginning of the "Era of Torah" as coinciding with Abraham's 52nd year—i.e., the year 2000 from creation. This is the point at which Abraham and Sarah began spreading the belief in the One G-d and the ethos of monotheism, as alluded to in the verse, ". . . the souls they made in Charan".
14 Cf. *Ethics of the Fathers* 5:2: "There were ten generations from Noah to Abraham . . . and Abraham reaped the reward for them all."
15 Complementing the kabbalistic equation of the seven millennia of history with the seven *sefirot* is the talmudic saying that, "The world exists for six thousand years: two millennia of *tohu* (chaos), two millennia of Torah, and two millennia of the days of Moshiach," followed by a seventh millennium of transcendent "annihilation" (Talmud, *Sanhedrin* 97a). In the teachings of kabbalah, *tohu* is a state of one-dimensionality, in which singular forces dominate without being mitigated by and integrated with the other forces of creation; ultimately, such a world collapses under its own weight, for nothing can be sustained in an absolute, untempered state. Thus, the millennium of *chesed* and its unequivocal benevolence, and the millennium of *gevurah* with its uncompromising judgment, both belong to the era of *tohu*; while the *tiferet* millennium, with its synthesis of benevolence and judgment, belongs to the era of Torah.

Yanki Tauber, *The Inside Story,* vol. 1 (Genesis) (Brooklyn: Meaningful Life Center, 2016), pp. 136–145

Lesson 3

JACOB AND ESAU

The Reunion of Jacob and Esau (detail), Virgil Solis. c. mid-1500s.

The epic struggle between the most famous twins in the Bible assumes many forms: the contest between sword and word, between matter and spirit, between self-realization and self-transcendence. We learn that Creation itself comes in two formats: a powerful yet unstable "World of Chaos," and a moderated and focused "World of Correction." In every area of life, we straddle both realms, and can look to the Jacob-Esau story for guidance in navigating this duality.

TEXT 1

GENESIS 25:22–28

THE STRUGGLE IN THE WOMB (25:22)

The children struggled within her
and she said, "If so, why am I thus?";
and she went to inquire of G-d.

THE PROPHECY (25:23)

G-d said to her:
"Two nations are in your womb
and two kingdoms from your insides will diverge;
kingdom will overpower kingdom
and the elder will serve the younger."

THE TWINS' BIRTH (25:24–26)

Her days to give birth were fulfilled
and behold, there were twins in her womb.
The first one came out ruddy
his entirety as a hairy mantle
and they called his name "Esau."
After that his brother came out
and his hand was grasping Esau's heel
and he called his name "Jacob." . . .

The World of Chaos Under Repair
A kabbalistic view of the Jacob-Esau saga
Rabbi Laibl Wolf:

MYJLI.COM/BIBLE

DIFFERENT NATURES (25:27)

The lads grew up;
Esau was a man who knows game
a man of the field
and Jacob was a wholesome man
a dweller of tents.

HOW THEIR PARENTS SAW THEM (25:28)

Isaac loved Esau for the game in his mouth
and Rebecca loved Jacob.

Illustration by Gustave Doré for
La Grande Bible de Tours, 1866.

TEXT 2

GENESIS 27:1–29

ISAAC DESIRES TO BLESS ESAU (27:1–4)

It came to pass when Isaac was old
and his eyes were dimmed of sight;
and he called his elder son Esau
and he said to him . . .
"Here, please, I have grown old;
I do not know the day of my death.
Now, please pick up your implement
your sword and your bow;
and go out to the field and trap game for me.
Make for me delicious food such as I love
and bring it to me, and I will eat;
in order that my soul should bless you before I die."

REBECCA INSTRUCTS JACOB TO STEAL THE BLESSINGS (27:5–13)

Rebecca was listening as Isaac spoke to his son Esau. . . .
And Rebecca said to her son Jacob:
". . . Listen to my voice
to that which I am commanding you.
Go now to the flock and take for me from there
two goodly goat-kids;
and I will prepare them as delicious food
for your father, such as he loves.
You will bring to your father and he will eat;

in order that he should bless you before his death."
Jacob said to his mother Rebecca:
"Here, my brother Esau is a hairy man
and I am a smooth man.
Perhaps my father will feel me
and I will be in his eyes as a trickster;
and I will bring upon myself a curse
and not a blessing."
And his mother said to him:
"Your curse is upon me, my son;
only listen to my voice and go take for me." . . .

JACOB'S DISGUISE (27:15–23)

Rebecca took the desirable garments of her elder son Esau. . .
and she dressed her younger son Jacob;
and she dressed the goat-kid skins on his hands
and upon the smoothness of his neck. . . .
He came to his father. . .
and he said . . . , "Who are you, my son?"
And Jacob said to his father:
"I am Esau your firstborn." . . .
Isaac said to Jacob:
"Please approach and I will feel you, my son;
are you this, my son Esau, or not?"

Jacob approached his father Isaac, and he felt him;
and he said: "The voice is the voice of Jacob
and the hands are the hands of Esau."
He did not recognize him
for his hands were
as the hands of his brother Esau, hairy;
and he blessed him. . . .

THE BLESSING (27:28–29)

"G-d shall give to you of the dew of the heavens
and the fat of the earth
and an abundance of grain and wine.
Nations will serve you, and kingdoms will bow to you;
you shall be a master over your brothers
and your mother's sons shall bow to you.
Those who curse you shall be cursed
and those who bless you shall be blessed."

Isaac and Jacob (detail), François-Robert Ingouf (engraver), Manuel de la Cruz Vasquez (draftsman), etching and engraving on wove paper, 1791. (Museo Nacional del Prado, Madrid)

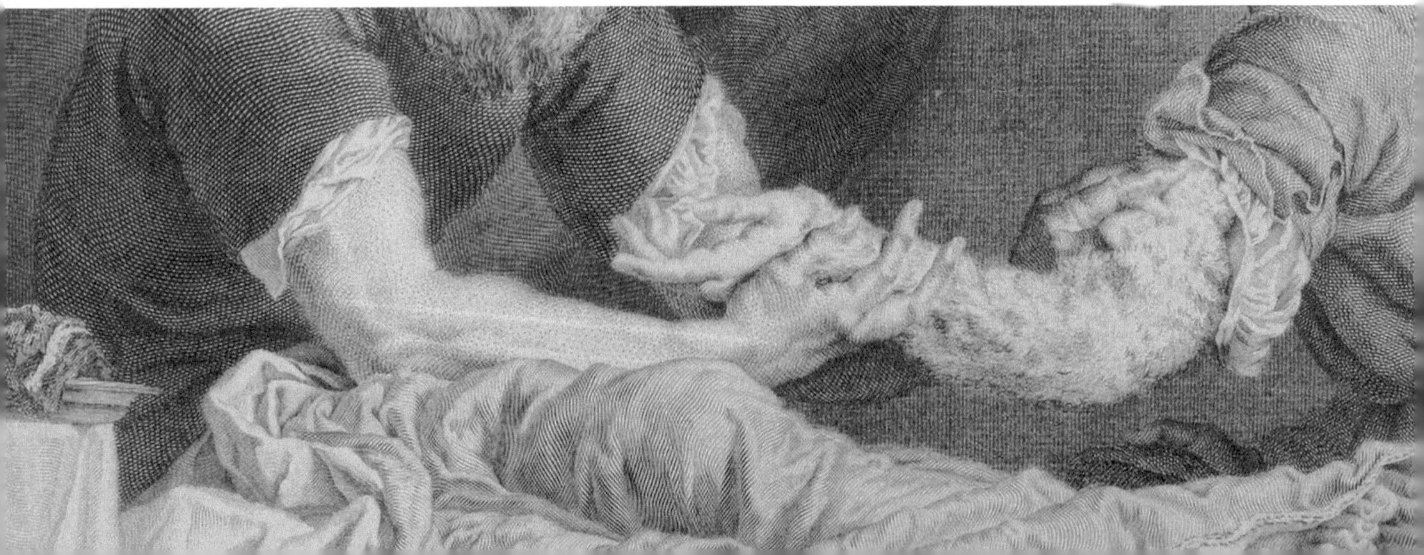

Figure 3.1

The Esau-Jacob Duality

	ESAU	JACOB
History	Rome	Judea
Daily Life	materialism	spirituality
Internal Self	self-realization	self-transcendence
Cosmic	*Tohu*	*Tikun*

QUESTIONS FOR DISCUSSION

1 What influences of historical "Rome" can you identify in American society today?

2 What influences of historical "Judea" can you identify in American society today?

3 Which is the more dominant influence in American society today?

The Conquest of Jerusalem by Emperor Titus (detail), Nicolas Poussin, oil on canvas, 1638. (Kunsthistorisches Museum Wien, Vienna)

TEXT 3

MIDRASH, SHEMOT RABAH 21:1

שְׁתֵּי יְרֻשּׁוֹת הִנְחִיל יִצְחָק לִשְׁנֵי בָנָיו. הִנְחִיל לְיַעֲקֹב הַקּוֹל, וְכֵן הוּא אוֹמֵר (בְּרֵאשִׁית כז, כב): "הַקֹּל קוֹל יַעֲקֹב". וְהִנְחִיל לְעֵשָׂו הַיָּדַיִם, שֶׁנֶּאֱמַר (שם): "וְהַיָּדַיִם יְדֵי עֵשָׂו".

Two legacies did Isaac bequeath to his two sons. To Jacob he gave the voice, as it is written, "the voice is the voice of Jacob" (GENESIS 27:22). And to Esau he gave the hands, as it is written, "and the hands are the hands of Esau" (IBID.).

SHEMOT RABAH

An early rabbinic commentary on the Book of Exodus. "Midrash" is the designation of a particular genre of rabbinic literature usually forming a running commentary on specific books of the Bible. *Shemot Rabah*, written mostly in Hebrew, provides textual exegeses, expounds upon the biblical narrative, and develops and illustrates moral principles. It was first printed in Constantinople in 1512 together with 4 other Midrashic works on the other 4 books of the Pentateuch.

TEXT 4

RABBI DOVBER OF LUBAVITCH, *TORAT CHAYIM*, BEREISHIT, P. 9A

> לְהָבִין בְּשֹׁרֶשׁ עִנְיַן הַהֶפְרֵשׁ שֶׁבֵּין בְּחִינַת הַתּוֹהוּ לִבְחִינַת הַתִּיקּוּן לְמַעְלָה וְאֵיךְ שֶׁבְּחִינַת הַתִּיקּוּן בָּא לְתַקֵּן וּלְבָרֵר לִבְחִינַת הַתּוֹהוּ . . . שֶׁהוּא כְּמוֹ הַצּוּרָה לַחוֹמֶר . . .
>
> דְהִנֵּה יָדוּעַ . . . שֶׁבְּחִינַת הָאוֹרוֹת דְתּוֹהוּ הָיוּ . . . אוֹרוֹת תַּקִּיפִים וַחֲזָקִים מְאוֹד, לִהְיוֹת שֶׁהָיָה הָאוֹר בְּרִיבּוּי וְהַכְּלִי בְּמִיעוּט . . . לְפִי שֶׁלֹּא יָכְלוּ הַכֵּלִים לִסְבּוֹל אֶת הָאוֹר, עַל כֵּן נָפְלוּ וְנִשְׁבְּרוּ . . .
>
> וְאַחַר כָּךְ נַעֲשָׂה בְּחִינַת הַתִּיקּוּן . . . עַל יְדֵי בְּחִינַת מִיעוּט הָאוֹר וְרִיבּוּי הַכֵּלִים, שֶׁעַל יְדֵי זֶה נִתְקַיֵּים הָאוֹרוֹת בַּכֵּלִים.

To understand the root of the difference between *Tohu* and *Tikun*, and how *Tikun* comes to rectify and refine *Tohu* . . . , serving as form to its substance. . . .

As is known . . . , the “lights” of *Tohu* were . . . extremely powerful and intense, as there prevailed a state of “abundant light and scant vessels.” . . . Because the vessels were unable to contain the light, they shattered and fell. . . .

Following that, the *Tikun* reality was made . . . with “scant light and abundant vessels,” with the result that the lights are sustained within the vessels.

Light = energy
vessel = executes energy

RABBI DOVBER OF LUBAVITCH (MITELER REBBE), 1773–1827

Rabbi Dovber was the eldest son of and successor to Rabbi Shne’ur Zalman of Liadi and greatly expanded upon and developed his father’s groundbreaking teachings. He was the first Chabad rebbe to live in the village of Lubavitch. Dedicated to the welfare of Russian Jewry, at that time confined to the Pale of Settlement, he established Jewish agricultural colonies. His most notable works on Chasidic thought include *Shaar Hayichud*, *Torat Chayim*, and *Imrei Binah*.

The Great Kaboom! A KabbalaToon ***Tzvi Freeman** and* ***Pilar Newton**:*

MYJLI.COM/BIBLE

Figure 3.2

Light and Vessel

	LIGHT	VESSEL
Book	ideas	words
Melody	emotions	musical notes
Business	vision and objectives	business strategy
Relationship	love	mutually supportive actions
Religion	beliefs and values	rituals and customs
	chaotic	orderly
	Essau	Jacob
	Tohu	Tikun

QUESTIONS FOR DISCUSSION

1 **a** What are the advantages of the *Tikun* model?
b What are the disadvantages of the *Tikun* model?

Tohu *and* Tikun
Rabbi Nochum Shapiro:

MYJLI.COM/BIBLE

2 **a** What are the advantages of the *Tohu* model?
b What are the disadvantages of the *Tohu* model?

3 If the *Tohu* model for Creation is prone to failure, why not skip the *Tohu* phase and go straight to *Tikun*?

Composition 8, Vasily Kandinsky, oil on canvas, 1923. (Guggenheim Museum, New York)

Exercise 3.1

What are the *Tohu* elements in our lives?

What are the *Tikun* elements in our lives?

QUESTION FOR DISCUSSION

Which are the more powerful forces in our lives—the *Tohu* elements or the *Tikun* elements?

TEXT 5

GENESIS 27:30–28:4

THE DECEPTION IS DISCOVERED (27:30–33)

And it was . . .
just as Jacob was going out from the presence of his father;
that his brother Esau came from his hunt. . . .
And he said to his father:
"My father should get up
and eat of the game of his son
in order that your soul should bless me."
And his father Isaac said to him:
"Who are you?"
And he said:
"I am your firstborn son Esau."
Isaac trembled an exceedingly great trembling
and he said:
"Who, then, is the one who trapped game
and brought it to me and I ate of it all
before you had come
and I blessed him?
Also blessed shall he be!"

ESAU BEGS TO ALSO BE BLESSED (27:34–40)

As Esau heard the words of his father
he cried an exceedingly great and bitter cry;
and he said to his father:

“Bless me too, my father!”
And he said:
“Your brother came with cunning and took your blessing.”
And he said:
“Is this why his name was called Jacob?
Twice he has deceived me:
he took my birthright
and here now he has taken my blessing!”
And he said:
“Have you not reserved a blessing for me?”
Isaac answered and said to Esau
“Here I have placed him master to you
and all his brothers I have given to him as servants
and with grain and wine I have supported him;
and for you, then, what shall I do, my son?”
And Esau said to his father:
“Have you only one blessing, my father?
Bless me, also me, my father!”;
and Esau raised his voice and he wept.
And his father Isaac answered and he said to him:
“Here, the fat of the land will be your settlement
and of the dew of the heavens above.
By your sword you will live
and your brother you will serve;

and it will be that when you are aggrieved
you will cast off his yoke from upon your neck."

JACOB RECEIVES ABRAHAM'S BLESSING (28:1–4)

Isaac called Jacob and he blessed him;
and he instructed him, and he said to him . . .
"Arise and go to Padan-Aram. . . .
and take yourself a wife from there
from the daughters of Laban, your mother's brother.
And the Almighty G-d will bless you
and make you fruitful and multiply you
and you will become a community of peoples.
And He will grant you the blessing of Abraham
to you and to your seed with you
to inherit you the land of your dwelling
which G-d has given to Abraham."

TEXT 6

RABBI SHNE'UR ZALMAN OF LIADI, *TORAH OR*, TOLEDOT, 20D–21B

יַעֲקֹב הוּא בְּחִינָה קְדוֹשָׁה, וּבְלַאו הָכִי נִמְשָׁכִים בּוֹ כָּל הָאוֹרוֹת עֶלְיוֹנִים . . . אַךְ הַבְּרָכָה הִיא בְּתוֹסֶפֶת וְרִבּוּי הַמְשָׁכָה מִלְמַעְלָה מִסֵּדֶר הַהִשְׁתַּלְשְׁלוּת . . . כְּדֵי לִהְיוֹת וְרֹב דָּגָן וְתִירוֹשׁ אֵלוּ הֲלָכוֹת וְאַגָּדוֹת שֶׁנִּתְלַבְּשׁוּ בִּלְבוּשִׁים גַּשְׁמִיִּים . . . [וּ]מַעֲשֵׂה הַמִּצְוֹת . . . מַה שֶּׁאֵין כֵּן אִלּוּ לֹא קִבֵּל יַעֲקֹב הַבְּרָכוֹת, הָיָה נִמְשַׁךְ מִן הַתּוֹרָה רַק בְּרוּחָנִיּוּת לְבָד.

Jacob is the realm of holiness; without all this, he still would have received all the supernal energies. . . . But the [first set of] blessings granted him an increase of powers from the highest levels to obtain "much grain and wine," referring to the laws and stories of the Torah that become embodied in material garments . . . and in the actions of the *mitzvot*. . . . However, had Jacob not received these blessings, the power of Torah would have extended only to the spiritual realm.

RABBI SHNE'UR ZALMAN OF LIADI (ALTER REBBE), 1745–1812

Chasidic rebbe, halachic authority, and founder of the Chabad movement. The Alter Rebbe was born in Liozna, Belarus, and was among the principal students of the Magid of Mezeritch. His numerous works include the *Tanya*, an early classic containing the fundamentals of Chabad Chasidism; and *Shulchan Aruch HaRav*, an expanded and reworked code of Jewish law.

Ayin Beis, Chapter 263
Text-based learning of a Chasidic discourse
Rabbi Simon Jacobson:

MYJLI.COM/BIBLE

TEXT 7

RABBI SHNE'UR ZALMAN OF LIADI, *TORAH OR*, TOLEDOT, 21B

וְהָיָה צָרִיךְ לָזֶה לְתַקֵּן חֵטְא עֵץ הַדַּעַת, שֶׁהָיָה גַּם כֵּן בְּמִרְמָה וּפִתּוּי שֶׁל נָחָשׁ, שֶׁעַל יָדוֹ נִתְגַּשְּׁמוּ הָעוֹלָמוֹת וְנַעֲשָׂה עֵירוּב גַּשְׁמִיּוּת בְּרוּחָנִיּוּת. וּלְתַקֵּן זֶה עָשָׂה מֵהָפוּךְ אֶל הָפוּךְ, וְהִמְשִׁיךְ רוּחָנִיּוּת וְאוֹרוֹת הָעֶלְיוֹנִים שֶׁיִּהְיֶה נִמְשָׁךְ גַּם לְגַשְׁמִיּוּת.

[Jacob's cunning] was necessary in order to correct the sin of the Tree of Knowledge, which also came about through the cunning and enticement of the serpent, and which caused the coarsening of all the worlds and the intermingling of materialism and spirituality. To rectify this, [Jacob] turned the tables, drawing down spirituality and supernal power into materialism.

Why Does Jacob Resort to Trickery in His Dealings with Esau, Isaac, and Laban?
Rabbi Lord Jonathan Sacks:

MYJLI.COM/BIBLE

QUESTIONS FOR DISCUSSION

1 Should we care about material success?

2 Is it possible to succeed in business—or in any endeavor requiring material resources—if one does not care?

1 The "two kingdoms" embodied by the biblical Jacob and Esau exist on many levels: as the historical nations of Judea and Rome; as the spiritual and material perspectives on life; as the altruistic and selfish instincts in the human psyche; and as the cosmic worlds of *Tikun* and *Tohu*.

2 Everything is composed of "light" and "vessels": the pure energy of the thing, and the structures and mechanisms through which it operates. But there are two models of existence. The *Tikun* model is one of "scant light and abundant vessels," meaning that the vessels contain and focus their energies. In the *Tohu* model there is "abundant light and scant vessels," meaning that the driving energy is constantly bursting free of the structures through which it is meant to operate.

3 Each model has its advantages and disadvantages: *Tikun* is harmonious and orderly but constrained. *Tohu* is innovative and limit-breaking, but also strife-ridden and unstable. An additional disadvantage to the *Tohu* model is that it is prone to corruption, resulting either in the dissipation of its energies or in their exploitation by evil.

4 Because *Tohu* preceded *Tikun*, we can tap the advantages of both models, drawing on the powerful *Tohu* elements present in our *Tikun* reality as remnants of an "earlier" world. But this is also the reason that the Jacob in us—our instincts for spirituality and altruism—faces an uphill battle in its efforts to master the more primordial *Tohu* forces of our internal Esau—the unbridled passions of the "Animal Soul," the uncontainable force of the human ego, and the unsatisfiable ambitions of a materialistic life.

5 Isaac believed that *Tohu* and *Tikun* could coexist side by side, each blessed with resources to fully develop its realm in accordance with the divine plan for Creation. Rebecca, however, understood that a material world that is ruled by materialists will not rise to its true purpose, but will descend into corruption. The powerful resources of *Tohu* can only be redeemed when "Jacob" is made the master of "Esau."

6 In our own lives, we need to internalize both sides of the "Isaac-Rebecca argument." Like Isaac, we need to recognize the powerful potential for good that lies in our *Tohu* self. Like Rebecca, we need to understand that in order to properly utilize this potential, we have to place our *Tikun* self firmly in control of our lives.

7 Every time we interact with the material world, we reenact the drama of the "stolen blessings." We become a spiritual Jacob who assumes the guise of a materialistic Esau in caring about material success for the ulterior motive of making our world a holier, more G-dly place.

Additional Readings

THE SUPERNAL ROOT OF ESAU

EXCERPT FROM *TORAT CHAYIM* BY RABBI DOVBER OF LUBAVITCH
TRANSLATION BY RABBI SHMUEL KLATZKIN

[To explain] the reason that Isaac loved Esau more than Jacob and truly wanted to bless him, and why this was to be achieved through Esau bringing Isaac hunted game from the field, as it is written (Genesis 27:3), "Take up your gear, your quiver and your bow, and go out to the field. . . .":

On the face of it, this is greatly astonishing. Isaac certainly knew that Jacob was a completely righteous man, "a wholesome man, a dweller of the tents" (Genesis 25:27)—"tents" in the plural to signify the study of the Written Torah and of the Oral Torah. It was specifically to Jacob that the blessing of Abraham—which is the Land of Israel—would be given. [For G-d had said to Isaac,] "Dwell in this land. . . . for to you and to your descendants I will give all these lands. And I will fulfill the oath which I swore to Abraham, your father, and I will multiply your seed" (Genesis 26:3–4). All this was referring to Jacob only, as the text proceeds to give the reason for this [blessing]: "Because Abraham listened to My voice, and he kept [My charge, My *mitzvot*, and My Torah]" (ibid., 26:5). This being so, how did it even cross Isaac's mind to give the blessing of Abraham to Esau, "the man of the field," who had no portion in the Land at all, as he was completely bereft of Torah and *mitzvot*?

RABBI DOVBER OF LUBAVITCH (MITELER REBBE), 1773–1827

Rabbi Dovber was the eldest son of and successor to Rabbi Shne'ur Zalman of Liadi and greatly expanded upon and developed his father's groundbreaking teachings. He was the first Chabad rebbe to live in the village of Lubavitch. Dedicated to the welfare of Russian Jewry, at that time confined to the Pale of Settlement, he established Jewish agricultural colonies. His most notable works on Chasidic thought include *Shaar Hayichud, Torat Chayim,* and *Imrei Binah.*

Also, consider what happened when Jacob came deceptively, wearing Esau's garments. Isaac did not recognize him, as his hands were hairy, and said, "The voice is the voice of Jacob. . . ." Isaac asked him again, "Are you really my son Esau?" And once he had smelled the aroma of his garments, identifying them as Esau's, he then blessed him (ibid., 27:18–28).

Why did Isaac not want to bless Jacob, "the wholesome man," as the Torah attests of him?

However, the matter is made clear [by the commentaries] elsewhere. Isaac already knew that the blessing of Abraham regarding the land of the seven Canaanite nations was something given exclusively to Jacob. As Isaac subsequently said to Jacob, "G-d Almighty will bless you . . . and grant you the blessing of Abraham, to you and to your descendants, to take as an inheritance the Land . . . which G-d gave to Abraham" (ibid., 28:3–4).

Isaac's desire to bless Esau, then, was not to give him the blessing of Abraham, for Esau had no portion in that at all. Rather, it was to give him the entire world, and all that it contains, outside of the Land of Israel. For the seventy nations will be refined in the future World to Come, as it is written (Zephaniah 3:9): "Then I will transform the nations to a refined language, to serve Him. . . ." In general, these are the seven primordial kings of *Tohu* who ruled in the land of Edom (see Genesis 36:31–39), which is the land of Esau, "the hairy man" (ibid., 27:11).

These "kings" are the supernal source of the seventy nations here below, and are not sublimated through the Torah study and the mitzvah actions of Israel in its Land in the manner of rectification (*Tikun*) achieved with the divine name *MaH* (45),[1] which pertains to the *sefirah* of *chochmah* (wisdom). For the divine name *MaH* only sublimates elements associated with the divine name *BaN* (52), namely the Land of Canaan, which is the Land of Israel, given as an inheritance to Israel alone. These elements are "refined through wisdom"—through the *mitzvot* that apply to the Land of Israel, such as the building of the Holy Temple and the sacrifices. All that is brought about by the Torah and *mitzvot* practiced by the people of Israel, which rectify the sin of the Tree of Knowledge of Good and Bad by separating between good and evil.

Torah and *mitzvot*, however, do not transform the complete evil of the completely profane *kelipot*. Those *kelipot* are remnants of the seven primordial kings, who are not sublimated through Torah and *mitzvot*, but only through *teshuvah*.

For *teshuvah* is a power greater and more powerful than wisdom; it transforms the evil itself into good. This is the concept of transforming the darkness itself into light—something that is beyond the capability of the light of wisdom, as is known regarding the concept of "the advantage of light coming from darkness" (Ecclesiastes 2:13).

In the supernal realm, this is the hiddenness within the essence of the Emanator, which is called "darkness is His hiding place," and is spoken of in the *Tikunei Zohar* as "the secret of all secrets, which no thought can grasp at all." This is higher than the hidden delight that will be revealed to the perfectly righteous in the World to Come. It is achieved only by means of *teshuvah*, which transforms the material darkness of the profane *kelipot* into good, which is like transforming death itself into life and curse into blessing, as already mentioned.

These are the remnants of the seven kings of *Tohu* that fell below into complete evil, which cannot be refined through the wisdom of the light of Torah, only through *teshuvah*, which "transforms deliberate sins into merits" (Talmud, Yoma 86b). For before Him, "even darkness does not darken" (Psalms 139:12), and darkness itself is transformed to light. This, however, is not in the power of the light of the supernal wisdom—to transform evil into good—but only to separate between good and evil, as already stated.

This is the reason that Isaac loved Esau, his older son. For the root of Esau's soul was from the aspect of *gevurah* of the seven kings of *Tohu* who fell down below into complete evil, but whose source on high is in the level of the supernal *gevurah* of "darkness is His hiding place." This is the level of the divine name *SaG* (63) of *Tohu*, which is higher than the aspect of *MaH* of *Tikun*. As it is written (regarding the seven kings of Edom, that they reigned) "before a king reigned over the Children of Israel" (Genesis 36:31).

Isaac himself is rooted in *gevurah* of *atik yomin*, in the flames of fire of the hidden delight that ascends above. Its power is very strong, as it transforms even the darkness into light, as in the resurrection of the dead (which relates to Isaac), as mentioned earlier. It brings about a very great profusion of refinements in *kelipat nogah*,[2] as well as in the realm of complete evil, elevating them all to the supernal holiness, as hinted at in the verse (ibid., 26:12–13): "Isaac sowed. . . . and he became great." This is as it will be in the World to Come, when "the nations [specifically] will say G-d has done great things" (Psalms 126:2), as we have earlier explained.

This is like Isaac's diggings that uncovered "a spring of living waters" (Genesis 26:19)—referred to as "the lower waters"—which ascend through the rebounding light of *teshuvah*, as mentioned earlier.

Therefore, Isaac desired, through *teshuvah*, to elevate Esau—who here below is the figure of the powerful and difficult forces of complete evil—to Esau's source in the supernal powerful forces of holiness. For the one who has fallen here below is able to ascend through *teshuvah* just as he is, without the rectification of Torah study and mitzvah practice, as in the case of Rabbi Elazar ben Durdaya, who acquired his World to Come in one moment (see Talmud, Avodah Zarah 17a), as we clarified previously when speaking about the idea of "the most impoverished of men will exult in the Holy One of Israel" (Isaiah 29:19).

This is why Isaac "loved Esau for the game in his mouth" (Genesis 25:28). This alludes to the sparks of holiness that fell in the "shattering of the vessels" of *kelipat nogah*, such as the souls of converts like Obadiah the Edomite convert, Shemaya and Avtalyon, Rabbi Akiva, and Rabbi Meir. In a similar way, all of the powerful lights of *Tohu* that fell into the difficult *gevurot* of *kelipat nogah* which then ascend are called "game," as when someone hunts wild animals or fowl in the wilderness.

Had Isaac succeeded in elevating Esau to be as he is on high, he would have been higher than Jacob, the "wholesome man, dwelling in tents," whose rectification (*Tikun*) is achieved with the light of the wisdom of Torah. For "in the place of masters of *teshuvah*, the completely righteous cannot stand" (Talmud, Berachot 34b). They ascend in the hiddenness of "the darkness of His concealment," higher than the light of the supernal primordial wisdom.

But had this come to pass, Jacob could not have established himself in the Land of Israel through Torah and *mitzvot*. (A proof of this comes from the *teshuvah* done by the people of Nineveh, which served as an indictment of Israel. That was why Jonah tried to avoid that mission. He was greatly pained that the nations of the world should come close through *teshuvah*.)

For this reason, Rebecca, who loved Jacob, devised a clever plan. She was of the aspect of *Tikun* of the truth of Torah and *mitzvot*, which, in their ultimate source, are higher even than the level of the hiddenness stemming from "the darkness of His concealment." [For Torah and *mitzvot*] are rooted within the very essence of the Infinite, which is higher even than the hiddenness of the delight of the "rebounding light" [of *teshuvah*].

(This is the deeper meaning of what Jacob said [Genesis 27:11], "I am a smooth [*chalak*] man," alluding to the verse [Deuteronomy 32:9], "For His people are a part [*cheilek*] of G-d," without the contraction or concealment alluded to by the concept of the "hairiness" of the rebounding light, as we shall explain.)

Rebecca took "Esau's desirable clothes" (Genesis 27:15), which were "the garments of skin (עור)" given to Adam (ibid., 3:21), and which after their sublimation are called "garments of light"—i.e., עור spelled with an *alef*, אור—when the hiddenness of the supernal darkness radiates light. She dressed Jacob in these garments, and placed "the skins of the kid goats on his [hands and on the smoothness of his] neck" (ibid., 27:16), with the result that "his hands were hairy" (ibid., 27:23). This is the concept of *teshuvah*, the rebounding light by which evil is sublimated into good.

Thus it is written that specifically when Isaac "smelled the aroma of his garments," that is when "he blessed [Jacob] and he said, 'The aroma of my son is like the aroma of the field [that G-d has blessed]" (ibid., 27:27)—as we will explain; and Jacob received the blessings of Esau from the supernal *gevurot* of *Tohu*.

The explanation of this is that in truth, also the sublimation of the seven kings of *Tohu* through *teshuvah* needs to accord exclusively with the wisdom of Torah (as we explained earlier regarding the idea that through the kindness and truth of Torah and *mitzvot*, sin is atoned by means of the Thirteen Attributes of Compassion on Yom Kippur). This is because the root of the wisdom of Torah on high derives from the very essence of the Infinite, which is higher than both the darkness and the light of the hiddenness and the revelation. This is why Rebecca wanted that the elevation through the *teshuvah* of Esau, "the hairy man," should be through Jacob only, who is a completely righteous person in Torah and *mitzvot*.

This was accomplished by means of deceit, by Jacob wearing the garments of Esau and saying, "I am Esau, your firstborn" (ibid., 27:19). In this, Jacob was like a completely righteous person who becomes a master of *teshuvah*, as in the teaching that "Mashiach comes to bring the righteous to do *teshuvah*" (*Zohar* 3:153b). The deeper meaning of this is that the whole of the souls of Israel, who are called "completely righteous" (Isaiah 60:21), should become masters of *teshuvah*, transforming darkness into light—a higher level than the light of Torah and *mitzvot*.

However, this is accomplished only through their being righteous and doing *teshuvah*. But *teshuvah* alone, without Torah and *mitzvot*, will not be effective, for Esau can only be refined through Jacob. This was accomplished when Jacob wore Esau's garments and took the blessings of Esau deceitfully, in such a way that Isaac thought that he was actually blessing Esau. As the text says, "He did not recognize him, for his hands were hairy, and he blessed him" (Genesis 27:23).

Had Isaac known that it was Jacob, he would not have given him these blessings. For the blessing ordained for Jacob was the blessing of Abraham, which was a drawing down of lights from the aspect of *Tikun* of the divine name *MaH*, which pertains only to the Torah and *mitzvot* of the Land of Israel, as earlier explained—not from the level of the lights of *Tohu*, which preceded the *Tikun*. That the sublimation and elevation of *Tohu*, in the manner of *teshuvah* and rebounding light, had to come exclusively through Jacob, was hidden from Isaac.

Furthermore, the ultimate elevation of Jacob through Torah and *mitzvot* in the future World to Come is also only through *teshuvah*. For in Torah and *mitzvot* without *teshuvah*, the light from the essence of the Infinite will not radiate in a genuine way, but only through the hiddenness of the supernal *chashmal*. And regarding the future World to Come, it is written (Isaiah 30:20), "No longer will your Master be garbed."

It is for this reason that it then will be said regarding Isaac, "For you are our father" (ibid., 63:16). For it was Isaac who elevated Jacob up to the *gevurot* of the rebounding light of *teshuvah*, so that it should illuminate the whole of the hiddenness of the essence of the Infinite with a greater revelation than the light of *Tikun* that flows through the measuring line after the *tsimtsum*. (Evidence is from the case of Moses, who did not merit to *teshuvah* until just before his death.)

Despite all this, the elevation through *teshuvah* is only by means of the Torah and *mitzvot* of Jacob, for the reasons set out above. This is the meaning of the statement (Berachot 17a), "The ultimate wisdom is *teshuvah* and good deeds"—both of them together. Likewise it is said, "One hour of *teshuvah* and good deeds in this world is better that the entire life of the World to Come" (*Ethics of the Fathers* 4:17). For the World to Come is only for the completely righteous through Torah and *mitzvot*, as was stated earlier.

Endnotes

1 *MaH*—the Hebrew letters מ"ה—refers to a certain configuration of the divine name *HaVaYaH* that produces a numerical value of 45. Other configurations yield values of *BaN* (52–ב"ן) and *SaG* (63–).

2 I.e., the mixture of good and evil identified with "the Tree of Knowledge of Good and Bad" discussed above.

Rabbi Dovber of Lubavitch, *Torat Chayim*, Toldot, Section 9

Lesson 4

JOSEPH AND HIS BROTHERS

Jozef Wordt door Zijn Broers uit Put Getrokken (Joseph Is Pulled out of the Well by His Brothers), Christoffel van Sichem (II) (printmaker), after Hans Holbein (II), woodcut, Amsterdam, c. 1645 and/or 1740. (Rijksmuseum, Amsterdam)

Our exploration of the deeper significance of the conflict between Joseph and his brothers takes us from a history of Jewish leadership, to the structure of the Holy Temple in Jerusalem, to an enigmatic debate recorded in the Talmud on the question: Which is greater, learning or action? We discover that there are two parallel quests embedded in the human soul, each of which—as well as the tension between them—is essential to our mission in life.

TEXT 1a

GENESIS 37:2–11

BROTHERS ARE JEALOUS OF JOSEPH (37:2–4)

Joseph was seventeen years old
shepherding with his brothers in the flocks . . .
and Joseph brought bad word of them to their father.
Israel loved Joseph more than all his sons
as he was a child-of-old-age to him;
and he made him a striped coat.
His brothers saw that their father loved him
more than all his brothers
and they hated him;
and they were not able to speak peaceably with him.

JOSEPH'S DREAMS (37:5–11)

Joseph dreamed a dream and told his brothers . . .
"Here, we were bundling sheaves
in the middle of the field
and here, my sheaf arose and also stood upright
and here, your sheaves surrounded
and they bowed to my sheaf."
His brothers said to him:
"Shall you then reign over us
or will you rule over us?"
And they hated him yet the more
for his dreams and for his words.
He again dreamed another dream

and related it to his brothers;
and he said:
"Here, I have dreamed another dream
and behold: the sun, the moon, and eleven stars
were bowing to me. . . ."
His brothers envied him
but his father guarded the matter.

The People v. Joseph's Brothers: A Courtroom Reenactment
Professor Michael A. Helfand, Hon. Andrew Kauffman,** and **Mr. Martin H. Pritikin:

MYJLI.COM/BIBLE

Illustration of Joseph's dream from the *Harrison Miscellany*. Corfu, first half of 18th century. (The Braginsky Collection)

TEXT 1b

GENESIS 37:18–34

BROTHERS SCHEME TO KILL JOSEPH (37:18–20)

They saw him from afar;
and when he had yet to come near to them
they schemed against him to put him to death.
And they said one to the other:
"Here comes the dreamer!
Now, let us go and kill him
and throw him into one of the pits
and we will say:
'An evil beast has devoured him';
and we shall see what will become of his dreams." . . .

BROTHERS THROW JOSEPH INTO A PIT (37:23–24)

When Joseph came to his brothers
they stripped Joseph of his coat
the striped coat that was on him.
And they took him and threw him into the pit. . . .

BROTHERS SELL JOSEPH (37:25–28)

They sat down to eat bread
and they lifted their eyes and they saw
behold, a caravan of Ishmaelites
was coming from Gilead. . . .

And Judah said to his brothers:
"What profit is there if we kill our brother
and cover up his blood?
Come, let us sell him to the Ishmaelites
but our hand shall not be upon him
as he is our brother, our flesh."
His brothers listened. . . .
And they sold Joseph to the Ishmaelites
for twenty pieces of silver;
and they brought Joseph to Egypt. . . .

BROTHERS MISLEAD JACOB (37:31–34)

They took Joseph's coat
and they slaughtered a hairy goat
and they dipped the coat in the blood.
They sent the striped coat and brought it to their father
and they said: "We found this;
please recognize: Is it your son's coat or not?"
He recognized it and he said: "My son's coat!
An evil beast has devoured him
torn! Joseph is torn." . . .
And he mourned his son many days.

TEXT 2

GENESIS 45:1–9

JOSEPH REVEALS IDENTITY TO BROTHERS (45:1–3)

Joseph was no longer able to constrain himself . . .
and he called:
"Remove every man from my presence!"
and no man stood with him
when Joseph made himself known to his brothers.
He put his voice to weeping;
and Egypt heard, and the house of Pharaoh heard.
And Joseph said to his brothers: "I am Joseph!
Is my father still alive?"
His brothers could not answer him
as they were bewildered before him.

NO ILL WILL TOWARD THEM (45:4–9)

And Joseph said to his brothers . . .
"Now, do not be distressed
and it should not upset you
that you sold me here;
for as a source of livelihood
G-d has sent me before you. . . .
It is not you who sent me here, but G-d. . . .
Hurry and go up to my father, and say to him:
'So said your son Joseph:
G-d has placed me master to all of Egypt;
come down to me, do not delay. . . .'"

Have Archaeologists Found Joseph's House in Egypt?

MYJLI.COM/BIBLE

TEXT 3

RABBI YESHAYAHU HOROWITZ, *SHENEI LUCHOT HABERIT* 2:298B

וְקֹדֶם שֶׁאֲבָאֵר אֵיךְ עִנְיַן מְכִירַת יוֹסֵף וְגִלְגּוּלוֹ הוּא קִיּוּם מַלְכוּת דָּוִד
וּמָשִׁיחַ, אֶתְעוֹרֵר עַל סְפֵקוֹת גְּדוֹלוֹת שֶׁרָאוּי לְהִתְעוֹרֵר עֲלֵיהֶם בְּעִנְיַן
יוֹסֵף עִם אֶחָיו. רִאשׁוֹן, הִיא קֻשְׁיָא כְּלָלִית, נוֹדַע מַעֲלַת הַשְּׁבָטִים גְּדוֹלָה
עַד מְאֹד, שֶׁבְּוַדַּאי מַעֲלָתָם יוֹתֵר מִמַּעֲלַת מַלְאֲכֵי הַשָּׁרֵת, וְהֵם בְּסוֹד י״ב
צֵרוּפֵי שֵׁם הֲוָיָ״ה, אֵיךְ יִתְפֹּס הַשֵּׂכֶל זֶה הַדָּבָר, שֶׁבְּנֵי עֲלִיָּה כָּאֵלּוּ יַעֲשׂוּ
בְּיַחַד הָעֲבֵרָה הַגְּדוֹלָה שֶׁבְּכָל הָעֲבֵרוֹת שֶׁבָּעוֹלָם, דְּהַיְינוּ רְצִיחָה?

Before explaining how the story of the selling of Joseph and all that happened with him is the basis for the kingdom of David and Mashiach, we must address the great difficulties [with this story]. First of all, a most general difficulty: The greatness of the sons of Jacob, the progenitors of the Twelve Tribes of Israel, is well known. Certainly, they were greater than the supernal angels, as they represent the mystical twelve configurations of the divine name *Havayah*. How, then, could the mind grasp the idea that these exalted individuals would join together to commit the most severe sin of all the sins in the world, namely the sin of murder?

RABBI YESHAYAHU HALEVI HOROWITZ *(SHALAH)* 1565–1630

Kabbalist and author. Rabbi Horowitz was born in Prague and served as rabbi in several prominent Jewish communities, including Frankfurt am Main and his native Prague. After the passing of his wife in 1620, he moved to Israel. In Tiberias, he completed his *Shenei Luchot Haberit*, an encyclopedic compilation of kabbalistic ideas. He is buried in Tiberias, next to Maimonides.

TEXT 4

TALMUD, SHABBAT 10B

לְעוֹלָם אַל יְשַׁנֶה אָדָם בְּנוֹ בֵּין הַבָּנִים. שֶׁבִּשְׁבִיל מִשְׁקַל שְׁנֵי סְלָעִים מֵילַת
שֶׁנָתַן יַעֲקֹב לְיוֹסֵף יוֹתֵר מִשְּׁאָר בָּנָיו, נִתְקַנְאוּ בּוֹ אֶחָיו, וְנִתְגַלְגֵל הַדָבָר
וְיָרְדוּ אֲבוֹתֵינוּ לְמִצְרַיִם.

A person should never discriminate between his children. Look what happened on account of two *selas*' weight of finespun wool that Jacob bestowed upon Joseph more than his other children, provoking their jealousy and causing our forefathers to end up in Egypt!

BABYLONIAN TALMUD

A literary work of monumental proportions that draws upon the legal, spiritual, intellectual, ethical, and historical traditions of Judaism. The 37 tractates of the Babylonian Talmud contain the teachings of the Jewish sages from the period after the destruction of the 2nd Temple through the 5th century CE. It has served as the primary vehicle for the transmission of the Oral Law and the education of Jews over the centuries; it is the entry point for all subsequent legal, ethical, and theological Jewish scholarship.

TEXT 5

RABBI OVADIAH BEN JACOB SEFORNO, COMMENTARY TO GENESIS 37:18

כִּי צִיְּירוּ בְּלִבָּם וְחָשְׁבוּ אֶת יוֹסֵף לְנוֹכֵל וּמִתְנַקֵּשׁ בְּנַפְשָׁם לַהֲמִיתָם בָּעוֹלָם הַזֶּה אוֹ בָּעוֹלָם הַבָּא אוֹ בִּשְׁנֵיהֶם. וְהַתּוֹרָה אָמְרָה "הַבָּא לְהָרְגְךָ כו'".

They saw Joseph as one who was plotting to destroy them, physically or spiritually or both together. And the Torah states (TALMUD, SANHEDRIN 72A): "One who is coming to kill you, [make haste to kill him first]."

RABBI OVADIAH SEFORNO
1475–1550

Biblical exegete, philosopher, and physician. Seforno was born in Cesena, Italy. After gaining a thorough knowledge of Talmud and the sciences, he moved to Rome, where he studied medicine and taught Hebrew to the German scholar Johannes Reuchlin. Seforno eventually settled in Bologna, where he founded and directed a yeshiva until his death. His magnum opus is a biblical commentary focused on the simple interpretation of the text, with an emphasis on philology and philosophy.

Joseph et Ses Frères (Joseph and His Brothers) (detail), from the *Bible Series*, Marc Chagall, etching, 1956. © 2020 Artists Rights Society (ARS), New York / ADAGP, Paris

TEXT 6

RABBI YITSCHAK BEN MOSHE ARAMA, *AKEIDAT YITSCHAK*, BEREISHIT, PORTAL 28

כַּאֲשֶׁר רָאוּ כִּי אוֹתוֹ אָהַב אֲבִיהֶם לְבַדּוֹ מִכָּל בָּנָיו . . . וּכְבָר חָשְׁבוּ שֶׁיִּקְרֶה לָהֶם כְּמוֹ שֶׁקָּרָה לְיִשְׁמָעֵאל וּבְנֵי קְטוּרָה עִם יִצְחָק, וּלְעֵשָׂו עִם יַעֲקֹב, וְכָל הַיָּמִים אֲשֶׁר הוּא חַי עַל הָאֲדָמָה לֹא יִהְיֶה לָהֶם חֵלֶק בֵּאלֹקֵי יִשְׂרָאֵל, וְלֹא לָהֶם יִהְיֶה הַזֶּרַע אֲשֶׁר נֶאֱמַר עָלָיו בִּרְכַּת אַבְרָהָם וְיִצְחָק לִהְיוֹת לְךָ לֵאלֹקִים וּלְזַרְעֲךָ אַחֲרֶיךָ וכו׳ (בְּרֵאשִׁית יז, ז). וְנִתְאַמְּתָה לָהֶם מַחְשָׁבָה זֹאת, כִּי רָאוּ עַד עַתָּה לֹא זָכָה בִּבְרָכָה זוּ כִּי אִם אֶחָד מִבְּנֵי הָאָבוֹת לְבָד.

When they saw that, of all his children, Jacob loved only Joseph, . . . they thought that what will happen to them will be the same as what happened to Ishmael and the children of Keturah vis-à-vis Isaac, and to Esau vis-à-vis Jacob. [They believed that] for as long as Joseph was alive, they would have no portion in the G-d of Israel, and their descendants would be excluded from the blessing given to Abraham and Isaac, "To be a G-d to you and to your descendants after you" (GENESIS 17:7). This belief was confirmed to them by the fact that they saw that until now, only one of the children of each of the patriarchs merited this blessing.

RABBI YITSCHAK ARAMA
1420–1494

Spanish rabbi and philosopher; known as "the Baal Akeidah," after his work *Akeidat Yitschak*, an influential philosophic and mystical commentary on the Torah. After initially serving as head of the yeshiva in Zamora, Spain, he was appointed as rabbi and preacher for the community of Tarragona. His writings were received favorably by his peers, including Rabbi Don Yitschak Abravanel. After the expulsion of 1492, Rabbi Arama ultimately settled in Naples, where he is buried.

Feelings and Choices
A lesson from the story of Joseph
Mrs. Sharon Freundel:

MYJLI.COM/BIBLE

TEXT 7

RABBI YESHAYAHU HOROWITZ, *SHENEI LUCHOT HABERIT* 2:298A–300A

כֶּתֶר מַלְכוּת זָכָה בּוֹ יְהוּדָה . . . וְאִלוּ לֹא הִקְדִים מְלוּכַת יוֹסֵף בְּמִצְרַיִם לֹא הָיָה מֵעוֹלָם מְלוּכַת יְהוּדָה, כִּי לֹא הָיוּ יִשְׂרָאֵל לְעַם חַס וְשָׁלוֹם . . . כִּי יוֹסֵף הוּא הַצִּנּוֹר . . .

וְהַשְּׁבָטִים לֹא הֵבִינוּ דָבָר זֶה, רַק הָיוּ סְבוּרִים אַךְ לוֹ הַמְּלוּכָה, שֶׁהוּא מְבַקֵּשׁ הַמְּלוּכָה בְּעֶצֶם לוֹ וּלְזַרְעוֹ. עַל כֵּן הָלְכוּ דֹתָיְנָה לְבַקֵּשׁ נִכְלֵי דָתוֹת, כְּלוֹמַר, לָדוּן אוֹתוֹ בְּדַת תּוֹרָה. וְהִסְכִּימוּ כֻּלָּם שֶׁהוּא בֶּן מָוֶת . . . מֵאַחַר שֶׁחוֹלֵק עַל מַלְכוּת בֵּית דָּוִד, וְכָל הַחוֹלֵק עַל מַלְכוּת בֵּית דָּוִד כְּחוֹלֵק עַל הַשְּׁכִינָה (רְאֵה סַנְהֶדְרִין קי א).

The crown of sovereignty was granted to Judah. . . . However, were it not to have been preceded by the kingship of Joseph in Egypt, the kingship of Judah would never have materialized, as the people of Israel would not have become a nation, G-d forbid. . . . For Joseph is the channel. . . .

Joseph's brothers failed to understand this. Rather, they thought that Joseph was seeking the sovereignty permanently and exclusively for himself and his descendants. . . . They therefore judged him by the law of the Torah, concluding that he is deserving of death . . . as one who is contesting the sovereignty of the House of David. For one who contests the sovereignty of the House of David, it is as if He contested the Divine Presence (SEE TALMUD, SANHEDRIN 110A).

TEXT 8

GENESIS 29:16–30

RACHEL AND LEAH (29:16–17)

Laban had two daughters;
the name of the elder was Leah
and the name of the younger was Rachel.
The eyes of Leah were tender;
and Rachel was of beautiful form
and beautiful appearance.

JACOB WORKS SEVEN YEARS TO MARRY RACHEL (29:18–21)

Jacob loved Rachel;
and he said: "I will serve you seven years
for Rachel your younger daughter."
Laban said: "Better I give her to you
than I give her to another man;
stay with me."
Jacob worked for Rachel seven years;
and they were in his eyes as a few days
in his love for her.
And Jacob said to Laban:
"Bring here my wife as my days are fulfilled
and I will come to her."

LABAN SUBSTITUTES LEAH FOR RACHEL (29:22–26)

Laban gathered all the people of the place
and made a feast.
It was in the evening
and he took his daughter Leah
and brought her in to him;
and he came to her. . . .
It was in the morning, and behold, she is Leah!
And he said to Laban:
“What is this you have done to me?
Have I not served with you for Rachel?
Why have you deceived me?”
And Laban said:
“It is not so done in our place
to give the younger before the firstborn.” . . .

JACOB ALSO MARRIES RACHEL (29:30)

He came also to Rachel
and he also loved Rachel more than Leah;
and he worked with him yet another seven years.

Covenant & Conversation: Joseph and His Brothers
Rabbi Lord Jonathan Sacks:

MYJLI.COM/BIBLE

QUESTION FOR DISCUSSION

What are the parallels between the incident of the "stolen blessings" and the bridal bait-and-switch that Laban perpetrated against Jacob?

TEXT 9

MIDRASH, *BEREISHIT RABAH* 70:19

הַהוּא לֵילְיָא הֲוָה צווֵחַ לָהּ "רָחֵל!" וְהִיא עַנְיָא לֵיהּ. בְּצַפְרָא - וְהִנֵּה הִיא לֵאָה. אָמַר לָהּ: "מָה רָמַיְיתָא בַּת רַמָּאָה! לַאו בְּלֵילְיָא הֲוָה קָרִינָא "רָחֵל" וְאַתְּ עָנִית לִי?" אָמְרָה לֵיהּ: "אִית סַפֵּר דְלֵית לֵיהּ תַּלְמִידִים? לֹא כָּךְ הָיָה צווֵחַ לְךָ אֲבוּךְ "עֵשָׂו" וְאַתְּ עָנֵי לֵיהּ?"

All that night, Jacob was calling to her, "Rachel!" and she responded in kind. Then, in the morning, she was Leah.

Said Jacob to her: "Deceiveress, the daughter of deceiver! Was I not calling you 'Rachel,' and you were answering me?"

Said she to him: "Every teacher has his pupils. When your father was calling you 'Esau,' did you not answer him in the same way?"

BEREISHIT RABAH

An early rabbinic commentary on the Book of Genesis. This Midrash bears the name of Rabbi Oshiya Rabah (Rabbi Oshiya "the Great"), whose teaching opens this work. This Midrash provides textual exegeses and stories, expounds upon the biblical narrative, and develops and illustrates moral principles. Produced by the sages of the Talmud in the Land of Israel, its use of Aramaic closely resembles that of the Jerusalem Talmud. It was first printed in Constantinople in 1512 together with 4 other Midrashic works on the other 4 books of the Pentateuch.

TEXT 10

RABBI ELIEZER ASHKENAZI, *MAASEI HASHEM*, VAYEITZEI

אָמַר לָבָן הַמְקַנְטֵר לְיַעֲקֹב, "לֹא יֵעָשֶׂה כֵן בִּמְקוֹמֵנוּ". כְּלוֹמַר, בִּמְקוֹמְךָ עוֹשִׂים מִן הַצָּעִיר בְּכוֹר, שֶׁלָּקַחְתָּ בְּכוֹרַת עֵשָׂיו. אֲבָל בִּמְקוֹמֵנוּ לֹא יִלָּקַח הַבְּכוֹרָה מִן הַגְּדוֹלָה לַצְּעִירָה.

Laban was taunting Jacob by saying to him, "It is not so done in our place. . . ." Laban was implying: In *your* place, the younger child is made into the firstborn, as you acted when you appropriated Esau's birthright. But in *our* place, the firstborn's rights won't be taken from the elder sister and given to the younger. . . .

RABBI ELIEZER ASHKENAZI
1515–1586

Talmudist, halachist, philosopher. Rabbi Eliezer served as rabbi in Egypt, Cyprus, Italy, and Poland, concluding his life in Cracow. He wrote many unpublished works; he published his commentary *Yosef Lekach* on the book of Esther, and his main work, *Maaseh Hashem*, a commentary on the Torah, was completed in Gniezno in 1580 and printed in Venice in 1583.

Illustration by Gustave Doré for *La Grande Bible de Tours* (detail), 1866.

TEXT 11

ZOHAR 1:185B

יַעֲקֹב עָבַד עוּבְדָא כְּדְקָא יָאוֹת . . . עִם כָּל דָּא, בְּגִין דְּאִיהוּ אַקְרִיב שָׂעִיר
וְאַכְחִישׁ לֵיהּ לַאֲבוּי דְּאִיהוּ סִטְרָא דִּילֵיהּ, אִתְעֲנַשׁ בְּהַאי שָׂעִיר אַחֲרָא
דְּאַקְרִיבוּ לֵיהּ בְּנוֹי דָּמָא דִּילֵיהּ. בְּאִיהוּ כְּתִיב, "וְאֵת עוֹרֹת גְּדָיֵי הָעִזִּים
הִלְבִּישָׁה עַל יָדָיו וְעַל חֶלְקַת צַוָּארָיו". בְּגִין כַּךְ, "וַיִּטְבְּלוּ אֶת הַכֻּתֹּנֶת בַּדָּם",
אַקְרִיבוּ לֵיהּ כֻּתּוֹנְתָּא לְאַכְחֲשָׁא לֵיהּ. וְכֹלָּא דָּא לָקֳבֵל דָּא.

Jacob was correct in acting as he did. . . . Nevertheless, because he presented a hairy goat to deceive his father that he is on his side, he was punished with another hairy goat, whose blood his children presented to him. Regarding [Jacob] it says, "And the skins of the goat-kids she dressed upon his hands, and upon the smoothness of his neck" (GENESIS 27:16). Because of this, "they dipped [Joseph's] coat in the blood" and presented him the coat to deceive him. It all corresponds, one to the other.

ZOHAR

The seminal work of kabbalah, Jewish mysticism. The *Zohar* is a mystical commentary on the Torah, written in Aramaic and Hebrew. According to the Arizal, the *Zohar* contains the teachings of Rabbi Shimon bar Yocha'i, who lived in the Land of Israel during the 2nd century. The *Zohar* has become one of the indispensable texts of traditional Judaism, alongside and nearly equal in stature to the Mishnah and Talmud.

TEXT 12

TALMUD, BAVA BATRA 123A

> שֶׁהָיְתָה שׁוֹמַעַת עַל פָּרָשַׁת דְרָכִים בְּנֵי אָדָם שֶׁהָיוּ אוֹמְרִים: שְׁנֵי בָנִים יֵשׁ לָהּ לְרִבְקָה, שְׁתֵּי בָנוֹת יֵשׁ לוֹ לְלָבָן. גְדוֹלָה לַגָדוֹל וּקְטַנָה לַקָטָן.
>
> וְהָיְתָה יוֹשֶׁבֶת עַל פָּרָשַׁת דְרָכִים וּמַשְׁאֶלֶת: "גָדוֹל מַה מַעֲשָׂיו?" "אִישׁ רַע הוּא מְלַסְטֵם בְּרִיוֹת". "קָטָן מַה מַעֲשָׂיו?" "אִישׁ תָּם יוֹשֵׁב אֹהָלִים" (בְּרֵאשִׁית כה, כז). וְהָיְתָה בוֹכָה עַד שֶׁנָשְׁרוּ רִיסֵי עֵינֶיהָ.

Leah heard people talking: Rebecca has two sons, and Laban has two daughters. The elder will marry the elder, and the younger will marry the younger.

She would sit at the crossroads and inquire, "How does the elder son conduct himself?"

"He is a wicked man, a highway robber."

"How does the younger son conduct himself?"

"A wholesome man dwelling in tents" (GENESIS 25:27). So she wept until her eyelashes fell out.

TEXT 13

THE REBBE, RABBI MENACHEM MENDEL SCHNEERSON,
LIKUTEI SICHOT 35, P. 153

שֶׁיְסוֹד הַחִילּוּק בֵּין עֲבוֹדַת הַשְּׁבָטִים, מַה שֶּׁבְּנֵי לֵאָה עִנְיָנָם (בְּעִיקָר) עֲבוֹדַת הַתְּשׁוּבָה, וְיוֹסֵף וּבִנְיָמִין עֲבוֹדַת הַצַּדִּיקִים, שָׁרְשׁוֹ בְּהָאִמָּהוֹת: דְלֵאָה שַׁיֶּיכֶת לַעֲבוֹדַת בַּעֲלֵי תְּשׁוּבָה וְרָחֵל לַעֲבוֹדַת הַצַּדִּיקִים.

וְעַל פִּי זֶה יֵשׁ לְפָרֵשׁ מַה שֶּׁנֶּאֱמַר, "... וְרָחֵל הָיְתָה יְפַת תֹּאַר וִיפַת מַרְאֶה". רָחֵל מוֹרָה עַל עֲבוֹדַת הַצַּדִּיקִים ... "יְפַת תֹּאַר וִיפַת מַרְאֶה" בְּלִי מוּם וּפְגָם ...

הִנֵּה בְּיַעֲקֹב נֶאֱמַר, "וַיֶּאֱהַב יַעֲקֹב אֶת רָחֵל", כִּי מִצַּד יַעֲקֹב עִיקַּר הָעֲבוֹדָה הִיא עֲבוֹדַת הַצַּדִּיקִים, כְּמוֹ שֶׁכָּתוּב "וְיַעֲקֹב אִישׁ תָּם יוֹשֵׁב אֹהָלִים", הָעֲבוֹדָה בִּ"פְנִים" בִּתְחוּם הַקְּדוּשָּׁה עַצְמָהּ, וְלֹא לָצֵאת לַחוּץ לְהַעֲלוֹת הַחוּץ לִקְדוּשָּׁה.

וְזֶהוּ הַפֵּירוּשׁ הַפְּנִימִי בְּמַאֲמַר רַבּוֹתֵינוּ זִכְרוֹנָם לִבְרָכָה: שֶׁהָיוּ הַכֹּל אוֹמְרִים: "שְׁנֵי בָנִים לְרִבְקָה, וּשְׁתֵּי בָנוֹת לְלָבָן. הַגְּדוֹלָה לַגָּדוֹל, וְהַקְּטַנָּה לַקָּטָן". דְּמִצַּד עֲבוֹדַת לֵאָה, שֶׁהִיא בְּחִינַת עֲבוֹדַת בַּעֲלֵי תְּשׁוּבָה, הֲרֵי הִיא שַׁיֶּיכֶת לְהַחְזִיר עֵשָׂו לְמוּטָב. מַה שֶּׁאֵין כֵּן רָחֵל, שֶׁעִנְיָנָהּ עֲבוֹדַת הַצַּדִּיקִים.

The essential difference between [the two groups within] the Tribes of Israel is that the primary focus of the Children of Leah is the service of *teshuvah*, and the focus of [Rachel's children], Joseph and Benjamin, is the service of *tsadikim*. This has its source in their mothers: Leah is connected with the service of the "masters of return," and Rachel is connected with the service of the perfectly righteous.

This is the meaning of the verse, "... Rachel was of beautiful form and beautiful appearance." Rachel indicates

RABBI MENACHEM MENDEL SCHNEERSON 1902–1994

The towering Jewish leader of the 20th century, known as "the Lubavitcher Rebbe," or simply as "the Rebbe." Born in southern Ukraine, the Rebbe escaped Nazi-occupied Europe, arriving in the U.S. in June 1941. The Rebbe inspired and guided the revival of traditional Judaism after the European devastation, impacting virtually every Jewish community the world over. The Rebbe often emphasized that the performance of just one additional good deed could usher in the era of Mashiach. The Rebbe's scholarly talks and writings have been printed in more than 200 volumes.

the service of the perfectly righteous . . . "of beautiful form and beautiful appearance" without blemish.

Regarding Jacob it is said, "Jacob loved Rachel." Because as far as Jacob himself is concerned, his primary task in life is the service of the perfectly righteous, as it says, "Jacob was a wholesome man, a dweller of tents." His achievements are in the "inside," within the realm of holiness, rather than in venturing out to elevate the "outside" to holiness.

This is the deeper meaning of what the sages relate that people were saying, "Rebecca has two sons, and Laban has two daughters. The elder will marry the elder, and the younger will marry the younger." Leah's life-mission, which is the service of the "masters of return," indicates that her task is to turn back Esau to goodness. Not so Rachel, whose mission is the service of the perfectly righteous.

TEXT 14

MAIMONIDES, *MISHNEH TORAH*, LAWS OF REPENTANCE 2:1

אֵי זוֹ הִיא תְּשׁוּבָה גְמוּרָה? זֶה שֶׁבָּא לְיָדוֹ דָּבָר שֶׁעָבַר בּוֹ וְאֶפְשָׁר בְּיָדוֹ לַעֲשׂוֹתוֹ וּפֵרַשׁ וְלֹא עָשָׂה . . . כֵּיצַד. הֲרֵי שֶׁבָּא עַל אִשָּׁה בַּעֲבֵרָה, וּלְאַחַר זְמַן נִתְיַחֵד עִמָּהּ, וְהוּא עוֹמֵד בְּאַהֲבָתוֹ בָּהּ, וּבְכֹחַ גּוּפוֹ, וּבַמְּדִינָה שֶׁעָבַר בָּהּ, וּפָרַשׁ וְלֹא עָבַר - זֶהוּ בַּעַל תְּשׁוּבָה גְמוּרָה.

What constitutes full *teshuvah* (repentance)? When a person is presented with the same sin they transgressed, and has the opportunity to again transgress, yet refrains from doing so. . . . For example: A person who engaged in forbidden relations with a woman, and is subsequently alone with her, and his love for her is just as strong, and his physical prowess has not diminished, and he is in the same surroundings as he was when he sinned, yet he refrains from transgressing—this is a person who has done a full *teshuvah*.

RABBI MOSHE BEN MAIMON (MAIMONIDES, RAMBAM) 1135–1204

Halachist, philosopher, author, and physician. Maimonides was born in Córdoba, Spain. After the conquest of Córdoba by the Almohads, he fled Spain and eventually settled in Cairo, Egypt. There, he became the leader of the Jewish community and served as court physician to the vizier of Egypt. He is most noted for authoring the *Mishneh Torah*, an encyclopedic arrangement of Jewish law; and for his philosophical work, *Guide for the Perplexed*. His rulings on Jewish law are integral to the formation of halachic consensus.

Figure 4.1

The Two Kingdoms

	SERVICE OF THE *TSADIK*	**SERVICE OF *TESHUVAH***
Primordial Origin	*Tikun*	*Tohu*
Primary Biblical Personalities	· Jacob (original) · Rachel · Joseph	· Jacob (after obtaining Esau's blessings) · Leah · Judah
Divine Dwelling	Tabernacle	Holy Temple
Judaism	Torah	*Mitzvot*
Activity	Learning	Action
Objective	Personal spiritual perfection	Repairing and transforming the world

The Ten Lost Tribes of Israel
Rabbi Moishe New:

MYJLI.COM/BIBLE

Figure 4.2

The Two Divine Dwellings

THE MISHKAN

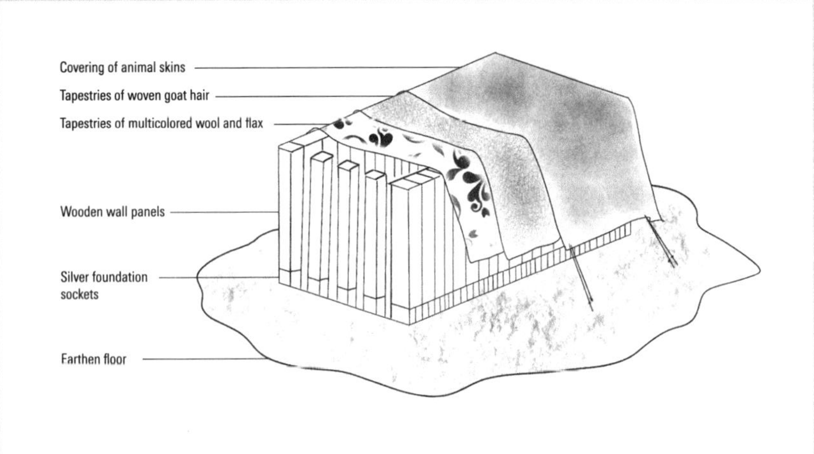

THE HOLY TEMPLE

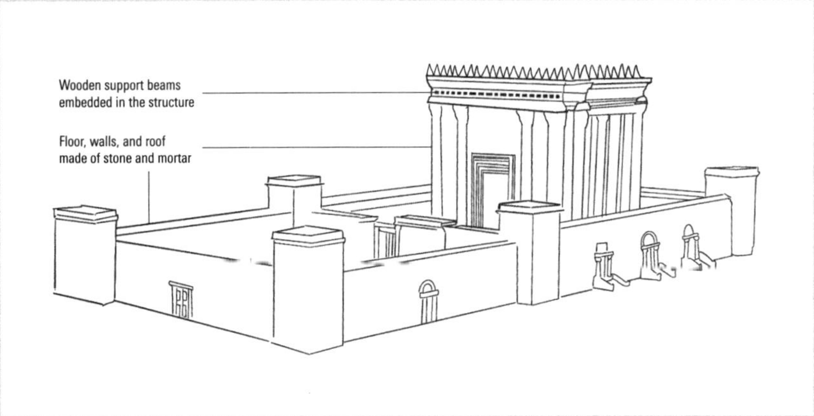

TEXT 15

RABBI YITSCHAK MEIR OF GER, CITED IN *LIKUTEI YEHUDAH*, VAYECHI

יוֹסֵף הוּא רַק הַקְדָּמָה. וְכֵן מָשִׁיחַ בֶּן יוֹסֵף הוּא קוֹדֶם מָשִׁיחַ בֶּן דָּוִד, שֶׁמְּתַקֵּן שֶׁיּוּכַל בֶּן דָּוִד לָבוֹא וּלְסַיֵּים הַגְּאוּלָּה, אֲבָל יוֹסֵף אֵינוֹ גוֹמֵר הַגְּאוּלָּה. וְכֵן רָחֵל, אַף שֶׁעִיקַּר הַמַּלְכוּת עַל שְׁמָהּ, מִכָּל מָקוֹם נִקְבְּרָה בַּדֶּרֶךְ, שֶׁאֵינָהּ גוֹמֶרֶת. וְזֶה הַפֵּירוּשׁ "בַּדֶּרֶךְ".

Joseph is only the preface. Accordingly, "Mashiach the son of Joseph" precedes "Mashiach the son of David," preparing the way for the Son of David to come and complete the Redemption; but Joseph does not complete the Redemption.

Similarly, although Rachel is the primary element of *Malchut* (the divine attribute of Kingship), nevertheless, she was buried on the roadside, as she does not complete the process. This is the deeper meaning of "on the road."

RABBI YITSCHAK MEIR ALTER *(CHIDUSHEI HARIM)* 1789–1866

Chasidic rebbe and Talmudist. Rabbi Yitschak Meir, the founder of the Chasidic dynasty of Ger, was a disciple of Rabbi Menachem Mendel of Kotsk and acknowledged by most as his successor. He followed the Kotsk approach of rigorously seeking unadulterated truth and continuously striving for self-perfection. His works include commentary and expositions on the Talmud and Shulchan Aruch, halachic responsa, and mystical teachings. In his private life, he experienced considerable suffering, losing his 13 children during his lifetime. He was succeeded by his grandson, better known as the *Sefat Emet*.

TEXT 16

TALMUD, KIDUSHIN 40B

> וּכְבָר הָיָה רַבִּי טַרְפוֹן וּזְקֵנִים מְסֻוּבִּין בַּעֲלִיַּת בֵּית נִתְזָה בְּלוּד. נִשְׁאֲלָה שְׁאֵילָה זוּ בִּפְנֵיהֶם: תַּלְמוּד גָּדוֹל אוֹ מַעֲשֶׂה גָּדוֹל?
>
> נַעֲנָה רַבִּי טַרְפוֹן וְאָמַר: "מַעֲשֶׂה גָּדוֹל".
>
> נַעֲנָה רַבִּי עֲקִיבָא וְאָמַר: "תַּלְמוּד גָּדוֹל".
>
> נַעֲנוּ כּוּלָּם וְאָמְרוּ: "תַּלְמוּד גָּדוֹל, שֶׁהַתַּלְמוּד מֵבִיא לִידֵי מַעֲשֶׂה".

It was already the case that Rabbi Tarfon and the sages were assembled in the loft of the Nitzah House in Lod, when the query came before them: Which is greater, learning or action?

Said Rabbi Tarfon: "Action is greater."

Said Rabbi Akiva: "Learning is greater."

Concluded all: "Learning is greater, because learning brings to action."

Is Tikun Olam *an Authentically Jewish Idea?*
***Rabbis Ari Sollish** and*
***Simon Jacobson**:*

MYJLI.COM/BIBLE

QUESTION FOR DISCUSSION

Did the Talmud settle the question, or did it only make things more complicated?

QUESTION FOR DISCUSSION

What should be the "mission statement" of Judaism?

Oil painting of family lighting Shabbat candles (detail). (Dobrik/Shutterstock.com)

KEY POINTS

1 The story of Joseph and his brothers presents us with two baffling mysteries: (a) What led the children of Jacob, who were righteous and holy men, to act in such a way, plotting to kill their own brother, and then selling him into slavery? (b) Since it is obvious from the narrative that Joseph bore no ill will toward his brothers, what was the purpose of the trials and tribulations to which he subjected them?

2 Both questions are resolved when we understand the deeper roots of the conflict between Joseph and his brothers—a division that runs as a seam throughout Jewish history, and exists as a dichotomy within our own lives.

3 There are a number of striking parallels between: (a) Jacob's deception of Isaac to receive the blessings intended for Esau; (b) Jacob being tricked into marrying Leah instead of Rachel; and (c) the brothers' selling of Joseph into slavery and misleading their father Jacob into believing that Joseph was killed by a wild animal. Indeed, these three events are interconnected.

4 Although Leah was Jacob's first wife and the mother of the majority of his children, Jacob regarded Rachel as his primary wife, and Rachel's children as his true progeny—something that the children of Leah refused to accept. This created the divide between the Children of Leah and the Children of Rachel within the formative family of the people of Israel.

5 On a deeper level, Rachel represents the "service of the *tsadik*"—the development of all that is spiritual and holy in ourselves and in the world. Leah represents the "service of *teshuvah*"—the mission to engage with the material world in order to transform it and sanctify it. In the original scheme of things, Rachel—the person as well as the lifestyle—was meant to be Jacob's only wife and role, while Leah was destined to marry Esau. However, when Jacob obtained mastery of the material world by "stealing" the blessings intended for Esau, he was compelled to marry Leah as well and to incorporate the "service of *teshuvah*" into his life's mission. But his first love remained Rachel and the path of spiritual perfection that Rachel represents.

6 The two paradigms of "the Children of Rachel" and "the Children of Leah" assume various forms. In the earlier periods of Jewish history, the people of Israel were governed by leaders and kings from the tribes of Joseph and Benjamin—i.e., the Children of Rachel. Subsequently, however, the leadership of Israel was entrusted to the tribe of Judah, of the Children of Leah. The same process is represented in the "Divine

Dwellings" created by the people of Israel. The portable Mishkan, which was made of organic materials and which stood in the territory of Joseph, represented the service of G-d through spiritual growth and self-perfection; whereas the Holy Temple, built of stone on its permanent site in the territory of Judah, represented the service of action in the material world. As these examples demonstrate, the "Rachel" paradigm always precedes and paves the way for the "Leah" paradigm.

7 The story of the selling of Joseph, and the sequence of events leading to Judah risking his life to save Benjamin and to the brothers' reconciliation, charts the process by which the Children of Leah came to accept the leadership of Joseph. Centuries later, the Children of Rachel would be challenged to accept the transition of the nation's leadership to the tribe of Judah.

8 The Talmud presents this dichotomy in the form of a debate: Which is greater: learning or action? The conclusion is that action is the ultimate goal, but one can reach it only through learning. Similarly, the many goals and objectives of Judaism may be described in terms of two general categories: (a) spiritual or "religious" objectives; (b) improving and perfecting the world. The latter cannot be achieved without the former. In the final analysis, we cannot fix the world without perfecting ourselves.

Additional Readings

THE KINGDOM OF JOSEPH AND THE KINGDOM OF JUDAH

EXCERPT FROM *SHENEI LUCHOT HABERIT* BY RABBI YESHAYAHU HOROWITZ
TRANSLATION BY RABBI SHMUEL KLATZKIN

I.

The Midrash *Bereishit Rabah* (85:1) comments on the verse (Genesis 38:1): "It was at that time that Judah went down from his brothers. . . .":

> *Rabbi Shmuel bar Nachman began his discourse by quoting the verse (Jeremiah 29:11): "For I knew the thoughts." The brothers were engaged in selling Joseph; Joseph was engaged in his sackcloth and fasting; Reuben was engaged in his sackcloth and fasting; Jacob was engaged in his sackcloth and fasting; Judah was engaged in taking a wife; and G-d was engaged in creating the light of Mashiach.*

The purpose of this passage is to explain the significance of the events surrounding the selling of Joseph. It is true that the brothers were engaged in the selling of Joseph in order to rid him from the world. Jacob, too, was engaged in his mourning and fasting and had despaired of him, saying (Genesis 37:35), "I will go down to my son to the grave mourning." The fact that Reuben was engaged in sackcloth and fasting (over his sin)[1] enabled Joseph to be sold, as he was not present at the time of the sale due to his penitential practices. Had he been present he would have prevented it, as the Torah testifies that when he saw Joseph was no longer in the pit, "He tore his garments" (Genesis 37:29).

Seemingly, all this happened for the worse; but G-d had planned it for the good. That is the meaning of "For I knew the thoughts": the chain of causation that brought about Joseph's sale eventually extended itself to be the chain of causation that will bring Mashiach.

One may ask: If this was all from G-d and was for the good, then it follows that the brothers were compelled to act as they did, and therefore why should they have been punished? Know this: G-d forbid to say that they were compelled! Everything was the result of free choice. It is only that the divine intent was brought about by means of their sin. This is consonant with the teaching in the Talmud (Shabbat 32a): "Merit is caused through the meritorious, and guilt through the guilty," even though the result was decreed by G-d. This is a matter that needs broad explanation, but here is not its place.

Before I explain how Joseph's sale and its consequences resulted in the establishment of David's kingship and that of Mashiach, I will address some major questions concerning Joseph and his brothers that properly need to be addressed.

First of all, a most general difficulty: The greatness of the sons of Jacob, the progenitors of the twelve tribes of Israel, is well known. Certainly they were greater than the supernal angels, as they represent the mystical twelve configurations of the divine name *Havayah*. How, then, could the mind grasp the idea that these exalted individuals would join together to commit the most severe sin of all the sins in the world, namely the sin of murder? How could they imagine murdering Joseph, particularly with Joseph being a righteous man, a pillar serving as the foundation of the world? Even someone who is a greatly evil person, transgressing several grave prohibitions, would

RABBI YESHAYAHU HALEVI HOROWITZ (*SHALAH*), 1565–1630

Kabbalist and author. Rabbi Horowitz was born in Prague and served as rabbi in several prominent Jewish communities, including Frankfurt am Main and his native Prague. After the passing of his wife in 1620, he moved to Israel. In Tiberias, he completed his *Shenei Luchot Haberit*, an encyclopedic compilation of kabbalistic ideas. He is buried in Tiberias, next to Maimonides.

refrain from murdering even a person of small stature from among his fellow Jews.

In *Bereishit Rabah, Parshat Vayigash* (93:9), the sages comment on the verse (Genesis 45:1), "Joseph was no longer able to constrain himself . . . [and he called, 'Remove every man from my presence!']":

> *Rabbi Chama bar Chanina says, "Joseph did not act prudently [in remaining alone with his brothers]. For had one of them kicked him, he would have died immediately." Rabbi Shmuel bar Nachman says, "He acted properly and prudently. He knew his brothers were righteous and said to himself, 'G-d forbid that my brothers should be suspect of plotting bloodshed.'"*

Now, if the brothers were not suspect of plotting to murder even an Egyptian who was charging them falsely, how could they have wanted to kill their brother, the righteous foundation of the world?

An even greater question: Even after they had repented and confessed their sin—as described in the verse (Genesis 42:21), "And they said, each one to his brother, 'Truly, we are guilty [over our brother . . .]"—we find in a Midrash (*Tanchuma,* Vayigash 5) that when Joseph revealed himself to his brothers, they sought to kill him, but an angel came and scattered them. We cannot explain this by saying that the power of shame is great and because of shame they acted this way. To the contrary: shame is needed by the penitent. As the rabbis said (Berachot 12b), "One who transgresses and is ashamed is forgiven. . . ." There is another verse that is apt (Jeremiah 31:18): "I am ashamed and mortified. . . ."

A second difficulty is that the sages say that the brothers made the Divine Presence their partner in the selling of Joseph (*Tanchuma*, Vayeishev 2). How could the Divine Presence be a partner with them? Did not our father Jacob, who was flesh and blood, say "May my soul not enter their council," referring to the act of Zimri? And did he not say, "Let my honor not unite with their assembly," in reference to the dispute of Korach? (Genesis 49:6, as expounded in *Bereishit Rabah* 99:7). [So even Jacob] did not wish to have his name associated with a sinful act! . . .

II.

In the Torah portion of *Vayigash*, when Joseph revealed himself to his brothers, we find several precise choices of words and several seemingly extraneous words. Joseph says (Genesis 45:5), "And now, do not be distressed." What is the meaning of "and now"? Wouldn't it have been more fitting to just say, "Do not be distressed"?

Another difficulty: Joseph mentions three times the mission of G-d in which he was sent before them: "As a source of livelihood, G-d has sent me before you" (ibid.); "G-d sent me before you to make for you a remnant in the land" (45:7); "And now, it is not you who sent me here, but G-d" (45:8)—three times.

Another difficulty: "He has made me as a father to Pharaoh" (ibid.). Was Joseph really a father to Pharaoh? To the contrary! Pharaoh was his superior. As Pharaoh himself said (Genesis 41:40), "Only the throne I will make greater than you."

A further difficulty: "He fell on Benjamin's neck and wept" (45:14). Rashi explains that Joseph was weeping over "the destruction of the Holy Temples" and "the destruction of Shiloh." How are these destructions relevant now, at a time of the joyous reunion of brothers recognizing and happily kissing one another?

III.

I have already written that G-d is *echad* ("one"), and so, too, Israel is *echad*. It is written (Job 23:13), "And He is *be-echad*"—G-d, who is *echad*, is tied to Israel, who are one. This is the meaning of *be-echad* (literally, "in one"), which hints at two *echads* (the letter *bet* signifying two). . . .

This attachment and bond is achieved by means of the Torah, as "the Torah is entirely names of G-d" (*Zohar* 2:87a). The Torah is the revelation of His divinity, and Israel's fulfillment of the Torah arouses the spiritualty of the Torah, which is the secret meaning of G-d's names, and thereby they are attached.

Therefore, Jacob, who is *echad*, is the master of the Torah—and so, too, is Joseph, as I have written. "Jacob was a wholesome man, dwelling in tents" (Genesis 25:27), and Joseph "was a child of sagacity to him" (37:3), which Rashi explains to mean: "All that Jacob had learned from Shem and Eber, he gave in its entirety over to Joseph" (Rashi, ad loc.; *Bereishit Rabah* 84:8).

Now, the crown of Torah has two other crowns related to it: the crown of priesthood and the crown of kingship.[2] For the Torah was given "to learn, to keep, and to do," which means the service of the *mitzvot* of action. The most essential of the *mitzvot* of action are the *korbanot* (sacrifices) brought in the Holy Temple, as taught in the Mishnah (Avot 1:2): "The world stands . . . on the study of Torah and on the service. . . ." The Temple offerings are simply called "the service" because they are the essence of our service of G-d. Thus, the crown of priesthood is for those to whom this service belongs.

The crown of kingship is also needed, so that the awe of the sovereign will guide the people to Torah and the actions it mandates, leading them to serve G-d in truth and wholeheartedness. This is how the righteous leaders of Israel acted, following in the way of the master of all the prophets. Our teacher Moses was called king—as it says (Deuteronomy 33:5), "There was a king in Jeshurun"—for he taught the Torah to all of Israel, reproved them, and led them in the path of truth to learn, do, and fulfill all the words of Torah.

Hence, these three crowns are ultimately one crown. Therefore, it is written about the giving of the Torah (Exodus 19:6), "And you will be for Me a kingdom of priests." The word "kingdom" alludes to the crown of kingship, and "priests" alludes to the crown of priesthood. For these two crowns are for the sake of the crown of Torah.

IV.

Joseph merited to the crown of Torah, for Jacob gave over to him all he had received from Shem and Eber. Levi merited to the crown of priesthood. When Levi was born, G-d sent the angel Gabriel to bring him before Him, and He gave him twenty-four gifts and "called his name Levi ('companion')," as is stated in the Torah portion of *Vayetsei* (Genesis 29:34, following Rashi). Judah merited to the crown of kingship, and the crown of kingship suited him, for he corresponds to the kingdom of heaven, which is the fourth leg [of the divine throne]. . . .

The Talmud teaches that one who contests the kingship of the House of David contests the Divine Presence (see Sanhedrin 110a). For the throne of the Divine Presence is the supernal "fourth leg," which is accomplished below by the kingship of the House of David; he is the vehicle for it, and he is the fourth.

The Patriarchs are three, and they are called the "divine chariots"; David is the fourth, completing the divine name י-ה-ו-ה (the four Hebrew letters *yud-hei-vav-hei*). For the root of the column[3] of benevolence (*chesed*) is the letter *yud*; the root of the column of strict judgment (*din*) is the first *hei*; and the column of compassion (*rachamim*) is the letter *vav*. The three Patriarchs are identified (in order) with benevolence, strict judgment, and compassion. The final *hei* of the divine name is kingship (*malchut*), through which David is connected to the chariot, and then the Name is complete.

In the future age of Mashiach, when David's kingship will be raised up and the sovereignty will be G-d's, the prophecy "On that day G-d will be one, and His name will be one" will be fulfilled (Zachariah 14:9). This is hinted at in the last of the letters of דוד ("David"). Look at the name יהודה ("Judah"), and you will see amazing things, for in it you have the divine name י-ה-ו-ה with an additional ד (from the name דוד), which hints at the fourth leg. It is necessarily through David's kingship that the Name is completed.

V.

I have already written that all attachment to G-d is by means of the Torah, and all the other crowns are for the sake of the crown of Torah. Therefore, you will find that they all incorporate Torah.

Regarding the tribe of Levi, to whom belongs the crown of priesthood, it is written (Deuteronomy 33:10), "They will teach your laws to Jacob and your instructions (*torah*) to Israel." Regarding the dynasty of the House of David, our sages explained that the verse (I Samuel 15:18) [speaking of King David] "G-d is with him" means that "the halachah (legal ruling of Torah law) follows his opinion in all cases" (Sanhedrin 93b).

The crown of kingship is included within the crown of priesthood, for the kingship of the descendants of

Judah came from Tamar, daughter of Shem, "who was a priest to G-d on high" (Genesis 14:18). So, too, you will find (*Bamidbar Rabah* 15:1) in Israel's conquest of the Holy Land that the two faithful spies sent to scout out the Land, Phineas and Caleb, were from these two tribes, Caleb from Judah and Phineas from the priesthood.

So too it will be in the future, when we will merit to the Land in its fullness and its goodness when our Mashiach comes: Elijah the Prophet will come [as the herald of Mashiach, who is from the House of David], and he is a priest, for Phineas and Elijah are the same person (*Targum Yonatan,* Shemot 6:18).

This was the error of the Hasmoneans, when during the time of the Second Temple they grasped the kingship. It was not hidden from them that the kingship was only for David and his descendants, as we will present later. But they thought that the kingship derived from the priesthood. They also reckoned the maternal line, and they assigned succession to the throne to the descendants of the mother of the king.

Thus, we have three crowns: Joseph's, Levi's, and Judah's. "But the crown of good name surmounts them all" (Avot 4:13). That refers to Jacob, who is their source. Nevertheless, Joseph was the head of all the crowns, which is the crown of Torah, because the two other crowns are for the sake of the crown of Torah. . . .

This is what is being hinted at in the text telling of Joseph's rise to greatness (Genesis 41:46): "Joseph was thirty years old. . . ." [Thirty is denoted by the letter *lamed*, and] the mystical secret of *lamed* is that it is the crown of Torah.[4] It is also written (Exodus 13:19), "Moses took the bones of Joseph with him"; meaning, that which was the essence[5] of Joseph, the crown of Torah, Moses took to himself, and through Moses, the Torah was given.

VI.

The sum of all this is: Jacob is the source of the [three] crowns; he is the "good name that surmounts them all." And Joseph is the head of the crowns. Thus, "Israel bowed at the head of the bed" (Genesis 47:31) in deference to Joseph, as explained by Rashi there. Levi is the crown of priesthood, and Judah is the crown of kingship.

The power of the crown of priesthood is only in the Holy Temple. It is in the Holy Temple that the kings of the House of David are elevated, as the Talmud teaches, "Only the kings of the Davidic line may sit in the Temple courtyard" (Yoma 25a). For David was the vehicle for the sovereignty of Heaven, which is the mystical secret of the heavenly Temple, as it is said (Habakkuk 2:2), "G-d is in His holy palace; all the world, be still (*hahs*) before Him!" The "palace" refers to the attribute of kingship; the divine name *Adonai* ("L-rd") has the same numerical value as the word *heichal* (palace), which has the same numerical value as the word *hahs* ("be still"), which is the mystical secret of the supernal Land.

But the Holy Temple is built in the portion belonging to Benjamin;[6] the eternal abode and its eternity is in the portion of the Land assigned to Benjamin. He, too, had the kingship, but only borrowed, and not on a permanent basis. This is the mystical secret to be read in the name of the Benjamite king, Saul (meaning "borrowed"). . . .

Also, in the time of the Destruction, when the Jewish people were exiled to Babylonia, Mordecai, who was a descendant of Benjamin, "did not bow and did not prostrate himself" (Esther 3:2). Thus, it was Mordecai, who raised Esther, who was the cause of Esther's son, Cyrus the Persian, building the Second Temple.

Hence, the Temple was in the portion of land belonging to Benjamin, even though his kingship did not last beyond the rule of Saul—it was living on borrowed time until David came. That is to say, it was borrowed until David would come, to whom the kingship justly belonged. . . .

VII.

The crown of kingship and the crown of priesthood are connected to each other, and both of them serve the crown of Torah—and that is Joseph, as I wrote earlier. He is the pillar upon which the world stands, for the world stands on a single pillar called *tsadik*—righteous—and our sages have said (Chagigah 12b), "Joseph is the righteous one."

The mystical secret is that the *tsadik* is the pillar of the world. All the energies and the channels of the *sefirot* converge in the *sefirah* of *yesod* ("foundation"),[7] and from *yesod*, a channel leads directly to *malchut*, as is explained in *Pardes* in *Shaar Hatsinorot*. The *sefirah* of *malchut* ("kingship") governs the worlds through the power of the *sefirot*, which carry the power of *Ein Sof* that energizes it. For that reason, *malchut* is called *olam*—world.

Which is the pillar through which our world derives its ongoing existence, which, as I have mentioned, is *malchut*? This is the pillar of the righteous foundation, that is to say, the channel that runs from *yesod* to *malchut*. From the perspective of the attribute of *malchut*—the crown of kingship and the Temple, which is the divine palace where the crown of priesthood resides—"Joseph is the ruler" (Genesis 42:6). Through him, all these elements are set aright. . . .

VIII.

Joseph is the matrix of Israel. Were it not for Joseph, we would still be enslaved. Joseph opened the doorway [for the liberation from Egypt], for his strength was great. G-d sent the cure before the plague; that is, he sent Joseph before Israel's slavery began. After the slavery, "they went out with a high hand" (Exodus 14:8). Then Israel became a unique people; G-d chose them as a people until they succeeded to having a kingship. David, our king, from the tribe of Judah, was the true king, but had Joseph not preceded him as ruler in Egypt, the kingship of Judah would never have come to be, for Israel would not have become a people, G-d forbid.

Similarly with respect to the holiness of the Temple. The Tabernacle at Shiloh, which was in the portion of Joseph, preceded the eternal Temple. Even though Shiloh was destroyed, nonetheless, through it, Joseph opened up the channel of holiness, and that holiness would survive and endure in the eternal Temple.

For Joseph is the channel. He is the pillar upon which the world stands, through his mystical quality of "the *tsadik* who is the foundation of the world" (Proverbs 10:25). All the various energies flow through this channel into *malchut*, which is called "world," even though afterward the kingship and the Temple were removed from him. . . .

"When Israel went out from Egypt" and was made a people, immediately "Judah was His holy portion, and Israel was His governance" (Psalms 114:2). So, too, with the tribal banners: the banner of the encampment of Judah was first, and similarly with the heads of the tribes. This extended even until after the inheritance of the Land in the days of Samuel, when the people said, "Give us a king" (I Samuel 8:5), and Saul was chosen from Benjamin, as I have written. But this was only a borrowed kingship; it was returned afterward to its owners—David and his descendants—until the end of time. "The scepter shall not depart from Judah" (Genesis 49:14).

However, when they sinned in the Land, the sin caused that the kingdom of the House of David should be split.[8] Joseph was the channel from above upon which the world stands, as I have explained, and he did not send his energy only to Jerusalem, that is, to the House of David, but rather sent energy outside Jerusalem as well. Then it was that the kingship was drawn to the descendants of Joseph.

This caused much evil, for "Their heart split apart; they now feel their guilt" (Hosea 10:2). From the force of that split, idolatry came about, Jeroboam beginning with the golden calves, and they served several kinds of idolatry. Afterward, the tribe of Judah learned also from their abominations, and the split continued to extend until they were exiled from the Land.

The matters were not returned to a correct state even when the Second Temple was built, because five of the choice features of the Holy Temple were lacking (see Yoma 21b). Nor was the kingship of the House of David there, only the kingship of the Hasmoneans, which G-d had not commanded, for G-d had commanded the kingship to David and his descendants forever. Thus, the Hasmoneans were punished for having taken the kingship, and Herod and his house arose and ruled in their place, as Nachmanides writes in his comment on the verse (Genesis 49:10), "The scepter shall not depart from Judah."

IX.

This breach will not be set aright until the messianic future. Then things will be restored, and once again, the kingship of the House of Joseph will precede that of the House of David. For Mashiach ben Joseph will come first, and only afterward Mashiach ben David. Then the House of Joseph will rectify what they ruined at the splitting apart of the kingdom of the House of David, for Mashiach ben Joseph will not come for his own need, but will come solely for the sake of Mashiach ben David. He will sacrifice his life for him and submit to death, and his blood will atone for the people of G-d in such a way that afterward the kingship of the House of David in the people of Israel will be eternal.

Then Joseph's two dreams will be fulfilled. [The two dreams refer to] (a) the precedence of Joseph's rulership in Egypt; (b) in the future, the precedence of his rulership to that of Mashiach ben David. Both of these two reigns are for the sake of the kingdom of Judah, and both of them are alike in their goodness. . . .

All of this comes by means of the Torah, which includes both learning and action: the learning using contemplative intellectual grasp, engaging the soul, and the action being done by the body. . . .[9]

X.

We will return to our subject. The rulership of Joseph was for the sake of Israel becoming a people and to establish the kingship of Judah. The tribes did not understand this, thinking rather that Joseph's ambition was for the kingship to be his, wanting to grasp it for himself and his descendants. Therefore they "went to Dothan" to design a plot against him, which really meant to judge him by Torah law.[10] They all agreed that he deserved death; even the sons of Bilhah and Zilpah who loved him agreed that this was justified by the law, because he was contesting the sovereignty of the House of David, and anyone who contests the kingship of the House of David is as if they disputed the authority of the Divine Presence (see Sanhedrin 110a).

(Note: One should not ask: Why were the brothers punished if they judged him by the law of the Torah? For it is regarding matters such as this that we are taught that "an error in learning is reckoned as guilt" [Avot 4:13; Bava Metsi'a 33b], as they should have known and comprehended the matter. But this was a case in which "hatred distorts the norm" [*Bereishit Rabah* 55:8]. Because they hated him, they did not reach the proper legal conclusion.)

This is the idea behind what the rabbis said (*Tanchuma,* Vayeishev 2), "They made the Divine Presence their partner." By this they meant that he was contesting the Divine Presence by contesting the kingship of the House of David. Therefore, when Joseph made himself known to his brothers, and they saw that he was a ruler, they wanted to kill him (as we quoted earlier from *Tanchuma,* Vayigash 5) because they saw that his thought had matured from mental planning into action, until G-d sent an angel and scattered them.

Then "Joseph said to his brothers, 'Please approach me'" (Genesis 48:4). For he wanted to reveal to them that the matter was not as they had thought, that he had usurped the crown of kingship. Quite to the contrary: G-d had sent him before them, that is to say, to prepare the way to cause that Israel should become a people and bring Judah to kingship. . . .

XI.

Three times, Joseph repeats the theme that "G-d has sent me before you." The first (Genesis 45:5) is understood in its simple sense: I was sent to provide sustenance in the face of the impending famine.

The second is that "G-d sent me before you to preserve a remnant in the land, and to keep alive for you a great salvation" (Genesis 45:7). The words of this verse are almost self-contradictory. For the word "remnant" denotes something small whereas "a great salvation" denotes a large amount. But rather than being a contradiction, this is really referring to the two missions for which Joseph was sent before them in setting up the kingdom of Judah. One was in this current world, so that Israel should be deserving and ready for the kingship, so that "When Israel left Egypt . . . Judah was His holy one" (Psalms 114:1–2). This extended all the way to the establishment of the kingship of the House of David. The second is for the future world to come, when Joseph will be sent before the kingship of Mashiach. For Mashiach ben Joseph will clear the way, and he will be killed for the sake of Israel while sanctifying G-d's blessed name. Then David will arise and there will be a reckoning for his blood.

An allusion to this came in the words of Reuben when he said (Genesis 42:22), "And behold, there is a reckoning for his blood." Although they did not understand this matter yet, a spark of a prophetic spirit glimmered in them on a number of occasions, and a true word was in their mouth. It was the holy spirit that put those words in Reuben's mouth. It is the mystical secret of the idea of Joseph that he is not just an agent sent before them, and not just that he will be killed in the future, but also that there will be a reckoning for his blood.

This is the meaning of what Joseph said to them: At the beginning, "G-d sent me before you to preserve a remnant," meaning the House of David in this world. But in the future, I will be an agent sent before you "for a great salvation," meaning the kingdom of Mashiach.

He said a third time: "And now, it is not you who have sent me here but G-d, and He has made me as a father to Pharaoh" (Genesis 45:8). Now he is coming to explain to them the matter of his mission and to clarify what it is all about and how it has caused Israel to be a people. He said that G-d has made him "a father to Pharaoh," that is to say, his ruler, for he rode in the second state chariot.

Now, Egypt was "the nakedness of the Land" (Genesis 42:9), the meaning of which I have explained, whereas Joseph was the guardian of the covenant [of circumcision], and it was of Joseph that Jacob had thought in his first seminal drop. Therefore, Joseph needed to be ruler there, and ride upon their governing angel. So at first Joseph was sold as a slave, by which he made a precedent for Israel when they would be slaves to Egypt. Afterward, the people of Israel "went out with a high hand," and G-d executed judgments against their gods, meaning their patron angel. "And Israel saw Egypt dead by the shore of the sea" (Exodus 14:30)—this refers to the angel of Egypt. Had all this not happened, we would still be enslaved in Egypt, G-d forbid.

And that is the very reason that in the future, Joseph will be sent before Mashiach.

Endnotes

1 See Genesis 35:22 and Rashi to Genesis 37:29.
2 See Avot 4:13: "There are three crowns: the crown of Torah, the crown of priesthood, and the crown of kingship. But the crown of good name surmounts them all."
3 The ten supernal *sefirot* (divine attributes) are arrayed in three columns of three, with the tenth *sefirah*, *malchut* ("kingship"), positioned beneath the middle column.
4 *Lamed* means "learning."
5 In Hebrew, the word עצם (*etsem*), "bone," also means "essence."
6 The Holy Temple in Jerusalem actually straddled the territories of the two tribes of Judah and Benjamin.
7 *Yesod* is the *sefirah* associated with Joseph.
8 After the death of King Solomon, ten of the twelve tribes broke away from the House of David to form the Northern Kingdom of Israel under the kingship of Jeroboam ben Nebat, a descendant of Joseph.
9 Joseph represents learning, and Judah represents action.
10 See Rashi to Genesis 37:17.

Rabbi Isaiah Horowitz, *Shenei Luchot Haberit* (*SHALAH*), 2:298b–301a (*Torah Shebichtav*, Vayeshev–Mikets–Vayigash)

THE ENCOUNTER OF JUDAH AND JOSEPH

EXCERPT FROM *TORAH OR* BY RABBI SHNE'UR ZALMAN OF LIADI
TRANSLATION BY RABBI SHMUEL KLATZKIN

I.

> *[It is written,] "And Judah approach him [Joseph], and he said, 'I beseech you, my master . . .'"* (Genesis 44:18).

It is written, "The roofbeams of our home are cedar . . ." (Song of Songs, 1:17). Now, we need to understand the distinction between the Mishkan (Tabernacle) and the Holy Temple. The Mishkan was built of cedar—as it is written, "[You shall make the wall panels for the Mishkan of] standing *shitim* wood" (Exodus 26:18)—and its roof-covering was made of sheets of goat hair, ram's skins and *tachash* skins, and so on. On the other hand, the Holy Temple was made only of stone and of earth. (Indeed, it was forbidden to build into the Temple any protruding wood or porticos of wood, as Maimonides writes in the first chapter of his *Laws of the Chosen House*; see also *Sefer Hachinuch*, mitzvah 492.) The only wood that was used in the Temple's construction were the cedar beams in the roof of the *ulam* (entrance hall).

We need to understand why the cedar wood was the main building material of the Mishkan, with earth being used only for the floor below, whereas the opposite was true of the Temple: the stones and the earth were the main building materials—even the roof was made from them—and wood was only in the cedar beams which played only a supporting role to the main structure.

RABBI SHNE'UR ZALMAN OF LIADI (ALTER REBBE), 1745–1812

Chasidic rebbe, halachic authority, and founder of the Chabad movement. The Alter Rebbe was born in Liozna, Belarus, and was among the principal students of the Magid of Mezeritch. His numerous works include the *Tanya*, an early classic containing the fundamentals of Chabad Chasidism; and *Shulchan Aruch HaRav*, an expanded and reworked code of Jewish law.

The idea can be grasped from the well-known teaching that all the beings of the world fall into four classes: inanimate, vegetative, animal, and human. The inanimate are lower than the vegetative, the vegetative are lower than the animal, and the highest of all is the human. But this raises the question: Given this hierarchy, why is it that only the earth brings forth vegetation? How can the vegetative proceed and extend from the "dust of the earth," being that it is higher than the inanimate dust in this hierarchy?

However, one is not dependent on the other. Although the inanimate is lower than the vegetative in this hierarchy of vitality, it has, nonetheless, a certain advantage over it, in that its source is from a higher place than all the others.

There is a well-known debate among the sages of the Mishnah found in the Talmud (Chagigah 12a): "One said that the heavens preceded the earth, as it is written, 'In the beginning G-d created the heavens and the earth' (Genesis 1:1). The other said that the earth preceded the heavens, as it is written, 'On the day that Almighty G-d made earth and heaven' (Genesis 2:4)."

Both these and these are the words of the living G-d. In thought, the earth preceded the heavens. But when G-d actually created them, He created the heavens first.

This idea is expressed in the statement, "The very final action was first in thought" (the mystical *Lechah Dodi* hymn). This means that because the earth was the last act of creation, it follows that its root in the divine thought was first; whereas the heavens, which were the first to actually be created, arose later in the divine thought. That is the rule: the last in action arises first in thought.

Therefore, in the system of the *seder hishtalshelut* (the "order of the devolution") of G-d's creation of the worlds, the vegetative is superior to the inanimate, and similarly, the animal is superior to the vegetative. In this order, the inanimate dust of the earth is the "final action"; the vegetative and animal levels are loftier than it in stature, just as the heavens precede the earth. However, from the perspective of their root in the primordial divine thought, the earth preceded all things. Therefore, it is precisely in the earth, on account of its superior source, that there is the power and the ability to bring forth vegetation; and for this reason, the vegetative, the animal, and the human all receive sustenance from it.

II.

Now, the Mishkan did not yet represent the ultimate perfection [for a Divine dwelling], as it was only a temporary dwelling for G-d; as it is written, "I went about in a tent and in a Tabernacle" (II Samuel 7:6). So it was made in a way that reflected the *seder hishtalshelut*, which was created in such an order that the heavens preceded the earth. Therefore, the walls of the Mishkan were wooden boards, part of the vegetative realm, while only the ground of the Mishkan was of earth. This reflected the process of devolution, in which the vegetative is higher than the inanimate. That is why the boards were made of cedar, since the cedar grows to a great height; it is the highest level of the vegetative world, far higher than the level of the inanimate, which does not grow at all.

This is also why the covering of the Mishkan was from sheets [of wool and goat hair] and skins of rams and *techashim,* which are of the animal realm—a realm higher than the vegetative. Thus the roof-coverings, whose mode was "encompassing," as they were spread out over the walls of the Mishkan, were from the animal realm, higher than the vegetative realm from which the walls of the Mishkan were built.

We thus find that everything in the Mishkan was made in accordance with the order of devolution, as creation preceded from above downward, reflected in the opinion that "the heavens came first."

The ultimate perfection, however, was embodied by the Holy Temple. For this was the permanent dwelling of G-d, as it is written, "This is My resting place for all eternity" (Psalms 132:14).

The Holy Temple, therefore, was a foretaste of the World to Come that will be in the seventh millennium, when there will be the tranquility of eternal life. At that time, the earth, which is the level of *malchut* of *atsilut*, will ascend to be above everything else. As it is written, "A woman of valor is the crown of her husband" (Proverbs 12:4). In the future, the feminine *malchut* will be the crown of her husband, *ze'eir anpin*, on account of its source, which arose first in the primordial divine thought—"earth preceded heaven."

Therefore, in the Holy Temple, which was modeled after the World to Come, the main part of the structure was made from stones and earth, which are of the level of the inanimate. Even the roof was made from stones and earth and not from cedar. This is as it will be in the World to Come—the earth preceding heaven, and "a woman of valor is the crown of her husband," all on account of its superior source. Only the beams in the roof were of cedar, and they served merely as support for the main part of the roof, which was made of inanimate material, paralleling the idea of "supporters of Torah."

III.

A clearly seen advantage that we discern in the earth is its selflessness: the earth allows itself to be stepped on by the sole of every foot. This humility is not present in the vegetative realm, which grow to a height, lifting themselves up. The earth derives its selflessness from its lofty source in the divine thought. The word for "thought" in Hebrew, *machshavah*, breaks down into two words, *chashav mah*, meaning literally "thought of 'what.'" This expresses an ultimate selflessness, as when our teacher Moses said, "And we, what are we?" From that source, that selflessness is drawn down and extended to the earth; and for that reason, in the World to Come, she will ascend to become the crown of her husband. Therefore, the Temple was built only from stones.

(This is similar to what is also written elsewhere, in explanation of Psalm 30, which speaks of the dedication of the Temple. The sages of the Talmud say that Cyrus of Persia spoiled things by revising his command and specifying that the vegetative realm should be incorporated into the Temple, laying "three tiers of hewn stone then one course of new wood," when the whole of the Temple needed to be made of stones only, for the reasons set forth above. In prayer, this is the aspect present in the bowing during the Amidah, which itself is modeled on the "murmuring small voice" heard by Elijah. This is the level of the inanimate, as are the letters of the prayer.)

This was not the case in the Mishkan, which was constructed in accordance with the current devolutionary order in which the realm of the vegetative is higher than the inanimate—"the heavens came first." Therefore, its walls were made of cedar, and the earth was only used as the ground beneath the Mishkan, as stated earlier.

IV.

This is also the idea behind [the encounter between] Joseph and Judah, which follows the paradigm of "heaven and earth" and "vegetative and inanimate."

The name "Joseph" [*Yosef* in Hebrew] denotes "addition" and "profusion"—one who continually adds on to his greatness and elevation, like the plants of the vegetative realm. This is true of the cedar in particular, which keeps growing to the highest heights; as it is written, "The righteous one will flourish like a palm; like a cedar in Lebanon, he will grow great" (Psalms 92:13).

(This is the aspect of *ze'eir anpin* [the emotional faculties] of *atsilut*, which is called "vegetative," in comparison to *malchut*, which is called "inanimate," as is written of elsewhere at length. The emotions flourish and grow, but the "letters" of the soul are in the inanimate mode. Emotions develop, growing from an immature to a mature, grown state. This is also seen in the relation between [two elements of the purification ceremony with the ashes of the red heifer] the cedar branch and the hyssop branch: the hyssop is small and the cedar is great—"like a cedar in Lebanon, he will grow great." This is true of Joseph in particular, who represents *yesod,* the concluding level of the emotional faculties, which ascends to the level of *daat*, and *daat* in turn ascends up to the super-intellectual realm of *keter*. As this "middle column" of the constellation of the *sefirot* extends higher and higher, it is called a "cedar in Lebanon.")

Judah, on the other hand, is of the aspect of earth: *malchut* of *atsilut*, which is the realm of the inanimate in *atsilut*. Therefore, the name "Judah" (*Yehudah*) denotes *hoda'ah*—submission—since the inanimate has the highest degree of selflessness, as stated earlier.

V.

In the current *seder hishtalshelut* ("devolutionary order"), Joseph is higher than Judah, as *malchut* receives its energy and life force from *ze'eir anpin*. Therefore, Joseph was king in Egypt, being of the level of the vegetative, that which grows and raises itself up—he was the provider and the leader of all; Judah was the recipient.

That is what is meant when the text says, "Judah approached him, and he said, 'I beseech you, my master.'" The term *bi* ("I beseech you") literally means "in me." Judah was saying that the vitality from the righteous Joseph should be extended into him. This follows the *Zohar*'s explanation that "he approached" (*vayigash*) implies "the drawing near of one world to another world." Meaning that the lower world, *malchut*, approaches and unites with the higher world, *ze'eir anpin*, to receive its vitality. That follows the model of the Mishkan, where the vegetative was higher than the inanimate, as already explained.

In the World to Come, however, Judah will ascend higher than Joseph, as signified in the statement "The woman of valor [*malchut*] is the crown of her husband [*ze'eir anpin*]," for the source [of *malchut*] arose first in the divine thought, as already explained. For *machshavah* ("thought") breaks down into the words *chashav mah*—"thought of 'what'"—indicating ultimate selflessness. This is the level of *chochmah* of *atsilut*, the word *chochmah* ("wisdom") also breaking down to two words, *koach mah*—"the power of 'what.'"

This is the meaning of the kabbalistic phrase, "the father founded the daughter" [i.e., *chochmah* is the foundation of *malchut*]. For the level of supernal wisdom (*chochmah*) is called "higher awe," and the lower wisdom, which is *malchut*, is the "lower awe." Hence, "the father founded the daughter"—the energy of *malchut*, the lower awe, is drawn down from the level of the higher awe of *chochmah*.

In the World to Come, however, the lower awe will ascend into the higher awe, its source, and will therefore become "the crown of her husband." For selflessness is loftier than both the emotions of love and awe of G-d, which are drawn out from *chesed* and *gevurah* of *ze'eir anpin*. Consequently, even now, the earth exhibits greater selflessness, as explained. This level of the selflessness of the higher awe is the level of Moses our teacher, who declared, "What are we?"

VI.

Thus, we find in the *haftarah* of the Torah portion of *Vayigash*:

> *"Take for yourself one branch and write upon it, 'For Judah.' . . . And take one branch and write upon it, 'For Joseph, the branch of Efraim.' . . . And bring close the one to the other. . . . Behold, I shall take the branch of Joseph . . . and I will place upon it the branch of Judah . . . and my servant David will be king over them" (Ezekiel 37).*

This means that in the present world, Joseph, who is compared to a cedar that continues to grow to the heights, is greater than Judah. Thus, ten tribes were under his rulership, as is written in the *haftarah* text, "The tribes of Israel, his fellows"—he had more tribes following him than Judah. For this reason, he is called Joseph ("to add"), for he is the level of the higher *daat*.

However, in the World to Come, when Joseph and Judah will rejoin in a true and ultimate union—this being the meaning of the verse, "Judah approached him" (Genesis 44:18), and as it says, "The one will approach the one" (Job 41:8)—then Judah will ascend higher than Joseph, as discussed earlier regarding the meaning of "a woman of valor is the crown of her husband." Therefore, at that time, "My servant David will be king" over all Israel.

Thus, the Torah relates, "Joseph was no longer able to constrain himself . . . when Joseph made himself known to his brothers" (45:1). Meaning that Joseph and Judah joined in an ultimate bond and unity, to become one within one.

VII.

From all that has been said above, it will be understood and explained that which is written in the Arizal's *Likutei Hashas,* when he explains what the sages taught: "G-d grasped hold of Jeroboam ben Nebat and said, 'Return, [and I and you and David the son of Jesse will stroll together in the Garden of Eden].' Jeroboam asked, 'Who will be at the head?' G-d said, 'The son of Jesse will be at the head.' Jeroboam replied to Him, 'If that is so, I don't want it'" (Sanhedrin 102a).

This is exactly the idea explained above. G-d wanted for Jeroboam [who was of the tribe of Joseph, and who rebelled against the House of David] to repent. Then that level of Joseph—"the branch of Efraim"—would shine through him. That is what is meant by, "I and you and the son of Jesse will stroll together in the Garden of Eden"—the light of the Infinite will radiate a great illumination through them, the level of the divine "I."

But Jeroboam asked, "Who will be at the head?" He wanted it to remain as it is now, with Joseph being higher than Judah. Therefore, he wanted to be the head, above David.

G-d, however, said to him that in the World to Come, Judah would be in the ascendant, and therefore, "The son of Jesse will be at the head." Jeroboam replied, "If that is so, I don't want it," as he did not have the selflessness and humility necessary to accept this. Regarding this, the sages said, "The pride of Jeroboam's spirit banished him."

This is similar to what is explained regarding the Spies [sent from the desert to scout out the Promised Land—Numbers 13–14]. They, too, lacked humility with respect to the higher Land. They imagined they did not need [the Land, which is feminine], as they belonged to the realm of the masculine; as Scripture says of them, "They were all men" (Numbers 13:3).

But Joseph the Righteous and Judah will join together in the World to Come in an ultimate state of union, to become "one within one."

Rabbi Shne'ur Zalman of Liadi, *Torah Or*, Vayigash, pp. 43c–44b

Lesson 5

THE BROKEN TABLETS

Depiction of Moses receiving the Torah on Mount Sinai, from the *Braginsky Leipnik Haggadah* (detail), copied and decorated by Joseph ben David of Leipnik, 1739. (The Braginsky Collection)

Can it be that the greatest divine revelation in human history failed to communicate its most basic message? Examining the dynamics behind the story of the Golden Calf and the Broken Tablets, we gain insight into some of the foundational underpinnings of the Jewish faith. What are "miracles" and "divine revelations," and what purpose do they serve? How was the Torah communicated to us, and why is so much of it open to human interpretation? And on a personal level: What should we do with the "broken pieces" of our past failures?

TEXT 1

EXODUS 19:1–20:15, 24:1–18, AND 31:18

ARRIVAL AT MOUNT SINAI (19:1–2)

In the third month of the Children of Israel's exodus
from the land of Egypt;
on this day, they arrived in the Sinai Desert . . .
and Israel encamped there, opposite the mountain.

ISRAEL WILL BE G-D'S CHOSEN PEOPLE (19:3–6)

Moses ascended to G-d;
and G-d called to him from the mountain, to say:
"So shall you say to the House of Jacob
and tell the Children of Israel:
'You have seen what I did to Egypt;
I carried you on the wings of eagles
and brought you to Me.
And now, if you will listen to My voice
and keep My covenant
you will be My own treasure
from among all peoples. . . .
You will be to Me a kingdom of priests
and a holy nation.' . . ."

WE EXPRESS OUR DESIRE TO RECEIVE THE TORAH (19:7–8)

Moses came and called the elders of Israel
and he placed before them all these words. . . .

And all the people replied in unison and they said:
"All that G-d has spoken we will do!" . . .

G-D APPEARS ON MOUNT SINAI (19:16–20)

It was on the third day, when it was morning
there were thunder and lightning
and a thick cloud upon the mountain
and the sound of the *shofar*, exceedingly strong. . . .
Moses brought the people out from the camp toward G-d
and they stood beneath the mountain. . . .
G-d descended upon Mount Sinai
to the top of the mountain. . . .

THE TEN COMMANDMENTS (20:1–14)

G-d spoke all these words, to say:
"I am G-d your G-d
who took you out from the land of Egypt
from the house of slavery.
Do not have any other gods before Me.
Do not make for yourselves a graven form
or an image of anything in the heaven above or on the earth below. . . .
Do not bow to them and do not serve them. . . .
Do not take the name of G-d your G-d in vain. . . .
Remember the Sabbath day to sanctify it. . . .
Honor your father and your mother. . . .
Do not murder.

Do not commit adultery.
Do not steal.
Do not bear false witness against your fellow.
Do not covet . . . anything that is your fellow's."

SIGHTS AND SOUNDS (20:15)

And all the people saw the sounds and the torches
and the sound of the *shofar* and the smoking mountain;
and the people saw and trembled
and they stood from afar. . . .

MOSES ASCENDS THE MOUNTAIN FOR FORTY DAYS (24:1–18)

And to Moses He said: "Come up to G-d. . . ."
Moses entered within the cloud
and he ascended the mountain;
and Moses was on the mountain
forty days and forty nights. . . .

THE FIRST TABLETS (31:18)

When He had finished speaking with him on Mount Sinai
He gave to Moses the two Tablets of the Testament:
tablets of stone inscribed by the finger of G-d.

QUESTION FOR DISCUSSION

If you had to name one event that changed the course of human history more than any other, what event would that be?

TEXT 2

DEUTERONOMY 4:32–33, 35

כִּי שְׁאַל נָא לְיָמִים רִאשֹׁנִים אֲשֶׁר הָיוּ לְפָנֶיךָ לְמִן הַיּוֹם אֲשֶׁר בָּרָא אֱלֹקִים אָדָם עַל הָאָרֶץ וּלְמִקְצֵה הַשָּׁמַיִם וְעַד קְצֵה הַשָּׁמָיִם הֲנִהְיָה כַּדָּבָר הַגָּדוֹל הַזֶּה אוֹ הֲנִשְׁמַע כָּמֹהוּ. הֲשָׁמַע עָם קוֹל אֱלֹקִים מְדַבֵּר מִתּוֹךְ הָאֵשׁ כַּאֲשֶׁר שָׁמַעְתָּ אַתָּה וַיֶּחִי . . .

אַתָּה הָרְאֵתָ לָדַעַת כִּי ה' הוּא הָאֱלֹקִים אֵין עוֹד מִלְּבַדּוֹ.

Ask, now, after the early days that came before you, from the day that G-d created man upon the earth, and from one end of the heavens to the other: Has there ever been the likes of this great thing, or has anything like it been heard? Has a people heard the voice of G-d speaking from within the fire, as you heard, and lived? . . .

You were made to see to know that G-d is the G-d; there is none else besides Him.

TEXT 3

RABBI YEHUDAH HALEVI, *THE KUZARI* 4:11

> לֹא כֵן מֹשֶׁה עָלָיו הַשָּׁלוֹם הַמַּנְהִיג הָרִאשׁוֹן. הוּא הֵבִיא אֶת כָּל הָעָם אֶל מַעֲמַד הַר סִינַי לְמַעַן יִרְאוּ בְּעֵינֵיהֶם, אִישׁ כְּפִי יְכָלְתּוֹ, אֶת הָאוֹר אֲשֶׁר רָאָה הוּא... כְּמוֹ שֶׁאָמַר הַכָּתוּב "וַיִּרְאוּ אֵת אֱלֹקֵי יִשְׂרָאֵל"... וְכָל אֵלֶּה הֵעִידוּ אִישׁ בִּפְנֵי רֵעֵהוּ עַל שֶׁרָאוּ וְעַל שֶׁשָּׁמְעוּ. וְכָךְ הִרְחִיק מִלֵּב הָאֻמָּה הַחֲשָׁד הָרַע: שֶׁמָּא אֵין זֹאת כִּי אִם טַעֲנַת יְחִידִים הַמִּתְפָּאֲרִים כִּי נִגְלְתָה אֲלֵיהֶם נְבוּאָה? כִּי לֹא תִּתָּכֵן כָּל קְנוּנְיָה בִּפְנֵי הַמּוֹנִים.

Moses, the first [Jewish] leader, was not like them [the founders of other religions]. He brought the entire people to stand at Mount Sinai, for them to see with their own eyes, each in accordance with their ability, the revelation that he saw. . . . As the verse states (EXODUS 24:10), "They saw the G-d of Israel." . . . They all could affirm to each other what they saw and heard. This removed from the heart of the nation the terrible suspicion: Perhaps all of this is just the claim of a few individuals that prophecy came to them? For it is not possible to create a conspiracy in full sight of the masses.

RABBI YEHUDAH HALEVI
C. 1075–1141

Noted author, physician, and poet. Rabbi Yehudah Halevi is best known as the author of the *Kuzari*, a philosophical work, written in the form of a discussion between a Jew, a Christian, and a Muslim before the King of the Khazars. In addition to the *Kuzari*, he wrote thousands of poems, of which only a few hundred survive today.

TEXT 4

MECHILTA, EXODUS 20:15

רוֹאִין אֶת הַנִשְׁמַע וְשׁוֹמְעִין אֶת הַנִרְאֶה.

They saw what is heard, and they heard what is seen.

מכילתא
נדפס
בווילנא

MECHILTA

A halachic Midrash to Exodus. Midrash is the designation of a particular genre of rabbinic literature usually forming a running commentary on specific books of the Bible. The name "*Mechilta*" means "rule" and was given to this Midrash because its comments and explanations are based on fixed rules of exegesis. This work is often attributed to Rabbi Yishmael ben Elisha, a contemporary of Rabbi Akiva, though there are some references to later sages in this work.

Wetgeving op de Berg Sinaï (Legislation on Mt. Sinai), Jan Luyken, etching, Amsterdam, 1712. (Rijksmuseum, Amsterdam)

QUESTION FOR DISCUSSION

Which is better, the movie or the book? What are the differences between "seeing" something and "hearing/understanding" it?

TEXT 5

THE REBBE, RABBI MENACHEM MENDEL SCHNEERSON,
LIKUTEI SICHOT (HEBREW EDITION) 6, P. 128

אֶת זֹאת חִידֵשׁ מַתַּן תּוֹרָה–"רוֹאִין אֶת הַנִּשְׁמָע וְשׁוֹמְעִין אֶת הַנִּרְאֶה".
הַ"נִּשְׁמָע", שֶׁאֶפְשָׁר לְקַבְּלוֹ רַק עַל יְדֵי שְׁמִיעָה - רוּחָנִיּוּת, אֱלֹקוּת - אוֹתוֹ קִבְּלוּ בְּנֵי יִשְׂרָאֵל בְּוַדָּאוּת וּבְאוֹפֶן מוּחָשִׁי שֶׁל רְאִיָּה. הֵם רָאוּ אֱלֹקוּת. וְהַדְּבָרִים הַגַּשְׁמִיִּים, שֶׁהָיוּ תָּמִיד בִּבְחִינַת "נִרְאֶה", הָיוּ אֶצְלָם אָז בְּאוֹפֶן שֶׁל "שׁוֹמְעִין"–כְּדָבָר שֶׁנִּקְלָט רַק עַל יְדֵי שְׁמִיעָה אוֹ הֲבָנָה שִׂכְלִית.

This is what the Giving of the Torah achieved: that "they saw what is heard, and they heard what is seen."

That which is ordinarily "heard"—i.e., spirituality and G-dliness, which can only be perceived through "hearing"—the people of Israel perceived with the certainty and tangibility of sight. They *saw* G-dliness. On the other hand, material things, which are ordinarily "seen," they now "heard." The materiality of the world was like something that is perceived by hearing or by logical deduction.

RABBI MENACHEM MENDEL SCHNEERSON 1902–1994

The towering Jewish leader of the 20th century, known as "the Lubavitcher Rebbe," or simply as "the Rebbe." Born in southern Ukraine, the Rebbe escaped Nazi-occupied Europe, arriving in the U.S. in June 1941. The Rebbe inspired and guided the revival of traditional Judaism after the European devastation, impacting virtually every Jewish community the world over. The Rebbe often emphasized that the performance of just one additional good deed could usher in the era of Mashiach. The Rebbe's scholarly talks and writings have been printed in more than 200 volumes.

TEXT 6

EXODUS 32:1–19

FEARING THAT MOSES IS GONE, THE PEOPLE ASK FOR AN IDOL (32:1)

The people saw that Moses delayed
in coming down from the mountain;
and the people massed upon Aaron
and they said to him:
"Arise, make us a god who will go before us;
for this man Moses
who brought us up from the land of Egypt
we do not know what has become of him."

THE MAKING OF THE GOLDEN CALF (32:2–6)

Aaron said to them:
"Remove the golden rings
that are on the ears of your wives
your sons, and your daughters
and bring them to me." . . .
He took them from their hand
and he formed it with a graving-tool
and he made it into a molten calf;
and they said: "This is your god, O Israel
who brought you up from the land of Egypt!" . . .
They arose early in the morrow
and they offered up burnt-offerings

Covenant & Conversation: Aaron's Role in the Making of the Golden Calf
Rabbi Lord Jonathan Sacks:

What Did the Golden Calf Represent? A Torah class
Rabbi Mendel Kaplan:

MYJLI.COM/BIBLE

Why Did Moses Break the Tablets? A Torah class
Rabbi Mendel Kaplan:

MYJLI.COM/BIBLE

and brought peace-offerings;
the people sat down to eat and to drink
and they got up to make merry. . . .

MOSES BREAKS THE TABLETS (32:15–19)

Moses turned and went down from the mountain
and the two Tablets of the Testament
were in his hand. . . .
The tablets were the handiwork of G-d
and the writing was the writing of G-d
engraved on the tablets. . . .
And it was, when he drew closer to the camp
and he saw the calf and the dances;
Moses's anger was kindled
and he threw the tablets from his hands
and he broke them beneath the mountain.

QUESTION FOR DISCUSSION

What other biblical story does the story of the Broken Tablets remind you of?

TEXT 7

MIDRASH, *SHEMOT RABAH* 32:1

הַדָא הוּא דִכְתִיב (תְּהִילִים פב, ו-ז), "אֲנִי אָמַרְתִּי אֱלֹקִים אַתֶּם [וּבְנֵי עֶלְיוֹן כֻּלְּכֶם. אָכֵן כְּאָדָם תְּמוּתוּן . . .]":

אִלּוּ הִמְתִּינוּ יִשְׂרָאֵל לְמֹשֶׁה וְלֹא הָיוּ עוֹשִׂים אוֹתוֹ מַעֲשֶׂה, לֹא הָיְתָה גָּלִיּוֹת וְלֹא מַלְאַךְ הַמָּוֶת שׁוֹלֵט בָּהֶן. וְכֵן הוּא אוֹמֵר, (שְׁמוֹת לב, טז) "וְהַמִּכְתָּב מִכְתַּב אֱלֹקִים הוּא, חָרוּת עַל הַלֻּחֹת". מַהוּ "חָרוּת"? . . . חֵירוּת מִן גָּלִיּוֹת . . . חֵירוּת מִמַּלְאַךְ הַמָּוֶת.

בְּשָׁעָה שֶׁאָמְרוּ יִשְׂרָאֵל, "כֹּל אֲשֶׁר דִּבֶּר ה' נַעֲשֶׂה וְנִשְׁמָע", אָמַר הַקָּדוֹשׁ בָּרוּךְ הוּא: אָדָם הָרִאשׁוֹן צִוִּיתִיו מִצְוָה אַחַת כְּדֵי שֶׁיְּקַיְּימֶנָּה, וְהִשְׁוִיתִיו לְמַלְאֲכֵי הַשָּׁרֵת . . . אֵלּוּ שֶׁהֵן עוֹשִׂין וּמְקַיְּימִין תרי"ג מִצְוֹת . . . אֵינוֹ דִּין שֶׁיִּהְיוּ הֵן חַיִּין וְקַיָּימִין לְעוֹלָם? . . . כֵּיוָן שֶׁאָמְרוּ, "אֵלֶּה אֱלֹהֶיךָ יִשְׂרָאֵל", בָּא מָוֶת עֲלֵיהֶן.

אָמַר הַקָּדוֹשׁ בָּרוּךְ הוּא: בְּשִׁיטָתוֹ שֶׁל אָדָם הָרִאשׁוֹן הֲלַכְתֶּם, שֶׁלֹּא עָמַד בְּנִסְיוֹנוֹ ג' שָׁעוֹת, וּבְתֵשַׁע שָׁעוֹת נִקְנְסָה עָלָיו מִיתָה. "אֲנִי אָמַרְתִּי אֱלֹקִים אַתֶּם", וַהֲלַכְתֶּם אַחַר מִדּוֹתָיו שֶׁל אָדָם הָרִאשׁוֹן, "אָכֵן כְּאָדָם תְּמוּתוּן".

This is the meaning of what is written (PSALMS 82:6–7), "I said you are divine, and that supernal beings you are all. Indeed, like Adam you will die. . . .":

Had the people of Israel waited for Moses and not done that deed, neither *galut* [the exiles of the Jewish people] nor the angel of death would have had any power over them. Thus, it is written (EXODUS 32:16), "The writing was the writing of G-d, *charut* (engraved) on the Tablets." What is the meaning of *charut*? . . . *Cheirut* (freedom) from exile . . . [and] *cheirut* from the angel of death.

When the people of Israel proclaimed, "All that G-d has spoken we will do and we will hear" (EXODUS

SHEMOT RABAH

An early rabbinic commentary on the Book of Exodus. "Midrash" is the designation of a particular genre of rabbinic literature usually forming a running commentary on specific books of the Bible. *Shemot Rabah*, written mostly in Hebrew, provides textual exegeses, expounds upon the biblical narrative, and develops and illustrates moral principles. It was first printed in Constantinople in 1512 together with 4 other Midrashic works on the other 4 books of the Pentateuch.

24:7), G-d said: "I commanded one mitzvah to Adam for him to fulfill, and I likened him to the ministering angels. . . . This people, who will fulfill 613 *mitzvot* . . . is it not fitting that they should live and exist forever? . . ." But when they proclaimed, "This is your god, O Israel," they became mortal.

Said G-d: "You followed in the ways of Adam, the first man, who did not hold out for three hours, and on the ninth hour of that day, death was decreed on him. 'I said you are divine,' but because you followed in Adam's path, 'Indeed, like Adam you will die.'"

Le Veau d'Or (The Golden Calf), from the *Bible Series*, Marc Chagall, etching, 1956.

TEXT 8

EXODUS 34:1–28

THE SECOND TABLETS

G-d said to Moses:
“Carve yourself two stone tablets like the first;
and I will write upon the tablets
the words that were on the first tablets
which you broke. . . .”
He carved two stone tablets like the first
and Moses rose early in the morning
and he ascended Mount Sinai
as G-d had commanded him;
and he took in his hand two stone tablets. . . .
And he was there with G-d
for forty days and forty nights . . .
and He wrote on the tablets
the words of the covenant, the Ten Commandments.

QUESTION FOR DISCUSSION

Based on the verses we just read, what differences can you find between the First Tablets and the Second Tablets?

Figure 5.1

First and Second Tablets

	FIRST TABLETS	**SECOND TABLETS**
State of the World	Restored state of Creation before Adam's sin	Reverted to world tainted by sin, death, and hardship
Source of the Tablets	*Content:* Divine *Medium:* Divine	*Content:* Divine *Medium:* human
Composition of Torah	Written Torah only	Written plus Oral Torah

TEXT 9

MIDRASH, *SHEMOT RABAH* 46:1

וְאָמַר לוֹ הַקָדוֹשׁ בָּרוּךְ הוּא: אַל תִּצְטַעֵר בְּלוּחוֹת הָרִאשׁוֹנוֹת, שֶׁלֹא הָיוּ
אֶלָא עֲשֶׂרֶת הַדִבְּרוֹת לְבָד, וּבְלוּחוֹת הַשְׁנִיִים אֲנִי נוֹתֵן לְךָ שֶׁיְהֵא בָּהֶם
הֲלָכוֹת מִדְרָשׁ וַאֲגָדוֹת.

Said G-d to [Moses]: "Do not be distressed over the First Tablets, which contained only the Ten Commandments. In the Second Tablets, I am giving you also Halachah, Midrash, and Agadah."

How Reliable Is the Oral Tradition? ***Mr. Howard P. Danzig** and **Rabbi Shlomo Yaffe**:*

MYJLI.COM/BIBLE

TEXT 10

TALMUD, NEDARIM 22B

אִלְמָלֵא חָטְאוּ יִשְׂרָאֵל, לֹא נִיתַּן לָהֶם אֶלָא חֲמִשָׁה חוּמְשֵׁי תּוֹרָה וְסֵפֶר
יְהוֹשֻׁעַ בִּלְבָד . . . מַאי טַעֲמָא? "כִּי בְּרוֹב חָכְמָה רָב כָּעַס".

Had Israel not sinned [with the Golden Calf], they would have received only the five books of Moses and the book of Joshua. . . . Why? Because, as the verse says (ECCLESIASTES 1:18), "Much wisdom comes through much grief."

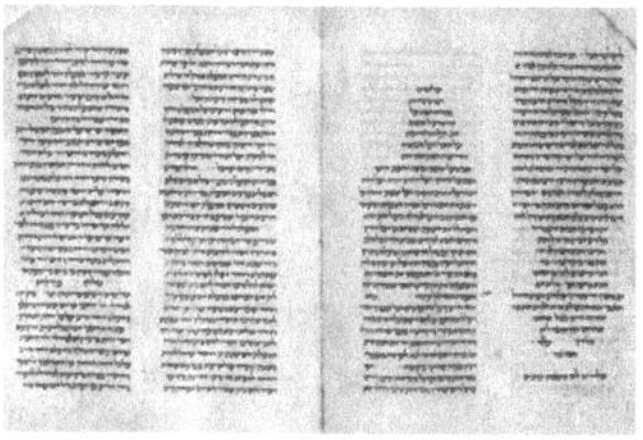

BABYLONIAN TALMUD

A literary work of monumental proportions that draws upon the legal, spiritual, intellectual, ethical, and historical traditions of Judaism. The 37 tractates of the Babylonian Talmud contain the teachings of the Jewish sages from the period after the destruction of the 2nd Temple through the 5th century CE. It has served as the primary vehicle for the transmission of the Oral Law and the education of Jews over the centuries; it is the entry point for all subsequent legal, ethical, and theological Jewish scholarship.

QUESTION FOR DISCUSSION

Why does the Torah consist of both a Written and an Oral component? If G-d wanted to communicate His will to us, why didn't He give us everything at Sinai?

QUESTION FOR DISCUSSION

Which is the best and most effective way to communicate the divine will to mankind:

A By divine revelation (the "First Tablets" method)?

B Through human extrapolation of a divine text (the "Second Tablets" method)?

Why Was the Torah Given in Two Parts—A Written Torah and an Oral Torah? ***Professor Lawrence Schiffman:***

MYJLI.COM/BIBLE

TEXT 11

TALMUD, SHABBAT 88A

> מְלַמֵּד שֶׁכָּפָה הַקָּדוֹשׁ בָּרוּךְ הוּא עֲלֵיהֶם אֶת הָהָר כְּגִיגִית, וְאָמַר לָהֶם:
> "אִם אַתֶּם מְקַבְּלִים הַתּוֹרָה, מוּטָב; וְאִם לַאו, שָׁם תְּהֵא קְבוּרַתְכֶם".

This teaches us that G-d overturned the mountain over them like a cask and said to them: "If you accept the Torah, fine; if not, there shall be your burial."

G-d's Judgment, Asher Brown Durand, oil on canvas, United States, c. 1851–1852. (Chrysler Museum of Art, Norfolk)

TEXT 12

THE REBBE, RABBI MENACHEM MENDEL SCHNEERSON,
LIKUTEI SICHOT 26, P. 424

אֵיךְ מַתְאִים מַאֲמַר רַבּוֹתֵינוּ זִכְרוֹנָם לִבְרָכָה "כָּפָה עֲלֵיהֶם כו'" . . . עִם הָעִנְיָן "נַעֲשֶׂה וְנִשְׁמָע"? . . .

וּבֵיאוּר פְּנִימִיּוּת הַפְּשַׁט בָּזֶה הוּא . . . בְּמַעֲמַד הַר סִינַי עָבְרוּ רַק נ' יוֹם מִיְּצִיאַת מִצְרַיִם, שֶׁהָיְתָה עֶרְוַת הָאָרֶץ בְּמִידּוֹת מוּשְׁחָתוֹת וכו' כַּיָּדוּעַ. וַעֲדַיִין לֹא הָיָ' שְׁהוּת שֶׁיָּבוֹאוּ בְּנֵי יִשְׂרָאֵל לְהַכָּרָה כָּזוּ שֶׁהוּא מִן הַקָּצֶה אֶל הַקָּצֶה לְגַבֵּי מַצָּבָם הַקּוֹדֶם. אֶלָּא שֶׁמִּלְמַעְלָה "כָּפוּ עֲלֵיהֶם" הַכָּרָה זוּ, עַל יְדֵי שֶׁהוֹפִיעַ עֲלֵיהֶם אוֹר הַכָּרַת הָאֱמֶת עַד כְּדֵי כַּךְ, שֶׁרָאוּ בְּמוּחָשׁ שֶׁהַתּוֹרָה וְהַמִּצְוֹות הֵם תַּכְלִית הַטּוֹב (גַּם בְּגַשְׁמִיּוּת), וּבְאִם לַאו אֵין חַיֵּיהֶם חַיִּים (גַּם בְּגַשְׁמִיּוּת). וְלָכֵן אָמְרוּ בְּכָל לֵב וָנֶפֶשׁ "נַעֲשֶׂה וְנִשְׁמָע".

אֲבָל כֵּיוָן שֶׁלֹּא בָּאוּ לְהַכָּרָה זוּ מֵעַצְמָם וּבְהַדְרָגָה, כִּי אִם בְּדֶרֶךְ מַתָּנָה וְהַבְרָקָה מִלְמַעֲלָה, הֲרֵי אַחֲרֵי מַעֲמַד הַר סִינַי לֹא נִשְׁאַר מִכָּל זֶה אֶלָּא רוֹשֶׁם בְּהֶעְלֵם.

How do we reconcile the saying of the sages that "G-d overturned the mountain over them like a cask" with the fact that the people willingly responded, "We will do and we will hear"? . . .

The deeper meaning is as follows. . . When the people of Israel stood at Mount Sinai, only fifty days had elapsed from their Exodus from Egypt, which was the most debased place in the world in terms of decadent character, as is well known. This was not sufficient time for them to make the transition, from one extreme to the other, and achieve a genuine recognition [of the value of the Torah]. Rather, this recognition was "forced" on

When Faith and Trust Break Down
A lesson from the story of the Golden Calf
Mrs. Sharon Freundel:

MYJLI.COM/BIBLE

them from Above, when the light of truth was revealed to them so powerfully that they could tangibly see that the Torah and the *mitzvot* were the ultimate good, and that without them, their lives were not worth living, in the most literal sense. They therefore proclaimed with all their heart and soul, "We will do and we will hear."

However, because they did not achieve this recognition in a progressive, methodical way by their own efforts, but rather as a gift and as a flash of illumination from above, once the moment of the revelation had passed, nothing but a faint impression of it remained.

TEXT 13

TALMUD, MENACHOT 99A

לוּחוֹת וְשִׁבְרֵי לוּחוֹת מוּנָּחִים בָּאָרוֹן.

Both the [Second] Tablets and the Broken Tablets were kept in the Ark.

more people understanding

miraculous moment (also - we all have broken, damaged things in our lives)

QUESTION FOR DISCUSSION

What "broken tablets" do you carry with you in your own life?

1 The Giving of the Torah at Mount Sinai, where the entire people of Israel directly experienced the most unequivocal divine revelation in history, is the foundational event of Judaism. At Sinai, we "saw what is heard, and heard what is seen": G-dliness and spirituality, which are ordinarily apprehended secondhand ("heard"), were perceived with the immediacy and veracity of sight; whereas the physical world, which is ordinarily "seen," was relegated to the lesser realism of something that is heard and understood. And yet, shortly thereafter, the people violated the first commandments they had heard directly from G-d by worshipping the Golden Calf, prompting Moses to break the Tablets. How was this possible?

2 At the Giving of the Torah, G-d restored for the people of Israel the state of tranquility and immortality that existed in the Garden of Eden. Worshipping the Golden Calf was essentially a repeat of Adam and Eve's transgression, and it resulted in the breakdown of this ideal state.

3 G-d granted the people the Second Tablets, but these differed from the First Tablets in a number of significant ways. This time, mortality and struggle were not abolished. In the First Tablets, both the content and the medium were from G-d, whereas in the Second Tablets, the content was divine but the medium was of human manufacture. The First Tablets embodied only the Written Torah—G-d's direct instructions to us; the Second Tablets incorporated also the Oral Torah—the process by which we expound the written text and apply it to our lives, making the Torah a partnership of divine revelation and human understanding.

4 Divine revelations and miraculous experiences shake us out of our complacency and set us in the right direction, but they do not truly change us. True and lasting transformation will only come by means of a "Second Tablets" process, in which we struggle to build a relationship with G-d. The First Tablets were a "seeing" experience—an overwhelming revelation to which we were the passive recipients. The Second Tablets are a "hearing" experience—something that we actively create, step-by-step, with our own faculties.

5 We need both sets of Tablets, as indicated by the fact that the Ark in the Holy Temple contained both. The First Tablets alone cannot create anything lasting in us, but they are the foundation for everything that we achieve.

6 There are two common reactions to the failures we experience in our lives: (a) despair; (b) a desire to "start from scratch" and leave our past behind. The fact that the Broken Tablets were preserved in the Ark presents us with a third option: to carry these "broken pieces" with us, connecting with the original passion and overwhelming energies they hold, and making them the foundation for our future achievements.

Appendix

TEXT 14

ZOHAR 2:93B

הָנֵי עַשַׂר אֲמִירָן דְאוֹרַיְיתָא, אִינוּן כְּלָלָא דְכָל פִּקוּדֵי אוֹרַיְיתָא. כְּלָלָא דְעֵילָא וְתַתָּא. כְּלָלָא דְכָל עַשַׂר אֲמִירָן דִבְרֵאשִׁית. אִלֵין אִתְחַקְקוּ עַל לוּחֵי אַבְנִין, וְכָל גִנְזִין דַהֲווֹ בְּהוּ, אִתְחַזוּן לְעֵינֵיהוֹן דְכֹלָּא, לְמִנְדַע וּלְאִסְתַּכְּלָא בְּרָזָא דְתרי"ג פִּקוּדִין דְאוֹרַיְיתָא דִכְלִילָן בְּהוּ.

These Ten Commandments encompass the whole of the Torah. They include all that is above and below. They incorporate the ten utterances with which G-d created the world. They were engraved on tablets of stone, and all the secrets they contain were revealed to all who looked upon them, to know and see in them the 613 commandments of the Torah which they include.

ZOHAR

The seminal work of kabbalah, Jewish mysticism. The *Zohar* is a mystical commentary on the Torah, written in Aramaic and Hebrew. According to the Arizal, the *Zohar* contains the teachings of Rabbi Shimon bar Yocha'i, who lived in the Land of Israel during the 2nd century. The *Zohar* has become one of the indispensable texts of traditional Judaism, alongside and nearly equal in stature to the Mishnah and Talmud.

Figure 5.2

The Ten Commandments and 613 *Mitzvot*

	COMMANDMENT	INCLUDES THE *MITZVOT*
1	I am G-d your G-d.	The love and awe of G-d; prayer; the service in the Holy Temple; the signs and reminders of our relationship with G-d: *tefilin*, *mezuzah*, *tsitsit*, etc.
2	Do not have other gods before Me.	All the prohibitions of idolatry and idolatrous practices; the laws of ritual purity
3	Do not take the name of G-d in vain.	Laws of prophecy, the sanctification of G-d's name, blasphemy, false oaths, and the fulfillment of vows; not to curse or insult one's fellow
4	Remember the day of Shabbat to sanctify it.	The festivals; the sabbatical and jubilee years
5	Honor your father and your mother.	Procreation, circumcision, mourning relatives, inheritance, charity and aiding a fellow in need, gifts to *Kohanim* and Levites
6	Do not murder.	The *mitzvot* governing preservation of life; the judging of capital cases; laws of warfare
7	Do not commit adultery.	Laws of marriage and divorce; forbidden relations
8	Do not steal.	All financial and property laws
9	Do not bear false witness unto your fellow.	Laws pertaining to the hearing of evidence and the proper execution of justice; prohibitions against slander, defamation, and gossip
10	Do not covet . . . anything that is your fellow's.	Love your fellow as yourself; laws pertaining to diet and dress

Additional Readings

YITRO

A DISCOURSE OF THE LUBAVITCHER REBBE; ADAPTED BY RABBI LORD JONATHAN SACKS

In this elaborate and profound Sicha, two disagreements in interpretation of events connected with the Giving of the Torah are explored. In both cases the disputants are Rabbi Akiva and Rabbi Ishmael; and their opinions reveal a deep underlying difference in their orientation towards the service of G-d. The two problems they confront are, what did the Israelites answer to G-d when they accepted the Ten Commandments, and, when the Torah tells us that they "saw the voices (of the thunder)," did they literally see a sound, or did they only hear it? From these apparently slight beginnings, the Rebbe uncovers fundamental themes; in particular, the difference in perception between the righteous man and the man of repentance.

1. The Answers of the Israelites

As a preliminary to the giving of the Ten Commandments the Torah tells us, "And G-d spoke all these things, saying."[1]

The usual meaning of the Hebrew word of "saying" is "to say to others."[2] For example, the meaning of "And G-d spoke to Moses, saying . . ." is that Moses should transmit the word of G-d to the Children of Israel. But this cannot be the meaning of the present verse, for at the time of the Giving of the Torah, G-d Himself spoke to all the Israelites. Nor can it mean "for transmission to the later generations," for we have a tradition that all Jewish souls, of past and future lives, were gathered at Sinai to witness the revelation.[3]

Therefore the Mechilta interprets "saying" as meaning that, for every commandment, the Children of Israel *answered* G-d saying that they would do what it demanded to them.

But the Mechilta cites two opinions as to the manner in which the Israelites answered. Rabbi Ishmael says that on the positive commandments they answered "yes" and on the negative, "no" (i.e., that they would do what G-d commanded, and would not do what He forbade). Rabbi Akiva, on the other hand, says that they answered "yes" to both positive and negative commands (i.e., that they would do G-d's will, whatever form it took). But what is the substance of the disagreement between the two opinions? Surely, they both, in essence, say the same thing?

2. The Voice of the Thunder

There is another disagreement between Rabbi Akiva and Rabbi Ishmael concerning the Giving of the Torah. We are told that "all the people saw the voices (of the thunder) and the lightning"[4]—a problem, for how can voices be *seen*?

RABBI MENACHEM MENDEL SCHNEERSON, 1902–1994

The towering Jewish leader of the 20th century, known as "the Lubavitcher Rebbe," or simply as "the Rebbe." Born in southern Ukraine, the Rebbe escaped Nazi-occupied Europe, arriving in the U.S. in June 1941. The Rebbe inspired and guided the revival of traditional Judaism after the European devastation, impacting virtually every Jewish community the world over. The Rebbe often emphasized that the performance of just one additional good deed could usher in the era of Mashiach. The Rebbe's scholarly talks and writings have been printed in more than 200 volumes.

RABBI LORD JONATHAN SACKS, 1948–

Former chief rabbi of the United Kingdom. Rabbi Sacks attended Cambridge University and received his doctorate from King's College, London. A prolific and influential author, his books include *Will We Have Jewish Grandchildren?* and *The Dignity of Difference.* He received the Jerusalem Prize in 1995 for his contributions to enhancing Jewish life in the Diaspora, was knighted and made a life peer in 2005, and became Baron Sacks of Aldridge in 2009.

Rabbi Ishmael says: "They saw what is (normally) seen and heard what is (normally) heard," taking the verb "saw" to apply not to the voices of the thunder, but to the lightning. But Rabbi Akiva says, "they saw what is (normally) heard, and heard what is (normally) seen," i.e., that they did indeed see the voices, and did not see, but *heard*, the lightning.

Now there is a general principle that G-d does not perform miracles for no reason. From which we can infer that the miracles that Rabbi Akiva describes were not *extraneous* to the Giving of the Torah, but were an essential part of it. So elevated were the Israelites by the revelation of the Ten Commandments that their senses took on miraculous powers. If so, we must understand the verse "they saw the voices (of the thunder) and the lightning" as relating to the ecstatic state of the Israelites. But now we cannot understand Rabbi Ishmael's opinion, for he interprets the verse as relating to a purely *natural* phenomenon.

3. Rashi's Quotations

Since these two disagreements relate to the same subject and are between the same protagonists, we can assume that their opinions on the answer of the Israelites are connected to their opinions on the seeing of the thunder (that one entails the other).

This would appear to be contradicted by the fact that Rashi, on the word "saying," quotes *Rabbi Ishmael's* opinion (the Israelites answered "yes" to the positive commands and "no" to the negative); while on the phrase "they saw the voices" he cites (part of) *Rabbi Akiva's* explanation (that they saw what is normally heard).

Since Rashi's commentary is consistent, it would seem that the two problems are not related if he can cite one side on one question, and the other on the other. This however, does not follow. For Rashi quotes only *half* of Rabbi Akiva's explanation, omitting "the Israelites heard what is normally seen." And it is this *second* half which forces Rabbi Akiva to his opinion that the Israelites answered "yes" to the negative command (i.e., his difference of opinion with Rabbi Ishmael). And the *reason* why Rashi selects Rabbi Ishmael's answer to one question and one half of Rabbi Akiva's to the other, is because these are the most appropriate to a *literal* understanding of the text (which is Rashi's concern). How this is so, will be explained later.

4. Sight and Sound

As a preliminary, we must understand the difference between "seeing" and "hearing."

Firstly the impression made on a man by seeing something happen is far stronger than that made by just hearing about it. So much so that "an eyewitness to an event cannot be a judge in a case about it"[5]—for no counter-argument could sway his fixed belief about what he saw. Whereas so long as he has only *heard* about it, he can be open to conflicting testimonies, and judge impartially between them.

Secondly, only a physical thing can be seen; while what can be heard is always less tangible (sounds, words, opinions).

These two points are connected. For man is a physical being, and it is natural that the physical should make the most indelible impression on him; while the spiritual is accessible only by "hearing" and understanding, hence its impression is weaker.

This explains the nature of the elevation that the Giving of the Torah worked on the Israelites. They saw what was normally heard—i.e., the spiritual became as tangible and certain as the familiar world of physical objects. Indeed, the *Essence* of G-d *was revealed* to their eyes, when they heard the words, "I (the Essence) the L-rd (who transcends the world) am thy G-d (who is immanent in the world)."

At a time of such revelations, the world is known for what it truly is—not an independently existent thing, but something entirely nullified before G-d. If so, how do we know that there is a world and not simply an *illusion* of one? One by *inference*, from the verse "In the beginning, G-d created heaven and earth." In other words, the Israelites "heard what was normally seen"—they had only an *intellectual* conviction (and not the testimony of the senses) that there was a physical world.

5. Rabbi Ishmael's Interpretation

But if this was so, what elevation was there in the Israelites according to Rabbi Ishmael, who holds that they only heard and saw what was normally heard and seen? How could this be, when the revelation was the greatest in all history?

The explanation is that the main revelation at the Giving of the Torah was that "the L-rd *came down* upon Mt. Sinai"[6]—the high came low; and the miracle was that G-d Himself should be revealed *within* the limits of nature. This is why it was so extraordinary that the Israelites should, *without any change* in their senses, perceive G-d in His Essence and so abdicate themselves that "they trembled and stood far off." [7]

6. The Priest and the Repentant

Why do Rabbi Ishmael and Rabbi Akiva hold opposing views as to the nature of the elevation brought about in the Israelites at Sinai?

Rabbi Ishmael was a High Priest (a *Kohen Gadol*)[8] and the nature of a priest is to be "sanctified to his G-d."[9] His service is that of the righteous, to transmit holiness to this world (to take the high and bring it low). This is why he saw the greatest miracle as being that G-d Himself came down to this world, so far as to be perceived by the *normal* senses ("they saw what is normally seen").

But Rabbi Akiva was a man of repentance (a *Ba'al Teshuvah*), whose descent was from converts[10] and who only started to learn Torah at the age of 40.[11] Repentance colors his whole manner of service: The desire to ascend higher than this world (and, as is known,[12] he longed *throughout his life* to be able to martyr himself in the cause of G-d). So that for him the greatest miracle was the transcending of all physical limitations ("they saw what is normally heard").

7. Two Faces of Commandment

There are two aspects to every commandment:

a. The element which is *common* to them all—that they are commands from G-d; and
b. The characteristics which are *individual* to each, each involving different human activities and sanctifying a different aspect of the world.

Rabbi Akiva and Rabbi Ishmael each attend to a different aspect. Rabbi Ishmael, who sees the ultimate achievement in translating G-dliness into this world, with all its limitations, sees principally the *details* of the commandments (how each sanctifies a different part of this world). And thus he holds that the Israelites answered "yes" to the positive ones and "no" to the negative—that they attended to what *distinguished* one kind of command from another.

But to Rabbi Akiva, what was important was the transcending of the world and its limitations, and hence in a commandment the essential element was what was *common to each*, that it embodies the will of G-d which has no limitations. Therefore he says that the Israelites responded primarily to this common element, they said "yes" to positive and negative alike.

8. The Positive in the Negative: The Character of Rabbi Akiva

We can in fact go deeper in our understanding of Rabbi Akiva's statement. When he says that the Israelites said "yes" to the negative commandments, this was not simply that they sensed in them the element common to all expressions of G-d's will; but more strongly, that they only saw what was *positive* even in a negative thing—the holiness that an act of restraint brings about.

And this follows from the second clause of his second explanation (which Rashi omits in his commentary) that the Israelites "heard what was normally seen." For since the physical world's existence was for them only an *intellectual* perception and the only sensed reality was the existence of G-d, they could not sense the existence of things which opposed holiness ("the other gods") but saw only the act of affirmation involved in "*thou shall have no* other gods."

We can see this orientation of Rabbi Akiva very clearly in the story related in the Talmud,[13] that Raban Gamliel, Rabbi Elazar ben Azariah, Rabbi Joshua and Rabbi Akiva were on a journey and decided to return to Jerusalem (after the destruction of the second Temple). When they reached Mt. Scopus they rent their garments. When they reached the Temple Mount, they saw a fox emerging from the Holy of Holies and they began to weep—but Rabbi Akiva *laughed*. They asked him, "Why are you laughing?" and he replied, "Why are you weeping?" They said, it is written, "the common man who goes near (to the Holy of Holies) shall die,"[14] and now *foxes* enter it—should we not cry?

He said, "This is why I laugh. For it is written, 'And I will take to Me faithful witnesses, Uriah the priest and Zechariah the son of Jeberechiah.'[15] Now what connection has Uriah with Zechariah? Uriah lived during the times of the First Temple, while Zechariah prophesied at the time of the second. But the Torah links the prophecies of both men. Uriah wrote, 'therefore shall Zion, because of you, be plowed like a field.' And Zechariah wrote, 'Yet shall old men and women sit in the broad places of Jerusalem.' So long as Uriah's prophecy had not been fulfilled, I was afraid that Zechariah's would not be. Now that it has, it is certain that Zechariah's will come true."

Even in the darkest moment of Jewish history—when foxes ran freely in the Holy of Holies—Rabbi Akiva saw only the good: That this was proof that the serene and hopeful vision of Zechariah would be vindicated.

9. The Meaning of Rashi

The two kinds of service which Rabbi Akiva and Rabbi Ishmael exemplify (the service of the righteous and the repentant) are relevant only to one who is already some way along the path to perfection. But to the "five-year-old"[16] (whether in years, or more generally to those at the beginning of the way) to whom Rashi addresses his commentary, he need only quote *part* of Rabbi Akiva's explanation, that "they saw what is normally heard." For the beginning of worship, stated in the *first* chapter of the Shulchan Aruch, is "I have set the L-rd before me continually." In other words, it is to strive to make G-dliness (normally only an intellectual notion, something "heard") as real for oneself as if one had literally seen Him with one's own eyes.

But Rashi does not quote the rest of the sentence, "they heard what was normally seen," for however real G-d may become for one; at the *beginning* of one's life of service, the world still seems like a tangible reality. And physical acts like eating and drinking are still prompted by physical desires, and are not unequivocally for the sake of Heaven.

And thus, since the physical world still has an independent reality for him, and he can still perceive the bad, Rashi gives Rabbi Ishmael's comment, that the Israelites answered "no" to the negative commandments.

Indeed, though Rashi cites Rabbi Akiva, that the Israelites "saw what was normally heard," this is consistent even with the opinion of Rabbi Ishmael. For his comment speaks to a man already at the level of righteousness when he can perceive G-dliness even within the constraints of the lowest of this world, symbolized by the expression that he "hears what is normally heard" (i.e., where G-dliness is so concealed that it is only affirmed as a result of intellectual proofs). But at the beginning of the path, one must relate to G-d only at a level, when he "sees what is normally heard" (i.e., where G-dliness is readily perceived).

The implication of Rashi for the conduct of the individual Jew, is that when the world still exercises its pull on him, he must strive to make his sense of the presence of G-d as clear as his sense of sight. But this is only a preliminary stage, from which he must take one of the two paths to perfection—Rabbi Ishmael's way of righteousness (bringing G-d into the lowest levels of this world) or Rabbi Akiva's way of repentance (bringing the world up to the highest level of perceiving G-d, so that this world is seen only as an expression of G-dliness). And since both are paths of Torah, both of them are true; therefore, one must combine aspects of both in his spiritual life.

Endnotes

1 *Shemot* 20:1.
2 Cf., e.g., *Rashi, Shemot* 19:12 and *Vayikra* 1:1.
3 *Pirkei deRabbi Eliezer*, ch. 41. *Shemot Rabbah*, 28:6; *Tanchuma*, *Yitro* 11. *Zohar*, Part I, 91a.
4 *Shemot* 20:15.
5 *Rosh Hashanah*, 26a.
6 *Shemot* 19:20.
7 *Shemot* 20:15.
8 *Chullin*, 49a, *Rashi* loc. cit.
9 *Vayikra* 21:7.
10 Cf. *Seder Hadorot. Rashi, Yoma*, 22b.
11 *Avot deRabbi Nathan*, 6:2. Cf. *Pesachim*, 49b; *Ketubot*, 62b.
12 *Berachot*, 61b.
13 At the conclusion of *Makkot*.
14 *Bamidbar* 1:51.
15 *Isaiah* 8:2.
16 The age when a child begins to learn Chumash (*Pirkei Avot*, end of ch. 5).

(Source: *Likkutei Sichot*, Vol. VI, pp. 119–129)

Rabbi Lord Jonathan Sacks, *Torah Studies* (Brooklyn: Kehot Publication Society, 1996), pp. 103–111

THE 120-DAY VERSION OF THE HUMAN STORY

BASED ON THE TEACHINGS OF THE LUBAVITCHER REBBE; ADAPTED BY RABBI YANKI TAUBER

> *Come see the doings of G-d, His fearsome plot on the children of man.* (Psalms 66:5)

> *On the 7th of Sivan, Moses went up onto the mountain. . . . On the 17th of Tammuz the Tablets were broken. On the 18th he burned the [Golden] Calf and judged the transgressors. On the 19th he went up for forty days and pleaded for mercy. On the 1st of Elul he went up to receive the Second Tablets, and was there for forty days. On the 10th of Tishrei G-d restored His goodwill with the Jewish people gladly and wholeheartedly, saying to Moses, "I have forgiven, as you ask," and gave Moses the Second Tablets.* (Rashi, Exodus 32:1 and 33:11)

Traversing the surface of time, we experience it as a succession of events and experiences. Each era is unique; each year, day, and moment distinct in content and character. But there are also time-vistas of a more inclusive nature. As we often recognize, the story of an individual life may tell the story of a century, and the events of a single generation may embody those of an entire era. Finally, there are stretches in the journey of an individual or a people in which a series of events offers a condensed version of the entire universe of time.

One such potent stretch of time was a 120-day period in the years 2448–9 from Creation (1313 BCE). The events of this period, experienced by the Jewish people soon after their birth as a nation, choreograph the essence of the human story—the basis, the process, and the end-goal of life on earth. The one hundred and twenty days from *Sivan* 6, 2448 to *Tishrei* 10, 2449 contained it all: the underpinnings of creation, the saga of human struggle, and the ultimate triumph which arises from man's imperfections and failings.

The Events

On *Sivan* 6, 2448, the entire people of Israel gathered at Mount Sinai to receive the Torah from the Almighty. There, they experienced the revelation of G-d, and heard the Ten Commandments which encapsulate the entire Torah. The following morning Moses ascended the mountain, where he communed with G-d for forty days and forty nights and received the Torah proper, the more detailed rendition of G-d's communication to humanity.

At the end of Moses' (first) forty days on Mount Sinai, G-d gave him two tablets of stone, "the handiwork of G-d,"[1] upon which the Ten Commandments were "engraved by the finger of G-d."[2] But in the camp below, the Jewish people were already abandoning their newly made covenant with G-d. Reverting to the paganism of Egypt, they made a calf of gold and, amidst feasting and hedonistic disport, proclaimed it the god of Israel.

RABBI MENACHEM MENDEL SCHNEERSON, 1902–1994

The towering Jewish leader of the 20th century, known as "the Lubavitcher Rebbe," or simply as "the Rebbe." Born in southern Ukraine, the Rebbe escaped Nazi-occupied Europe, arriving in the U.S. in June 1941. The Rebbe inspired and guided the revival of traditional Judaism after the European devastation, impacting virtually every Jewish community the world over. The Rebbe often emphasized that the performance of just one additional good deed could usher in the era of Mashiach. The Rebbe's scholarly talks and writings have been printed in more than 200 volumes.

RABBI YANKI TAUBER, 1965–

Chasidic scholar and author. A native of Brooklyn, N.Y., Rabbi Tauber is an internationally renowned author who specializes in adapting the teachings of the Lubavitcher Rebbe. He is a member of the JLI curriculum development team and has written numerous articles and books, including *Once Upon a Chassid* and *Beyond the Letter of the Law.*

> *G-d said to Moses: Descend, for your people, whom you have brought up from the land of Egypt, have corrupted; they have quickly turned from the path that I have commanded them. . . .*
> *And Moses turned and went down from the mountain, with the two Tablets of Testimony in his hand. . . . And when Moses approached the camp and saw the calf and the dancing . . . he threw the tablets from his hands and shattered them at the foot of the mountain.*[3]

It was the 17th of *Tammuz.*

Moses destroyed the idol and rehabilitated the errant nation. He then returned to Sinai for a second forty days, to plead before G-d for the forgiveness of Israel. G-d acquiesced, and agreed to provide a second set of tablets to replace those which had been broken in the wake of Israel's sin. These tablets, however, were to be not the "handiwork of G-d," but of human construction:

> *G-d said to Moses: "Carve yourself two tablets of stone, like the first; and I will inscribe upon them the words that were on the first tablets which you have broken. . . . Come up in the morning to Mount Sinai, and present yourself there to Me on the top of the mountain.*[4]

Moses ascended Sinai for his third and final forty days atop the mountain on the 1st of *Elul*. G-d had already forgiven Israel's sin, and now a new and invigorated relationship between Him and His people was to be rebuilt on the ruins of the old. On *Tishrei* 10, we received our second set of the Ten Commandments, inscribed by G-d upon the tablets carved by Moses' hand.[5]

Thus, we have three forty-day periods, and three corresponding states of Torah: the First Tablets, the Broken Tablets, and the Second Tablets. These embody the foundation of our existence, the challenge of life, and the ultimate achievement of man.

The Plot

Our sages point out that the opening verse of the Torah's account of creation, "*Bereishit bara Elokim. . . .*" ("In the beginning G-d created the heavens and earth. . . .") begins with the letter *bet*, the *second* letter of the Hebrew *alef-bet*. This is to teach us that there is an *alef* that comes before the *bet* of the created existence; that creation is not an end in itself, but comes to serve a principle which precedes it in sequence and substance.

The pre-Genesis *alef* is the *alef* of "*Anochi Hashem Elokecha. . . .*" ("I Am G-d your G-d. . . .")—the first letter of the Ten Commandments. Torah is G-d's preconception of what life on earth should be like. The basis and *raison d'être* of creation is that we develop ourselves and our environment to this ideal.

But G-d wanted more. More than the realization of His original blueprint for existence, more than the falling into place of a pre-programmed perfection. More than a "First Tablets" world that is wholly the handiwork of G-d.

A created entity, by definition, has nothing that is truly its own: all the tools, potentials, and possibilities it possesses have been *given* to it by its Creator. But G-d desired that the human experience should yield a profit beyond what is projected—or even warranted—by His initial investment in us. So G-d created us with the vulnerabilities of the human condition.

He created us with the freedom to choose, and thus with the possibility for failure. When we act rightly and constructively, we are behaving "according to plan" and realizing the potential invested within us by our Creator. When we choose to act wrongly and destructively, we enter into a state of being that is not part of the plan of Torah—indeed, it is the antithesis of what Torah prescribes. Yet this state of being is the springboard for *teshuvah* ("return")—the power to rise from the ruins of our fall to a new dimension of perfection, one that is beyond the scope of an untarnished life.

This is how Chassidic teaching explains G-d's creation of the possibility of evil. This is G-d's "fearsome plot upon the children of man."[6] The soul of man is a spark of G-dliness, inherently and utterly good; in and of itself, it is not in any way susceptible to corruption. Its human frailties are nothing less than a contrived plot, imposed upon it in total contrast to its essential nature.

If the "First Tablets" are the divine vision of creation, the "Broken Tablets" are our all-too-familiar world—a world that tolerates imperfection, failure, even outright evil. It is a world whose First Tablets have been shattered—a world gone awry of its foundation and its true self, a world wrenched out of sync with its inherent goodness.

The Broken Tablets are a plot contrived by the Author of existence to allow the possibility for a "Second Tablets." Every failing, every decline, can be exploited and redirected as a positive force. Every breakdown of the soul's First Tablets perfection is an opportunity for us to "carve for yourself" a second set, in which the divine script is chiseled upon the tablets of human initiative and creation: a second set which includes an entire vista of potentials that were beyond the scope of the first, wholly divine set.

> *G-d said to Moses: "Do not be distressed over the First Tablets, which contained only the Ten Commandments. In the Second Tablets I am giving you also Halachah, Midrash and Aggadah."*[7]

"Had Israel not sinned with the Golden Calf," our sages conclude, "they would have received only the Five Books of Moses and the book of Joshua. For as the verse says, 'Much wisdom comes through much grief.'"[8]

Remembered and Enacted

These 120 days have left a lasting imprint on our experience of time. For the Jewish calendar does far more than measure and mark time; in the words of the Book of Esther, "These days are remembered and enacted."[9] The festivals and commemorative dates that mark our annual journey through time are opportunities to reenact the events and achievements which they commemorate.

Every Shavuot, we once again experience the revelation at Sinai and our acquisition of the blueprint and foundation of our lives. Every year on the 17th of *Tammuz* we once again deal with the setbacks and breakdowns epitomized by the events of the day.[10] The month of *Elul* and the first ten days of *Tishrei*, corresponding to Moses' third 40-day stay on Mount Sinai, are today, as they were then, days of "goodwill" between G-d and man—days in which the Almighty is that much more accessible to all who seek Him.

And Yom Kippur, the holiest and most potent day of the year, marks the climax of this 120-day saga. Ever since the day that G-d gave the Second Tablets to the people of Israel, this day is a fountainhead of *teshuvah*: the source of our capacity to reclaim the deficiencies of the past as fuel and momentum for the attainment of new, unprecedented heights; the source of our capacity to exact a "profit" from G-d's perilous investment in human life.

Endnotes

1 Exodus 32:16.
2 Exodus 31:18.
3 Exodus 32:7–19.
4 Exodus 34:1–2.
5 Exodus chapters 19 and 20, 24:12–18, 32:1–19, and 34:1–2; Rashi to Exodus 32:1 and 33:11.
6 Psalms 66:5. See Midrash Tanchuma, Vayeishev 4; Talmud, Berachot 31b and Rashi ad loc.
7 Midrash Rabbah, Shemot 46:1.
8 Ecclesiastes 1:18; Talmud, Nedarim 22b.
9 Esther 9:28.
10 The 17th of Tammuz is observed as a fast day in commemoration of five tragedies that occurred on this day, the first of which is the breaking of the First Tablets (Talmud, Taanit 26a–b).

Yanki Tauber, *Inside Time*, vol. 2 (Brooklyn: Meaningful Life Center, 2015), pp. 37–43

Lesson 6

KORACH'S REBELLION

Korach, Datan en Abiram en Hun Gezinnen Worden door de Aarde Verzwolgen (Korach, Datan and Abiram and Their Families Are Swallowed by the Earth) (detail), Jan Luyken, etching, Amsterdam, 1708. (Rijksmuseum, Amsterdam)

The story of Korach's rebellion against the leadership of Moses addresses a number of fundamental questions on the variety of paths we follow through life. If every individual has a direct relationship with G-d, why are there "hierarchies of holiness" in the communal structure established by the Torah? If the purpose of Creation lies in the sanctification of physical life, why is the spiritual deemed "higher" than the material? What determines when our differences devolve into conflict, and when they become the ingredients of harmony?

TEXT 1

NUMBERS 16:1–35

KORACH'S ARGUMENT (16:1–4)

Korach, the son of Yizhar the son of Levi, took up
and Dathan and Abiram, the sons of Eliab
and On the son of Peleth
children of Reuben.
They rose up before Moses
with two hundred and fifty men
from the Children of Israel:
chieftains of the congregation
those called to the assembly
men of renown.
They congregated upon Moses and Aaron
and said to them:
"Enough! The entire community is holy
and G-d is amongst them;
why do you raise yourselves above the
congregation of G-d?"
Moses heard and he fell on his face.

MOSES'S RESPONSE (16:5–7)

He spoke to Korach and to all his company, saying:
"Come morning, and G-d will make known
who is His and who is holy
and will bring them near to Him

and the one whom He will choose
He will bring near to Him.
Do this:
Take yourselves pans, Korach and all his company.
Put fire in them, and place incense upon them
before G-d tomorrow
and the man whom G-d chooses, he is the holy one;
you have taken too much upon yourselves,
sons of Levi!" . . .

THE ROLE OF THE LEVITES (16:8–10)

"Please listen, sons of Levi.
Is it not enough
that the G-d of Israel has distinguished you
from the congregation of Israel
to draw you near to Him
to perform the service in the Tabernacle of G-d
and to stand before the congregation
to minister to them?
He drew you near
and all your brothers the sons of Levi with you
and you seek also the priesthood?"

The Great Debate
The Itche Kadoozy Show
Dovid Taub *and*
***Jonathan Goorvich*:**

MYJLI.COM/BIBLE

SWALLOWED BY EARTH, CONSUMED BY FIRE (16:31–35)

. . . The ground split beneath them.
The earth opened her mouth

and swallowed them and their houses.
They and all they possessed
descended alive into the abyss;
the earth covered them up
and they were lost to the community. . . .
And a fire came forth from G-d
and consumed the two hundred and fifty men
who had offered up the incense.

TEXT 2

TALMUD, SANHEDRIN 110A

כָּל הַמַּחֲזִיק בְּמַחְלוֹקֶת עוֹבֵר בְּלָאו, שֶׁנֶּאֱמַר (בַּמִּדְבָּר יז, ה): "וְלֹא יִהְיֶה כְקֹרַח וְכַעֲדָתוֹ".

Anyone who engages in divisiveness transgresses a biblical prohibition, as it is written (NUMBERS 17:5), "And he shall not be as Korach and his company."

BABYLONIAN TALMUD

A literary work of monumental proportions that draws upon the legal, spiritual, intellectual, ethical, and historical traditions of Judaism. The 37 tractates of the Babylonian Talmud contain the teachings of the Jewish sages from the period after the destruction of the 2nd Temple through the 5th century CE. It has served as the primary vehicle for the transmission of the Oral Law and the education of Jews over the centuries; it is the entry point for all subsequent legal, ethical, and theological Jewish scholarship.

TEXT 3

MIDRASH, *TANCHUMA*, KORACH 4

כִּי כָל הָעֵדָה כֻּלָּם קְדֹשִׁים, וְכֻלָּם שָׁמְעוּ בְּסִינַי, "אָנֹכִי ה' אֱלֹקֶיךָ" וּמַדּוּעַ תִּתְנַשְּׂאוּ?

The entire community is holy. At Mount Sinai, everyone heard G-d proclaim, "I am G-d your G-d." So why do you elevate yourselves?

MIDRASH TANCHUMA

A Midrashic work bearing the name of Rabbi Tanchuma, a 4th-century Talmudic sage quoted often in this work. "Midrash" is the designation of a particular genre of rabbinic literature usually forming a running commentary on specific books of the Bible. *Midrash Tanchuma* provides textual exegeses, expounds upon the biblical narrative, and develops and illustrates moral principles. *Tanchuma* is unique in that many of its sections commence with a halachic discussion, which subsequently leads into nonhalachic teachings.

Aäron, Johann Sadeler (I) (printmaker), after Crispijn van den Broeck, engraving, Antwerp, 1575. (Rijksmuseum, Amsterdam)

TEXT 4

RASHI, NUMBERS 16:1

עָמַד וְכָנַס מָאתַיִם וַחֲמִישִּׁים רָאשֵׁי סַנְהֶדְרָאוֹת, רוּבָּן מִשֵּׁבֶט רְאוּבֵן שְׁכֵנָיו . . . וְהִלְבִּישָׁן טַלִיתוֹת שֶׁכּוּלָּן תְּכֵלֶת, בָּאוּ וְעָמְדוּ לִפְנֵי מֹשֶׁה. אָמְרוּ לוֹ: "טַלִית שֶׁכּוּלָּהּ שֶׁל תְּכֵלֶת, חַיֶּיבֶת בְּצִיצִית אוֹ פְּטוּרָה?" אָמַר לָהֶם: "חַיֶּיבֶת". הִתְחִילוּ לִשְׂחֹק עָלָיו: "אֶפְשָׁר טַלִית שֶׁל מִין אַחֵר, חוּט אֶחָד שֶׁל תְּכֵלֶת פּוֹטְרָהּ, זוֹ שֶׁכּוּלָּהּ תְּכֵלֶת, לֹא תִּפְטוֹר אֶת עַצְמָהּ?"

[Korach] gathered two hundred and fifty magistrates, most of them from the tribe of Reuben, his neighbors. . . . He dressed them in garments that were entirely of blue wool. They came and stood before Moses and asked him: "If a garment is made entirely of blue wool, does it require *tsitsit* or is it absolved?"

Moses answered them: "It requires *tsitsit*."

They began to laugh at him. "If a garment of another sort is absolved by a single thread of blue wool, this garment, composed wholly of blue wool, cannot absolve itself?"

RABBI SHLOMO YITSCHAKI (RASHI), 1040–1105

Most noted biblical and Talmudic commentator. Born in Troyes, France, Rashi studied in the famed *yeshivot* of Mainz and Worms. His commentaries on the Pentateuch and the Talmud, which focus on the straightforward meaning of the text, appear in virtually every edition of the Talmud and Bible.

TEXT 5

MIDRASH, *BAMIDBAR RABAH*, 18:3

קָפַץ קֹרַח וְאָמַר לְמֹשֶׁה . . . "בַּיִת מָלֵא סְפָרִים, מַהוּ שֶׁיְּהֵא פָּטוּר מִן הַמְזוּזָה?" אָמַר לוֹ: "חַיָּיב בִּמְזוּזָה". אָמַר לוֹ: "כָּל הַתּוֹרָה כֻּלָּהּ מָאתַיִם וְשִׁבְעִים וְחָמֵשׁ פָּרָשִׁיּוֹת אֵינָהּ פּוֹטֶרֶת אֶת הַבַּיִת, פָּרָשָׁה אַחַת שֶׁבַּמְזוּזָה פּוֹטֶרֶת אֶת הַבַּיִת? . . . דְבָרִים אֵלּוּ לֹא נִצְטַוֵּיתָ עֲלֵיהֶן, וּמִלִּבְּךָ אַתָּה בּוֹדְאָן!"

Korach sprang up and said to Moses . . . , "If a house is full of Torah scrolls, is it absolved from the obligation to affix a *mezuzah* on its doorpost?"

Replied Moses: "It requires a *mezuzah*."

Said Korach: "The entire Torah, consisting of 275 chapters, does not absolve this house, and the two chapters in the *mezuzah* absolve it? . . . G-d did not command you these things—you have invented them yourself!"

BAMIDBAR RABAH

An exegetical commentary on the first 7 chapters of the book of Numbers and a homiletic commentary on the rest of the book. The first part of *Bamidbar Rabah* is notable for its inclusion of esoteric material; the second half is essentially identical to *Midrash Tanchuma* on the book of Numbers. It was first printed in Constantinople in 1512, together with 4 other midrashic works on the other 4 books of the Pentateuch.

Looking for Leadership
***Rabbi Michoel Gourarie*:**

MYJLI.COM/BIBLE

TEXT 6

MIDRASH TEHILIM, PSALM 1

וַיַּקְהֵל עֲלֵיהֶם קֹרַח אֶת כָּל הָעֵדָה (בַּמִדְבָּר טז, יט). הִתְחִיל לוֹמַר לֵיצָנוּת, וְאוֹמֵר לָהֶן:

אַלְמָנָה אַחַת הָיְתָה בִּשְׁכוּנָתִי וְעִמָּהּ שְׁתֵּי נְעָרוֹת יְתוֹמוֹת וְהָיְתָה לָהּ שָׂדֶה אַחַת.

בָּאתָה לַחֲרוֹשׁ, אָמַר לָהּ מֹשֶׁה: "לֹא תַחֲרוֹשׁ בְּשׁוֹר וּבַחֲמוֹר יַחְדָו" (דְבָרִים כב, י).

בָּאתָה לִזְרוֹעַ, אָמַר לָהּ מֹשֶׁה: "שָׂדְךָ לֹא תִזְרַע כִּלְאָיִם" (וַיִקְרָא יט, יט).

בָּאתָה לִקְצוֹר וְלַעֲשׂוֹת עֲרֵימָה, אָמַר לָהּ: הַנִיחִי לֶקֶט, שִׁכְחָה וּפֵאָה.

בָּאתָה לַעֲשׂוֹת גוֹרֶן, אָמַר לָהּ: תְּנִי תְּרוּמָה וּתְרוּמַת מַעֲשֵׂר וּמַעֲשֵׂר רִאשׁוֹן וּמַעֲשֵׂר שֵׁנִי. הִצְדִיקָה עָלֶיהָ אֶת הַדִין וְנָתְנָה לוֹ.

מַה עָשְׂתָה? מָכְרָה אֶת הַשָּׂדֶה וְלָקְחָה שְׁנֵי כְבָשׂוֹת לִלְבּוֹשׁ מִגִזוֹתֵיהֶן וְלֵיהָנוֹת מִפֵּירוֹתֵיהֶן. כֵּיוָן שֶׁיָלְדוּ, בָּא אַהֲרֹן וְאָמַר לָהּ: תְּנִי לִי אֶת הַבְּכוֹרוֹת, שֶׁכַּךְ אָמַר לִי הַקָבָּ"ה: "כָּל הַבְּכוֹר אֲשֶׁר יִוָלֵד בִּבְקָרְךָ וּבְצֹאנְךָ הַזָכָר" (דְבָרִים טו, יט). הִצְדִיקָה עָלֶיהָ אֶת הַדִין וְנָתְנָה לוֹ. הִגִיעַ זְמַן גִיזָה וְגָזְזָה אוֹתָן, אָמַר לָהּ: תְּנִי לִי רֵאשִׁית הַגֵז, שֶׁכֵּן אָמַר לִי הַקָבָּ"ה: "וְרֵאשִׁית גֵז צֹאנְךָ תִּתֶּן לוֹ" (שָׁם יח, ד).

אָמְרָה: אֵין לִי כֹּחַ לַעֲמוֹד בָּאִישׁ הַזֶה. הֲרֵי אֲנִי שׁוֹחֵט אוֹתָן וְאוֹכַלְתָּן. כֵּיוָן שֶׁשְּׁחָטָן, אָמַר לָהּ: תְּנִי לִי הַזְרוֹעַ וְהַלְחָיַיִם וְהַקֵיבָה. אָמְרָה לוֹ: אֲפִילוּ שֶׁשְּׁחַטְתִּי אוֹתָן לֹא נִצַלְתִּי מִיָדוֹ. הֵן עָלַי חֵרֶם! אָמַר לָהּ: תְּנָה לִי, שֶׁכַּךְ אָמַר הַכָּתוּב: "כָּל חֵרֶם בְּיִשְׂרָאֵל לְךָ יִהְיֶה" (בַּמִדְבָּר יח, יד). נְטָלָהּ וְהָלַךְ לוֹ. הִנִיחָהּ בּוֹכָה, הִיא וּשְׁתֵּי בְנוֹתֶיהָ.

אַרִיךְ כְּדִין הָא בִּיזְתָּא עֲלוּבְתָּא. כָּל כָּךְ הֵם עוֹשִׂים וְתוֹלִין בְּהַקָבָּ"ה.

MIDRASH TEHILIM

A rabbinic commentary on the Book of Psalms. "Midrash" is the designation of a particular genre of rabbinic literature usually forming a running commentary on specific books of the Bible. This particular Midrash provides textual exegeses and develops and illustrates the principles of the Book of Psalms.

"Korach gathered the congregation against them" (NUMBERS 16:19). He began to speak mockery, saying to the people:

There was a widow in my neighborhood with two orphaned girls, and she had one field. When she came to plow, Moses said to her, "Do not plow with an ox and a donkey together" (DEUTERONOMY 22:10). When she came to sow, Moses said to her, "Do not sow your field with mixed seeds" (LEVITICUS 19:19).

When she came to harvest and to stack heaps of cut grain, Moses said to her, "Leave the gleanings, forgotten sheaf, and edges of the field [for the poor]." When she came to bring the grain into storage, he said to her, "Contribute the priest's due, the priest's due from the tithe, and the first and second tithes." She accepted the judgment and gave it to him.

What did she do? She sold her field and bought two sheep so that she could clothe herself with their shearings and benefit from what they brought forth. But when the sheep gave birth, Aaron came and said to her, "Give me the firstborns, for thus has G-d said to me, 'Every male firstborn from your cattle and from your flocks [you shall consecrate to G-d]' (DEUTERONOMY 15:19)." She accepted the judgment and gave it to him.

The time came to shear them, and Aaron said to her, "Give me the first of the shearing, for thus has G-d said to me, 'The first of the shearing of your flock you should give to Me' (DEUTERONOMY 18:4)."

The woman said, "I don't have the strength to resist this man. I will slaughter them and eat them." As soon as she had slaughtered them, Aaron said to her, "Give me the shoulder, the cheeks, and the stomach."

The woman said to him, "Even when I have slaughtered them, I have not escaped your hand. I take an oath upon myself that they should be *cherem* [off limits to everyone]!"

Said Aaron to her, "Give them to me, for this is what Scripture says, 'Every *cherem* in Israel shall be yours' (NUMBERS 18:14)." Saying this, he took them and went off, leaving her and her two daughters crying.

How contemptuously do they treat these poor people! All this they do, and they attribute it to G-d.

QUESTION FOR DISCUSSION

What messages was Korach communicating through these three demonstrations?

QUESTION FOR DISCUSSION

If Korach is against the "hierarchy," why is he seeking a higher place in it?

New Year's postcard, Germany, c. late 19th–early 20th century. (*The Jewish World*)

וְהָאֲבָנִים עַל שְׁמֹות בְּנֵי יִשְׂרָאֵל הֵנָּה
לשנה טובה תכתבו

Is Life an Optical Illusion?
Chana Weisberg:

MYJLI.COM/BIBLE

Figure 6.1

The Hierarchy of Divine Service

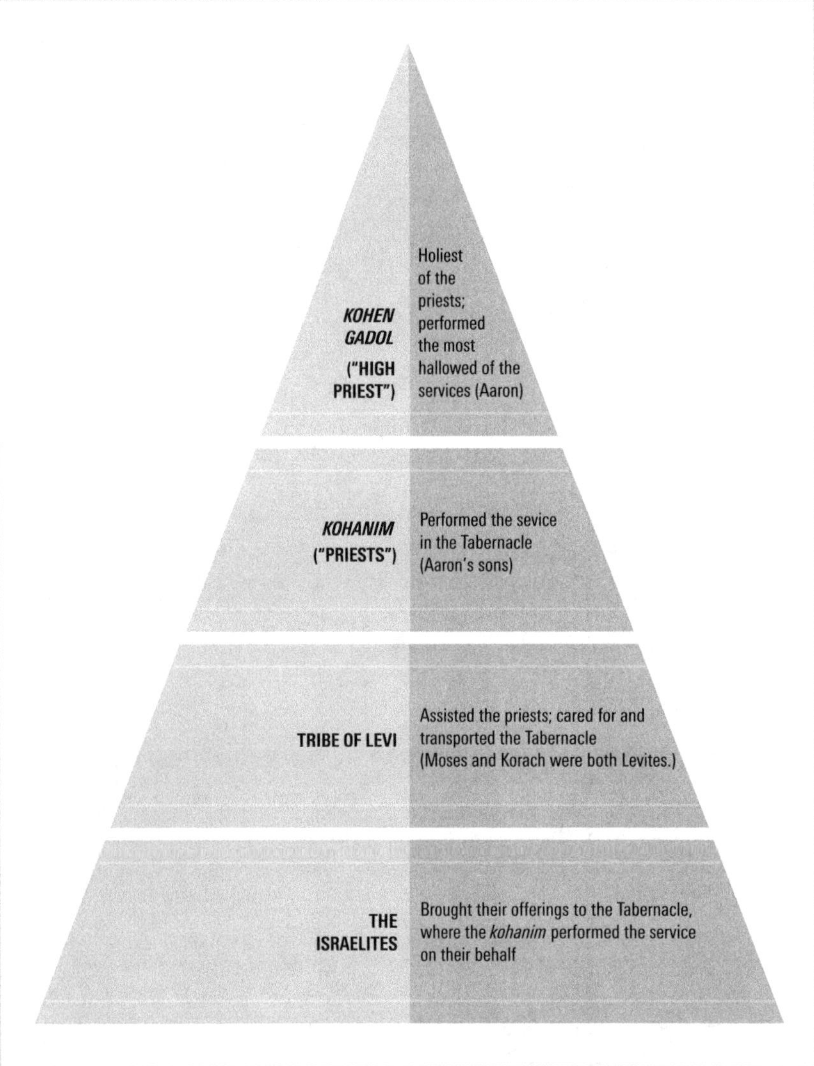
KOHEN GADOL
("HIGH PRIEST")
Holiest of the priests; performed the most hallowed of the services (Aaron)
KOHANIM
("PRIESTS")
Performed the sevice in the Tabernacle (Aaron's sons)
TRIBE OF LEVI
Assisted the priests; cared for and transported the Tabernacle (Moses and Korach were both Levites.)
THE ISRAELITES
Brought their offerings to the Tabernacle, where the *kohanim* performed the service on their behalf

TEXT 7

MAIMONIDES, *MISHNEH TORAH*, LAWS OF SABBATICAL AND JUBILEE YEARS 13:13

וְלֹא שֵׁבֶט לֵוִי בִּלְבָד, אֶלָּא כָּל אִישׁ וְאִישׁ מִכָּל בָּאֵי הָעוֹלָם, אֲשֶׁר נָדְבָה רוּחוֹ אוֹתוֹ וֶהֱבִינוֹ מַדָּעוֹ לְהִבָּדֵל לַעֲמוֹד לִפְנֵי ה' לְשָׁרְתוֹ וּלְעָבְדוֹ לְדֵעָה אֶת ה' וְהָלַךְ יָשָׁר כְּמוֹ שֶׁעֲשָׂהוּ הָאֱלֹקִים וּפָרַק מֵעַל צַוָּארוֹ עוֹל הַחֶשְׁבּוֹנוֹת הָרַבִּים אֲשֶׁר בִּקְשׁוּ בְּנֵי הָאָדָם - הֲרֵי זֶה נִתְקַדֵּשׁ קֹדֶשׁ קָדָשִׁים. וְיִהְיֶה ה' חֶלְקוֹ וְנַחֲלָתוֹ לְעוֹלָם וּלְעוֹלְמֵי עוֹלָמִים, וְיִזְכֶּה לוֹ בָּעוֹלָם הַזֶּה דָּבָר הַמַּסְפִּיק לוֹ, כְּמוֹ שֶׁזָּכָה לַכֹּהֲנִים לַלְוִיִּם.

Not only the tribe of Levi, but any individual of any of the inhabitants of the world whose generosity of spirit motivates them, and who understand with their wisdom to set themselves aside to stand before G-d, to serve Him and minister to Him, to know G-d, proceeding justly as G-d made them; and they cast off from their neck the yoke of the many calculations that people seek—that person is sanctified as a "holy of holies." G-d will be their portion and heritage forever, and will provide their needs for them in this world, as He provided for the *kohanim* and the Levites.

RABBI MOSHE BEN MAIMON (MAIMONIDES, RAMBAM), 1135–1204

Halachist, philosopher, author, and physician. Maimonides was born in Córdoba, Spain. After the conquest of Córdoba by the Almohads, he fled Spain and eventually settled in Cairo, Egypt. There, he became the leader of the Jewish community and served as court physician to the vizier of Egypt. He is most noted for authoring the *Mishneh Torah*, an encyclopedic arrangement of Jewish law; and for his philosophical work, *Guide for the Perplexed*. His rulings on Jewish law are integral to the formation of halachic consensus.

Defying Labels
A lesson from the story of Korach's mutiny
Mrs. Sara Blau:

MYJLI.COM/BIBLE

TEXT 8

THE REBBE, RABBI MENACHEM MENDEL SCHNEERSON,
LIKUTEI SICHOT (HEBREW EDITION) 4, PP. 24–25

נֶאֱמַר בְּתוֹרַת הַחֲסִידוּת סִיבַּת הַדָּבָר שֶׁלֹּא רָצוּ הַמְרַגְּלִים לְהִכָּנֵס לְאֶרֶץ יִשְׂרָאֵל אֶלָּא לְהִשָּׁאֵר בַּמִּדְבָּר הִיא מִשּׁוּם שֶׁלֹּא רָצוּ לְהַשְׁפִּיל עַצְמָם וּלְהִתְעַסֵּק בְּגַשְׁמִיּוּת.

בִּהְיוֹתָם בַּמִּדְבָּר הָיוּ בְּנֵי יִשְׂרָאֵל מְסוּגָּרִים וּמְנוּתָּקִים מִן הָעוֹלָם. גַּם אֲכִילָתָם וּשְׁתִיָּיתָם הַגַּשְׁמִיִּים הָיוּ נַעֲלִית מִן אַרְצִיּוּת. הַמָּן הָיָה לֶחֶם מִן הַשָּׁמַיִם, מַיִם מִבְּאֵרָהּ שֶׁל מִרְיָם. וַאֲפִילוּ בִּגְדֵיהֶם . . . גָּדְלוּ יַחַד עִם הַגּוּפִים . . . וְאִילוּ בִּכְנִיסָתָם לְאֶרֶץ יִשְׂרָאֵל . . . נֶאֶלְצוּ לֶאֱכוֹל לֶחֶם מִן הָאָרֶץ, וּבִכְדֵי לְהַשִּׂיגוֹ דְּרוּשָׁה הָיְתָה הִתְעַסְּקוּת בְּעִנְיָנֵי הָעוֹלָם בִּמְלָאכוֹת שֶׁל חֲרִישָׁה וּזְרִיעָה וְכוּ' . . .

לְפִיכָךְ לֹא רָצוּ הַמְרַגְּלִים לְהִכָּנֵס לְאֶרֶץ יִשְׂרָאֵל בְּטַעֲנָה שֶׁהִיא "אֹכֶלֶת יוֹשְׁבֶיהָ"–הִיא אוֹכֶלֶת אֶת הַיּוֹשְׁבִים עָלֶיהָ, שֶׁנַּעֲשִׂים בְּחִינַת "אֶרֶץ", גַּשְׁמִיּוּת בִּלְבָד, וְלֹא עִנְיָנִים רוּחָנִיִּים שֶׁנִּיתַּן לְהַגִּיעַ אֲלֵיהֶם בְּהִסְתַּגְּרוּת מִן הָעוֹלָם, כְּשֶׁמִּתְעַסְּקִים רַק בְּרוּחָנִיּוּת . . .

אֲבָל לַאֲמִתּוֹ שֶׁל דָּבָר טָעוּ הַמְרַגְּלִים בָּזֶה. שֶׁכֵּן תַּכְלִית הַכַּוָּונָה הִיא לַעֲשׂוֹת לְהַקָּבָּ"ה כִּבְיָכוֹל "דִּירָה בַּתַּחְתּוֹנִים"–לַעֲסוֹק בְּעִנְיָנֵי הָעוֹלָם וְלַעֲשׂוֹת מֵהֶם כְּלִי לֶאֱלֹקוּת. וְשֶׁהוּתָם שֶׁל בְּנֵי יִשְׂרָאֵל בַּמִּדְבָּר לֹא הָיְתָה אֶלָּא רַק הֲכָנָה לְ"דִירָה בַּתַּחְתּוֹנִים", אוֹתָהּ עָשׂוּ רַק בְּבוֹאָם לְאֶרֶץ יִשְׂרָאֵל.

The teachings of *Chasidut* explain the reason that the Spies wanted to remain in the desert and not enter the Land of Israel. It was because they did not want to lower themselves to engage with material things.

When they were in the desert, the Children of Israel were secluded and disconnected from the material world. Even their physical food and drink were elevated above the earthly and the mundane. The manna served them as "bread from heaven"; their water came from the

RABBI MENACHEM MENDEL SCHNEERSON 1902–1994

The towering Jewish leader of the 20th century, known as "the Lubavitcher Rebbe," or simply as "the Rebbe." Born in southern Ukraine, the Rebbe escaped Nazi-occupied Europe, arriving in the U.S. in June 1941. The Rebbe inspired and guided the revival of traditional Judaism after the European devastation, impacting virtually every Jewish community the world over. The Rebbe often emphasized that the performance of just one additional good deed could usher in the era of Mashiach. The Rebbe's scholarly talks and writings have been printed in more than 200 volumes.

"Well of Miriam"; even their clothes . . . [miraculously] grew with their bodies. . . . But upon their entry into the Land of Israel, . . . they would be required to eat bread from the earth, and in order to obtain it, they would be required to occupy themselves in worldly matters: in the labors of plowing, sowing, and so on. . . .

This is why the Spies did not want to enter the Land of Israel. They argued that it is "a land that consumes its inhabitants": it "consumes" those who dwell in it by turning them into "earthly"—i.e., materialistic—beings, depriving them of the spiritual achievements that can be attained only by secluding oneself from the world and occupying oneself solely with spiritual pursuits. . . .

In truth, however, the Spies erred in their approach. For the ultimate purpose is to make for G-d, so to speak, "a dwelling in the lowly realms"—to engage with worldly things and make them a receptacle for G-dliness. The period that the people of Israel were in the desert was only in preparation for the "dwelling in the lowly realms" that they would make when they entered the Land of Israel.

TEXT 9

RABBI SHNE'UR ZALMAN OF LIADI, *TANYA*, CHAPTER 33

וְזֶה כָּל הָאָדָם, וְתַכְלִית בְּרִיאָתוֹ, וּבְרִיאַת כָּל הָעוֹלָמוֹת עֶלְיוֹנִים וְתַחְתּוֹנִים:
לִהְיוֹת לוֹ דִירָה זוּ בַּתַּחְתּוֹנִים.

This is what man is all about; this is the purpose of man's creation, and of the creation of all the worlds, both the lofty and the lowly: that G-d should have this dwelling in the lowly realms.

RABBI SHNE'UR ZALMAN OF LIADI (ALTER REBBE), 1745–1812

Chasidic rebbe, halachic authority, and founder of the Chabad movement. The Alter Rebbe was born in Liozna, Belarus, and was among the principal students of the Magid of Mezeritch. His numerous works include the *Tanya*, an early classic containing the fundamentals of Chabad Chasidism; and *Shulchan Aruch HaRav*, an expanded and reworked code of Jewish law.

A girls' "*Kheyder*" (traditional school), Biala Bilits, 1926. (Photo credit: Alter Kacyzne, YIVO Institute for Jewish Research, New York)

TEXT 10

MIDRASH, *TANCHUMA*, VA'ERA 15

מָשָׁל לְמָה הַדָּבָר דּוֹמֶה? לְמֶלֶךְ שֶׁגָּזַר וְאָמַר: "בְּנֵי רוֹמִי לֹא יֵרְדוּ לְסוּרְיָא, וּבְנֵי סוּרְיָא לֹא יַעֲלוּ לְרוֹמִי". כַּךְ, כְּשֶׁבָּרָא הַקָּבָּ"ה אֶת הָעוֹלָם גָּזַר וְאָמַר (תְּהִילִים קטו, טז): "הַשָּׁמַיִם שָׁמַיִם לַה' וְהָאָרֶץ נָתַן לִבְנֵי אָדָם". כְּשֶׁבִּקֵּשׁ לִיתֵּן אֶת הַתּוֹרָה, בִּטֵּל אֶת הַגְּזֵרָה הָרִאשׁוֹנָה, וְאָמַר: "הַתַּחְתּוֹנִים יַעֲלוּ לָעֶלְיוֹנִים, וְהָעֶלְיוֹנִים יֵרְדוּ לַתַּחְתּוֹנִים". וַאֲנִי הַמַּתְחִיל, שֶׁנֶּאֱמַר (שְׁמוֹת יט, כ), "וַיֵּרֶד ה' עַל הַר סִינַי וגו'", וּכְתִיב (שָׁם כד, א), "וְאֶל מֹשֶׁה אָמַר עֲלֵה אֶל ה'".

This can be compared to the following parable: There was a king who decreed, "The people of Rome may not go down to Syria, and the people of Syria may not go up to Rome."

Likewise, when G-d created the world, He decreed (PSALMS 115:16): "The heavens are G-d's, and the earth is given to humanity." But when G-d wished to give the Torah, He rescinded His original decree and declared: "The lowly realms should ascend to the higher realms, and the higher realms should descend to the lowly realms." [G-d also said,] "And I shall begin." As it is written (EXODUS 19:20), "G-d descended on Mount Sinai"; and then it says (IBID., 24:1), "And to Moses He said: Go up to G-d."

QUESTIONS FOR DISCUSSION

1 What does it mean that "The higher realms should descend to the lowly realms"?

2 What does it mean that "The lowly realms should ascend to the higher realms"?

The Messianic Nature of Korach's Campaign
Rabbi Moishe New:

MYJLI.COM/BIBLE

3 Why are both steps necessary in order to make "a dwelling for G-d in the lowly realms"?

Figure 6.2

What Is Your Primary Occupation?

MATERIAL OCCUPATIONS	SPIRITUAL OCCUPATIONS

QUESTIONS FOR DISCUSSION

For "Material Occupations":

1 Do you have feelings of inferiority because you are engaged, for the most part of your day, in a material occupation?

2 Do you believe these feelings to be a positive thing or a negative thing?

3 Why would such a feeling be a good thing?

4 Why would it not be good?

5 What would you like to do to make your life more spiritual?

For "Spiritual Occupations":

1 Do you have feelings of superiority because you are engaged, for the most part of your day, in a spiritual occupation?

2 Do you believe these feelings to be a positive thing or a negative thing?

3 Why would such a feeling be a good thing?

4 Why would it not be good?

5 What would you like to do in order to have a greater impact on the material world?

QUESTION FOR DISCUSSION

Why is there so much conflict in the world? Why is there so much animosity toward the "other"?

Tragic Conflict, Leonardo Dudreville, oil on canvas, 1913.

Figure 6.3

Two Paths to Unity

KORACH'S MODEL	MOSES'S MODEL
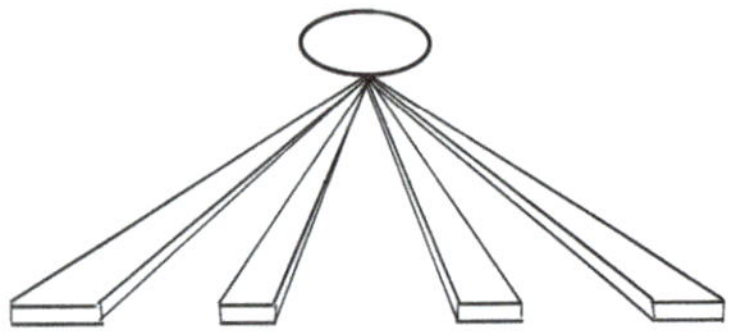	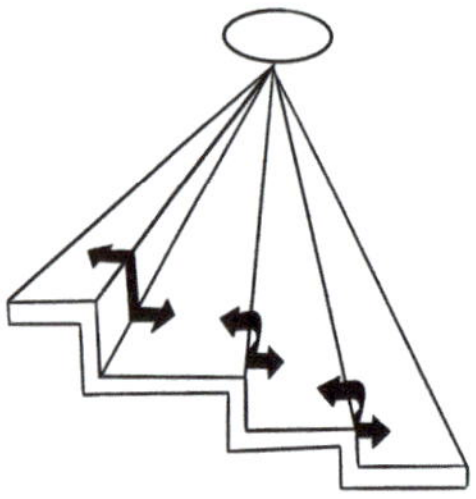
PARALLEL TRACKS (Pluralism)	**RECIPROCAL RELATIONSHIPS**
1. Equality	1. Hierarchy
2. Independence	2. Interdependence
3. Alienation	3. Harmony
4. Conflict	4. Unity

QUESTION FOR DISCUSSION

What would be a modern-day equivalent of the "priestly gifts"?

1 Korach challenged the leadership of Moses and Aaron. He objected to the "hierarchy" that Moses had instituted, which implied that those who dedicate their lives exclusively to serving G-d were holier than those who occupied themselves with the material world. In Korach's view, spiritual and material life are parallel tracks to serving the divine purpose, neither of which should be regarded as holier or "higher" than the other.

2 Korach's rebellion was preceded by the incident of the Spies, who dissuaded the people from conquering and settling the Promised Land. Chasidic teaching explains that the Spies wished to maintain their spiritual way of life in the desert rather than engage with the material world. The error of the Spies lay in their failure to appreciate that while there is the need for a spiritual component in our lives, the purpose of life on earth—and of Creation as a whole—is "to make a dwelling for G-d in the lowly realms" of the material world.

3 Two central questions arise from these two accounts: If the ultimate purpose of Creation is fulfilled within the material world, why was Korach wrong in arguing that the spiritual is not higher than the material? And why is

Korach regarded as a prototype of divisiveness, when he advocated against elitism and for equality?

4 A famous Midrashic parable describes two conditions for making a home for G-d in the material world: (a) "the higher realms should descend to the lower realms"; (b) "the lower realms should ascend to the higher realms." This means that those who are living a spiritual life need to "descend" to instruct and inspire those who are engaged with the material world. It also means that those who are materially engaged need to "ascend" by constantly striving to become more spiritual. Without this striving, a person will become enmeshed in and consumed by the material world, instead of refining it and making it receptive to G-dliness.

5 Korach's "parallel tracks" approach seems to be a recipe for harmony. In truth, however, this form of equality, in which the various groups exist independently from each other, ultimately devolves into divisiveness and conflict. On the other hand, Moses's "reciprocal relationships" approach, which fosters interdependence between the groups, leads to harmony and unity.

Additional Readings

KORACH

A DISCOURSE OF THE LUBAVITCHER REBBE; ADAPTED BY RABBI LORD JONATHAN SACKS

The Sidra of Korach concerns the revolt of Korach and his followers against the Priesthood of Aaron and his sons. But what exactly was Korach's aim? On the one hand, he voiced protest against the whole institution of priesthood or at least against its carrying any special status. On the other, it is clear from the narrative that he was seeking the High Priesthood for himself. Can we make sense of his apparently contradictory aims? This is the central point of the Sicha's inquiry. And as a result of its analysis we can understand two further difficulties: Why "Korach," the name of an inciter to dissent, is eternalized by making it the name of one of the sections of the Torah, and why this one Sidra contains two such seemingly opposite themes: Korach's revolt, and the conferring of the "twenty-four Gifts of Priesthood" on Aaron.

1. Themes and Oppositions

Each of the 53 Sidrot of the Five Books of Moses has a central theme: One that is carried through each of its verses, from first to last, and which is suggested in the name it bears.[1] This connecting motif is so strong, that the thematic link between the first and last verses of a Sidra is stronger than that between the ending of one Sidra and the beginning of the next, even though it may continue what appears to be the same narrative. In fact, the very existence of a break between two Sidrot indicates that there is some *discontinuity* between them sometimes going so far as to point out an *opposition*: As we see in the ending of Behaalotecha, where Miriam was punished for her evil report against Moses; and the beginning of Shelach, where the spies who are about to be sent to Israel saw the punishment and did not take heed of it, ultimately to repeat the sin.[2]

On the face of it, this general rule seems hard to apply to the Sidra of Korach, which begins with the accusation of Korach and his followers against Aaron and the priesthood, and ends with G-d giving the "twenty-four Gifts of Priesthood." The initial accusation and the ultimate validation seem to stand as opposites to one another; and yet it is not merely that the latter is the *outcome* of the former. Rather, we must search for a way in which the "Gifts of Priesthood" are an *integral part* of the story of Korach. For the Sidra is called by his name—and this is where the core of the Sidra lies.

But the search is beset by this problem: The insurrection of Korach was an opposition to the priesthood, as it stood in the hands of Aaron; while the "twenty-four Gifts" were, as Rashi says, a way of "writing and

RABBI MENACHEM MENDEL SCHNEERSON, 1902–1994

The towering Jewish leader of the 20th century, known as "the Lubavitcher Rebbe," or simply as "the Rebbe." Born in southern Ukraine, the Rebbe escaped Nazi-occupied Europe, arriving in the U.S. in June 1941. The Rebbe inspired and guided the revival of traditional Judaism after the European devastation, impacting virtually every Jewish community the world over. The Rebbe often emphasized that the performance of just one additional good deed could usher in the era of Mashiach. The Rebbe's scholarly talks and writings have been printed in more than 200 volumes.

RABBI LORD JONATHAN SACKS, 1948–

Former chief rabbi of the United Kingdom. Rabbi Sacks attended Cambridge University and received his doctorate from King's College, London. A prolific and influential author, his books include *Will We Have Jewish Grandchildren?* and *The Dignity of Difference*. He received the Jerusalem Prize in 1995 for his contributions to enhancing Jewish life in the Diaspora, was knighted and made a life peer in 2005, and became Baron Sacks of Aldridge in 2009.

sealing and recording in the court" the gift of priesthood to him.

2. The Name of Korach

There is an additional difficulty. How did the Sidra come to be called Korach in the first place? For, on the verse[3] "The name of the wicked shall rot" the Talmud[4] comments, "Their names shall decay for we do not mention (the wicked) by name." If *we* should not mention the wicked by name in ordinary conversation, still less should a Sidra of the Torah be named after one of them, for this is a way of *perpetuating* a name.

And there is no saving grace in Korach, for though, as Rashi tells us, his sons repented, he himself did not. In the name itself there is no hint of righteousness: It means a bald spot,[5] and as the Midrash[6] explains, it has the connotation of *making divisions*—creating a bald spot between two factions where previously there had been unity.

Rambam writes[7] that the Torah "was given to make peace in the world." How then should a portion of it be called by a name that suggests divisiveness?

3. Korach's Claim

And finally, there is an apparent inconsistency in the very claim that Korach made. On the one hand it appears that he was set against the very institution of the priesthood, or at least its special status, for he said:[8] "For all the congregation is holy, and the L-rd dwells in their midst; and why therefore do you elevate yourselves above the congregation of the L-rd?" On the other hand, it was apparent that Korach and his followers sought the priesthood for themselves, as Moses explicitly says to them.[9]

One explanation is that they did not want the status of the priesthood to be abolished, merely that they did not want it confined to Aaron. They wanted *many* High Priests; they sought to be included in that rank. And yet it is clear from Rashi's commentary[10] that Korach sought the High Priesthood for himself alone: He thought that he alone would be vindicated in the trial that the accusers were to undergo. If he had this ambition, why then did he say, "Why do you elevate yourselves?"—for he had reason to wish to see the priesthood elevated.

4. The Firmament Which Divides the Waters

The opening words of our Sidra, "And Korach took," are translated in the *Targum* as "And Korach *divided*," and in the book *Noam Elimelech*, Rabbi Elimelech of Liszensk compares Korach's dissension to the firmament which G-d created on the second day to divide between the higher and lower waters.

What is the analogy? One difference between the priests and the rest of the Children of Israel was that the priests were withdrawn from the affairs of the world and entirely taken up with their holy office. Especially the High Priest (against whom Korach's accusation was primarily intended), of whom it is written[11] that "he shall not depart from the Sanctuary."

But despite this, he was not uninvolved with the rest of the people: On the contrary, he exercised his influence over them *all*, drawing them up to his own level of holiness. This was symbolized by the kindling of the seven branches of the Menorah.[12] Aaron's special attribute was "Great, or everlasting Love"—and he drew the people near to this service.

But Korach did not see this. He saw only the *separation* between priest and people. And viewed in this light, he saw that just as the priests had their special role, so too did the people, in enacting G-d's will in the *practical* world, which was, indeed, the whole purpose of the Torah. Seen as separate entities, the people had at least as much right to honor and elevation as the priests.

And this removes the inconsistency from his claim. He sought the priesthood, but as an office entirely remote from the people. Hence his accusation, "Why do you elevate yourselves?" In his eyes, the two groups, utterly distinct, each had their special status. In this way Korach was like the firmament: His aim was to divide the people, like the waters, and sever the connection between the Sanctuary and the ordinary world.

5. Division and Peace

On the second day of creation we find that G-d did not say: "And it was good." The Rabbis explain[13] that this was because division (the firmament) was created on that day. It was not until the third day that this judgment was pronounced and repeated, once for the creation of that day, and once for the firmament,[14] which was purified and its division healed.[15] Thus we learn that in the Divine scheme, there has to be a division between the things of heaven and those of earth, but that its consummation is in their re-uniting. And just as on the third day, so too in the third millennium Torah was given to bring together heaven and earth, G-d descending and Israel ascending to union.[16]

The same applies to the Children of Israel. Although there are those who are totally involved in holy service and "do not depart from the Sanctuary," and those whose service is in the practical world ("In all your ways, know Him"[17]); the one must not be separate from the other, but the former must lead the latter, in the manner of Aaron, ever closer to G-d. This is the man of the world, the businessman etc., who reaches through setting regular times for study of Torah. And this study should be of such intense concentration, that he is, at that time, as one who never departs from the Sanctuary!

And just as the work of the second day was consummated on the third, so did G-d allow the division caused by Korach, so that it would reach its fulfillment in the "twenty-four Gifts of Priesthood." For the priesthood was established as an everlasting covenant in a way that could not have happened had Korach not raised dissent about it previously. *This* is the connection between the beginning and the end of our Sidra. The dissension, although it seems on the face of it to be opposed to the covenant of priesthood, was in fact a precondition of it.

And this is why the name of Korach is perpetuated by standing as the name of the Sidra. Even though Korach represents division and Torah represents peace, the peace and union which Torah brings comes not merely in spite of, but *through*, the medium of division: That though there is a heaven and an earth, worship and service bring them together until G-d Himself dwells in our midst.

Endnotes

1 Cf. supra, p. 10.
2 *Rashi, Bamidbar* 13:2.
3 *Proverbs* 10:7.
4 *Yoma,* 38b.
5 *Sanhedrin,* 109b.
6 Cf. *Yalkut Shimoni, Re'eh,* Remez 891.
7 End of *Hilchot Chanukah*. Cf. *Gittin*, 59b; *Sifri*, 6:26.
8 *Bamidbar* 16:3.
9 Ibid., v. 10.
10 *Bamidbar* 16:7.
11 *Vayikra* 21:12, Cf. *Rambam, Hilchot Klei Hamikdash,* 5:7; *Hilchot Bi'at Hamikdash,* 1:10.
12 Cf. supra, p. 235 ff.
13 *Bereishit Rabbah*, 4:6. Cf. *Zohar*, Part I, 46a.
14 *Bereishit Rabbah,* Ibid. *Rashi, Bereishit* 1:7.
15 *Or Hatorah, Bereishit* 34a. Cf. *Zohar*, Ibid.
16 *Shemot Rabbah*, 12:3. *Tanchuma, Vaera,* 15.
17 *Proverbs* 3:6.

(Source: *Likkutei Sichot*, Vol. Viii pp. 114–9.)

Rabbi Lord Jonathan Sacks, *Torah Studies* (Brooklyn: Kehot Publication Society, 1996), pp. 252–257

THE GAP

BASED ON THE TEACHINGS OF THE LUBAVITCHER REBBE; ADAPTED BY YANKI TAUBER

> *"These are the progeny of the heavens and the earth when they were created" (Genesis 2:4). Do not read it as* behibar'am, *"when they were created"; rather, read it as* be'hei bera'am, *"with a* hei, *He created them." Meaning: This world was created with the letter* hei. (Talmud, *Menachot* 29b)

We all nurture in our minds a vision of an ideal world—a world as defined by our purest instincts and by our knowledge of the potential for goodness and perfection invested in it by its Creator. Yet as a rule, the world to which we wake up each morning, the world with which we grapple in the course of our lives, falls short of this ideal.

How should we deal with this dissonance? Should we retreat into a world of ideas? Should we become "realistic," accept the world for what it is, and adjust our ideals accordingly? Should we ignore the discordance and go about our business as if it didn't exist?

The *Hei*

An answer to this dilemma can be found in the talmudic passage cited above. The world in which we live, says the Talmud, has the form of the Hebrew letter *hei*. The Talmud deduces this from the verse, "These are the progeny of the heavens and the earth when they were created." The Hebrew word *behibar'am*, "when they were created," can also be read as *be'hei bera'am*, "with a *hei*, He created them,"[1] to imply that G-d created this world with the letter *hei*.[2]

The Hebrew letter *hei* is comprised of three lines: an upper, horizontal line which forms the "roof" of the letter; and two vertical lines, one to the right and the other to the left, which form its walls or "legs." The right leg is connected to the right end of the roof and extends downward to the bottom of the written line. The left leg extends along the left side of the *hei*, but is not connected to the roof, leaving a gap between the upper and left lines. The fourth, bottom side of the *hei* is completely open (see figure 1).

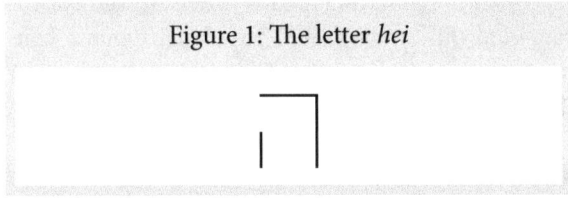

Figure 1: The letter *hei*

The three lines of the *hei* represent three realms of our positive endeavors: thought, speech, and action. The bottom, open side of the *hei* represents the vacuum of evil.[3]

The upper line of the *hei* represents the "thought" dimension of reality—the ideal world we hold in our minds. "Speech," the endeavor to articulate this vision to ourselves and to our fellow human beings, is the right leg of the *hei*: by studying, teaching, and communicating the ideals contained in the world of thought, we create a world of words that draws the lofty but abstract upper line of the *hei* downward into the more tactual dimension of speech.

RABBI MENACHEM MENDEL SCHNEERSON, 1902–1994

The towering Jewish leader of the 20th century, known as "the Lubavitcher Rebbe," or simply as "the Rebbe." Born in southern Ukraine, the Rebbe escaped Nazi-occupied Europe, arriving in the U.S. in June 1941. The Rebbe inspired and guided the revival of traditional Judaism after the European devastation, impacting virtually every Jewish community the world over. The Rebbe often emphasized that the performance of just one additional good deed could usher in the era of Mashiach. The Rebbe's scholarly talks and writings have been printed in more than 200 volumes.

RABBI YANKI TAUBER, 1965–

Chasidic scholar and author. A native of Brooklyn, N.Y., Rabbi Tauber is an internationally renowned author who specializes in adapting the teachings of the Lubavitcher Rebbe. He is a member of the JLI curriculum development team and has written numerous articles and books, including *Once Upon a Chassid* and *Beyond the Letter of the Law.*

The left leg of the *hei* is the world of "action." This is the realm of our interaction with the physical world to mold it and transform it in accordance with the vision we hold in our minds. Like speech, action is a downward extension from the realm of thought, a drawing down of its ideals into a more concrete reality. In both cases, the downward extension must beware the pitfall of the "bottom opening" of a still unperfected world, where even the best-intentioned efforts are vulnerable to corruption.

There is, however, a significant difference between speech and action, illustrated by the difference between the *hei*'s right and left legs. In the realm of speech, we can forge a reality that is a direct extension of the reality we inhabit in the realm of thought. We can express an idea as we understand it, communicate a vision as we see it, convey a belief as we believe it. But when we seek to apply our ideals to the world of action, we encounter a "gap"—an inherent inconsistency between the ideal and the real. We act upon the physical world, we change it and transform it, but sooner or later we encounter resistance. Time and again, we are confronted with an unbridgeable breech between our inner truth and an obstinate external reality.

The gap between thought and action is an intrinsic part of the created reality. This is what our sages are telling us when they say that G-d created the world in the form of a *hei*: that this gap is real. It is not an illusion; it is not a subjective projection of our personal deficiencies or our lack of determination. Rather, it was put in place by the Creator of the world, who desired that the breach between thought and action should be a real and inescapable feature of our existence. For it is this dichotomy, this tension between the ideal and the real, which lends challenge, significance, and fulfillment to our lives.

Three Alterations

One way to gain a better understanding of the significance of the *hei* as the inner form of our world is to look at other Hebrew letters that approximate the shape *hei*, but also differ from it in subtle—and not so subtle—ways. We will look at three such letters: the *kuf*, the *reish*, and the *chet* (fig. 2).

Figure 2: The three Hebrew letters (from right to left): *kuf*, *reish*, *chet*

As the above illustration shows, these three letters are similar in form to the letter *hei*. The *kuf* is a *hei* whose left leg extends below the written line. The *reish* is a *hei* that lacks a left leg altogether. And the *chet* is a *hei* without the "gap"—a *hei* whose left leg is joined to its roof.

On the face of it, these are more "harmonious" letters than the fractured *hei*. The dissonance between thought and speech on the one hand, and deed on the other, is resolved, or at least allowed to take its natural course. Ultimately, however, modeling our lives after any of these three approaches actually results in greater conflict and disharmony. For each of these letters is a distortion of the *hei*—a corruption of the manner in which the Creator desires that we perceive and deal with His creation.

The Realist *Kuf*

The first distorted perception is that of the ultra-realist. This is a person who not only recognizes the gap between thought and action, but also accepts it. To this person, the world is a *kuf*—a world whose left flank is not only disconnected from its other two lines, but also drops below the area delineated by them.

In a world described by the letter *kuf*, a different set of standards governs the world of action than those which govern the realms of thought and speech. "Certainly, I have my ideals," argues this approach to life. "I have my inner truth; I know what's right and what's wrong. This is the world I inhabit in my thoughts, these are the ideals I discuss with and advocate to others, these are the truths which I teach my children. But I'm not so naive as to believe that these truths can be applied, without compromise and equivocation, to the world of action. What is right as an abstract or verbalized ideal simply won't work in the reality of a material and materialistic world. Can I negotiate a business deal with the same integrity I demand from myself when I address G-d in my prayers? Should I assess my physical needs and wants by the same criteria I apply to my spiritual aspirations? These are two different domains, and an unbridgeable gap separates the two. I would never compromise my convictions, but the way we think and speak about our world will always be of a higher standard than the way we act in it."

The Idealistic *Reish*

At the other extreme from the ultra-realist is the ultra-idealist. This is a person who, if they cannot inhabit a world where their actions play out as an unbroken continuum of their thoughts and words, prefers not to deal with it at all. Why sully our lives by venturing into an arena which, if it does not corrupt us outright, will at the very least coarsen our higher sensitivities?

The Torah provides us with a historical failing by the people of Israel that derived from this attitude. The Book of Numbers (chapters 13 and 14) relates the story of the spies sent by Moses to scout the Holy Land, who were loath to leave their spiritual life in the desert for a material existence of life on the land. This led them to spurn the land promised by G-d as Israel's eternal heritage, delaying the people's settlement of the Holy Land by a full generation.

The ultra-idealist's response to the gap between the *hei*'s left leg and its other two lines is to jettison that leg entirely: to shun the world of action and devote all their energies and resources to the worlds of thoughts and words, which comprise the higher two strata of creation. The reality they inhabit is in the form of a *reish*—a two-dimensional world of theory and polemic, devoid of all regard for the state of the physical universe.

The Delusional *Chet*

The third corruption of the *hei* is the *chet*, which represents a more subtle, but no less destructive, form of idealism.

Rather than disavowing the left leg of the *hei*, the *chet*-perspective disavows the gap, claiming that no true separation exists between the various realms of G-d's creation. The material, says this world-view, is no less sacred than the spiritual; actions are no less pure than words; both "legs" are equally connected with the "upper line" and can equally bring down its ideals into their respective realities.

The problem with this vision of reality is that, lacking a proper awareness of the true state of the world of action, one is far too easily satisfied. While the *reish* thinks that thoughts and words can take the place of actions, the *chet*-persona deludes themselves that their thoughts and words *are* actions, or that a few vague, symbolic deeds suffice to transform the world into a harmonious actualization of its highest potentials.

Harmony through Tension

True harmony in life can be achieved only in recognizing, confronting, and grappling with the intrinsic dissonance between thought and action.

If we succumb to the gap, we end up with a *kuf*—a physical world that has slipped "below the line" and gone awry from the principles upon which it is founded. If we escape the gap by renouncing all that lies beyond it, we end up with a *reish*—a world lacking its most real and important dimension.[4] If we ignore or make light of the gap, we end up with a *chet*—a fool's paradise in which nothing has changed and nothing has been achieved save in one's own imagination. Because they fail to deal with the world as it has been forged by its Creator, each of the three approaches ultimately breaks down into chaos and conflict.

This is alluded to by the fact that the three letters *kuf*, *reish*, and *chet* spell the Hebrew name קרח—"Korach"—which is the name of the person whose ill-fated challenge to Moses and Aaron's leadership is recounted in the sixteenth chapter of Numbers. The very name "Korach" is seen to represent conflict and discord. As the the Talmud states, "Whoever engages in divisiveness transgresses a prohibition of the Torah, as it is written: 'And[5] he shall not be like Korach and his company.'"[6]

On the other hand, the *hei* perspective on life is the formula for true and enduring harmony. The *hei* approach acknowledges that the world of action is disconnected from the worlds of thought and speech, yet insists that it must be confined to the boundaries delineated by them. In other words, the gap between the ideal and the real exists, but this does not mean that we cannot profoundly transform the physical world with our actions and bring it "in line" with the ideals which we contemplate and propagate.

The gap is a source of dissonance and tension, but this is a constructive tension which drives the aspirations, challenges, and achievements of life. For it is our knowledge of our imperfections which fuels our striving to improve ourselves and our world. It is our sensitivity to the distance between what we are and what we ought to be which makes us aware and productive partners in the divine endeavor of Creation.

The Final *Mem*

Ultimately, our efforts in the present *hei* phase of existence will yield the future world of Moshiach, when G-d will "annihilate death forever"[7] and "banish the spirit of impurity from the world."[8] That future world is represented by the letter "final *mem*,"[9] whose form is that of a closed square (see fig. 3).[10]

Figure 3: The "final *mem*"

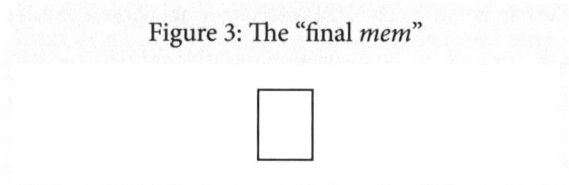

In this future world of divine perfection, not only will the gap between spirit and matter be closed, but also the negative "fourth side" will be transformed into good, as the whole of the created existence will reflect the goodness and perfection of its Creator.

Endnotes

1 In the Torah scroll, the word בהבראם is written with an undersized ה, indicating that the word can be split in two, and read as בראם .

2 The kabbalists teach that the 22 letters of the Holy Tongue, and the words they form, are the building blocks of creation (as expounded in the ancient kabbalistic work, *Sefer Yetzirah*; also see *Tanya*, part II, chapter 1). The *hei*, whose phonetic sound is a simple expulsion of breath, is the most primary of these phonetic elements.

3 Cf. Genesis 4:7: "Sin lurks at the opening."

4 In the words of the *Tanya*: "This is what man is all about, this is the purpose of his creation and of the creation of all worlds, the lofty and the lowly—to make for G-d a dwelling in the lowly realms [i.e., the world of physical action]" (*Tanya*, chapter 33).

5 Numbers 17:5.

6 Talmud, *Sanhedrin* 110a.

7 Isaiah 25:8.

8 Zachariah 13:2.

9 The form that the letter *mem* takes when it appears at the end of a word.

10 As alluded to in the verse, "For the increase of the realm and for peace without end" (Isaiah 9:6), in which the letter *mem* uncharacteristically appears in its closed form in the middle of a word.

Yanki Tauber, *The Inside Story,* vol. 1 (Genesis) (Brooklyn: Meaningful Life Center, 2016), pp. 32–40

Acknowledgments

We are grateful to the following individuals for helping shape this innovative course:

Rabbis Mordechai Dinerman and **Naftali Silberberg,** who codirect the JLI Curriculum Department and the Flagship editorial team; **Rabbi Dr. Shmuel Klatzkin,** JLI's senior editor; and **Rabbi Zalman Abraham,** who skillfully provides the vision and strategic planning of JLI course offerings.

Rabbi Yanki Tauber designed and authored this course.

Rabbis Menachem Feldman, Dovid Labkowski, Yossi Mendelson, and **Benjy Silverman,** the Instructor Advisory Board for this course, spent many hours reviewing the course materials with the JLI team. Their invaluable suggestions have enhanced the course and ensured its suitability for a wide range of students.

Rivki Mockin directed the content production, ensuring its smoothness and timeliness, and **Chana Dechter,** JLI Flagship's administrator, capably oversaw the entire project. **Mushka Grossbaum** provided editorial assistance, and **Rakefet Orobona, Mimi Palace, Shmuel Telsner,** and **Ya'akovah Weber** enhanced the quality and accuracy of the writing with their proofreading. **Rivky Fieldsteel, Shayna Grosh, Rabbi Zalman Korf,** and **Shternie Zaltzman** designed the textbooks with taste and expertise, and the textbook images were researched and selected by **Rabbi Zalman Abraham. Rabbi Mendel Sirota** directed the book's publication and distribution.

We thank **Rabbi Zalman Abraham** for leading the vision for the marketing of this course, and **Shevi Rivkin** for creating and designing the course marketing materials.

Chany Block, Mushka Druk, and **Mimi Rabinowitz** designed the aesthetically pleasing PowerPoint presentations. **Baila Goldstein** and **Aliza Mayteles** created the illustrations for the artistically crafted lesson videos, skillfully produced by **Moshe Raskin** and **Getzy Raskin.**

We are immensely grateful for the encouragement of JLI's visionary chairman, and vice-chairman of *Merkos L'Inyonei Chinuch*—Lubavitch World Headquarters, **Rabbi Moshe Kotlarsky**. Rabbi Kotlarsky has been highly instrumental in building the infrastructure for the expansion of Chabad's international network and is also the architect of scores of initiatives and services to help Chabad representatives across the globe succeed in their mission. We are blessed to have the unwavering support of JLI's principal benefactor, **Mr. George Rohr,** who is fully invested in our work, continues to be instrumental in JLI's monumental growth and expansion, and is largely responsible for the Jewish renaissance that is being spearheaded by JLI and its affiliates across the globe.

The commitment and sage direction of JLI's dedicated Executive Board—**Rabbis Chaim Block, Hesh Epstein, Ronnie Fine, Yosef Gansburg, Shmuel Kaplan, Yisrael Rice,** and **Avrohom Sternberg**—and the countless hours they devote to the development of JLI are what drive the vision, growth, and tremendous success of the organization.

Finally, JLI represents an incredible partnership of more than 1,600 *shluchim* and *shluchot* in more than 1,000 locations across the globe, who contribute their time and talent to further Jewish adult education. We thank them for generously sharing feedback and making suggestions that steer JLI's development and growth. They are our most valuable critics and our most cherished contributors.

Inspired by the call of the **Lubavitcher Rebbe**, of righteous memory, it is the mandate of the Rohr JLI to **provide a community of learning** for all Jews throughout the world where they can participate in their precious heritage of Torah learning and experience its rewards. May this course succeed in fulfilling this sacred charge.

On behalf of the Rohr Jewish Learning Institute,

RABBI EFRAIM MINTZ
Executive Director

RABBI YISRAEL RICE
Chairman, Editorial Board

10 Shevat, 5780

The Rohr Jewish Learning Institute

AN AFFILIATE OF MERKOS L'INYONEI CHINUCH,
THE EDUCATIONAL ARM OF THE CHABAD-LUBAVITCH MOVEMENT
822 EASTERN PARKWAY, BROOKLYN, NY 11213

JLI INTERNATIONAL

Rabbi Avrohom Sternberg
CHAIRMAN

Rabbi Dubi Rabinowitz
DIRECTOR

Rabbi Berry Piekarski
ADMINISTRATOR

Rabbi Eli Wolf
ADMINISTRATOR, JLI IN THE CIS
IN PARTNERSHIP WITH
THE FEDERATION OF JEWISH
COMMUNITIES OF THE CIS

Rabbi Shevach Zlatopolsky
EDITOR, JLI IN THE CIS

Rabbi Nochum Schapiro
REGIONAL REPRESENTATIVE,
AUSTRALIA

Rabbi Avraham Golovacheov
REGIONAL REPRESENTATIVE,
GERMANY

Rabbi Shmuel Katzman
REGIONAL REPRESENTATIVE,
NETHERLANDS

Rabbi Avrohom Steinmetz
REGIONAL REPRESENTATIVE,
BRAZIL

Rabbi Bentzi Sudak
REGIONAL REPRESENTATIVE,
UNITED KINGDOM

Rabbi Shlomo Cohen
FRENCH COORDINATOR,
REGIONAL REPRESENTITIVE

NATIONAL JEWISH RETREAT

Rabbi Hesh Epstein
CHAIRMAN

Mrs. Shaina B. Mintz
DIRECTOR

Bruce Backman
HOTEL LIAISON

Rabbi Menachem Klein
PROGRAM COORDINATOR

Rabbi Shmuly Karp
SHLUCHIM LIAISON

Rabbi Mendel Rosenfeld
LOGISTICS COORDINATOR

Mrs. Mussi Abelsky
Ms. Rochel Karp
Ms. Zehavah Krafchik
Mrs. Aliza Mayteles
SERVICE AND SUPPORT

JLI LAND & SPIRIT

ISRAEL EXPERIENCE

Rabbi Shmuly Karp
DIRECTOR

Mrs. Shaina B. Mintz
ADMINISTRATOR

Rabbi Yechiel Baitelman
Rabbi Dovid Flinkenstein
Rabbi Chanoch Kaplan
Rabbi Levi Klein
Rabbi Mendel Lifshitz
Rabbi Mendy Mangel
Rabbi Sholom Raichik
Rabbi Ephraim Silverman
STEERING COMMITTEE

SHABBAT IN THE HEIGHTS

Rabbi Shmuly Karp
DIRECTOR

Mrs. Shulamis Nadler
SERVICE AND SUPPORT

Rabbi Chaim Hanoka
CHAIRMAN

Rabbi Mordechai Dinerman
Rabbi Zalman Marcus
STEERING COMMITTEE

MYSHIUR

ADVANCED LEARNING INITIATIVE

Rabbi Shmuel Kaplan
CHAIRMAN

Rabbi Shlomie Tenenbaum
ADMINISTRATOR

TORAHCAFE.COM

ONLINE LEARNING

Rabbi Mendy Elishevitz
WEBSITE DEVELOPMENT

Moshe Levin
CONTENT MANAGER

Avrohom Shimon Ezagui
FILMING

MACHON SHMUEL

THE SAMI ROHR RESEARCH INSTITUTE

Rabbi Zalman Korf
ADMINISTRATOR

Rabbi Gedalya Oberlander
Rabbi Chaim Rapoport
Rabbi Levi Yitzchak Raskin
Rabbi Chaim Schapiro
Rabbi Moshe Miller
RABBINIC ADVISORY BOARD

Rabbi Yakov Gershon
RESEARCH FELLOW

FOUNDING DEPARTMENT HEADS

Rabbi Mendel Bell
Rabbi Zalman Charytan
Rabbi Mendel Druk
Rabbi Menachem Gansburg
Rabbi Meir Hecht
Rabbi Levi Kaplan
Rabbi Yoni Katz
Rabbi Chaim Zalman Levy
Rabbi Benny Rapoport
Dr. Chana Silberstein
Rabbi Elchonon Tenenbaum
Rabbi Mendy Weg

Faculty Directory

ALABAMA

BIRMINGHAM
Rabbi Yossi Friedman 205.970.0100

MOBILE
Rabbi Yosef Goldwasser 251.265.1213

ALASKA

ANCHORAGE
Rabbi Yosef Greenberg
Rabbi Mendy Greenberg 907.357.8770

ARIZONA

CHANDLER
Rabbi Mendy Deitsch 480.855.4333

FLAGSTAFF
Rabbi Dovie Shapiro 928.255.5756

FOUNTAIN HILLS
Rabbi Mendy Lipskier 480.776.4763

ORO VALLEY
Rabbi Ephraim Zimmerman 520.477.8672

PHOENIX
Rabbi Zalman Levertov
Rabbi Yossi Friedman 602.944.2753

SCOTTSDALE
Rabbi Yossi Levertov 480.998.1410

TUCSON
Rabbi Yehuda Ceitlin 520.881.7956

ARKANSAS

LITTLE ROCK
Rabbi Pinchus Ciment 501.217.0053

CALIFORNIA

AGOURA HILLS
Rabbi Moshe Bryski
Rabbi Yisroel Levine 818.991.0991

BAKERSFIELD
Rabbi Shmuli Schlanger
Mrs. Esther Schlanger 661.331.1695

BEL AIR
Rabbi Chaim Mentz 310.475.5311

BURBANK
Rabbi Shmuly Kornfeld 818.954.0070

CARLSBAD
Rabbi Yeruchem Eilfort
Mrs. Nechama Eilfort 760.943.8891

CHATSWORTH
Rabbi Yossi Spritzer 818.718.0777

CONTRA COSTA
Rabbi Dovber Berkowitz 925.937.4101

CORONADO
Rabbi Eli Fradkin 619.365.4728

DANVILLE
Rabbi Shmuli Raitman 213.447.6694

ENCINO
Rabbi Aryeh Herzog 818.784.9986
Chapter founded by Rabbi Joshua Gordon, OBM

FOLSOM
Rabbi Yossi Grossbaum 916.608.9811

FREMONT
Rabbi Moshe Fuss 510.300.4090

GLENDALE
Rabbi Simcha Backman 818.240.2750

HUNTINGTON BEACH
Rabbi Aron David Berkowitz 714.846.2285

LA JOLLA
Rabbi Baruch Shalom Ezagui 858.455.5433

LAGUNA BEACH
Rabbi Elimelech Gurevitch 949.499.0770

LAGUNA NIGUEL
Rabbi Mendy Paltiel 949.831.8475

LOMITA
Rabbi Eli Hecht
Rabbi Sholom Pinson 310.326.8234

LONG BEACH
Rabbi Abba Perelmuter 562.621.9828

LOS ANGELES
Rabbi Leibel Korf 323.660.5177
Rabbi Dovid Liberow 424.261.8770

MALIBU
Rabbi Levi Cunin 310.456.6588

MARINA DEL REY
Rabbi Danny Yiftach-Hashem
Rabbi Dovid Yiftach 310.859.0770

NEWHALL
Rabbi Choni Marosov 661.254.3434

NORTH HOLLYWOOD
Rabbi Nachman Abend 818.989.9539

NORTHRIDGE
Rabbi Eli Rivkin 818.368.3937

OJAI
Rabbi Mordechai Nemtzov 805.613.7181

PACIFIC PALISADES
Rabbi Zushe Cunin 310.454.7783

PALO ALTO
Rabbi Menachem Landa 415.418.4768
Rabbi Yosef Levin
Rabbi Ber Rosenblatt 650.424.9800

PASADENA
Rabbi Chaim Hanoka
Rabbi Sholom Stiefel 626.539.4578

PLEASANTON
Rabbi Josh Zebberman 925.846.0700

POWAY
Rabbi Mendel Goldstein 858.208.6613

RANCHO CUCAMONGA
Rabbi Sholom B. Harlig 909.949.4553

RANCHO MIRAGE
Rabbi Shimon H. Posner 760.770.7785

RANCHO PALOS VERDES
Rabbi Yitzchok Magalnic 310.544.5544

RANCHO S. FE
Rabbi Levi Raskin 858.756.7571

REDONDO BEACH
Rabbi Yossi Mintz
Rabbi Zalman Gordon 310.214.4999

RIVERSIDE
Rabbi Shmuel Fuss 951.329.2747

S. CLEMENTE
Rabbi Menachem M. Slavin 949.489.0723

S. CRUZ
Rabbi Yochanan Friedman 831.454.0101

S. DIEGO
Rabbi Rafi Andrusier 619.387.8770
Rabbi Motte Fradkin 858.547.0076

S. FRANCISCO
Rabbi Gedalia Potash 415.648.8000
Rabbi Shlomo Zarchi 415.752.2866

S. MATEO
Rabbi Yossi Marcus 650.341.4510

S. MONICA
Rabbi Boruch Rabinowitz 310.394.5699

S. RAFAEL
Rabbi Yisrael Rice 415.492.1666

SOUTH LAKE TAHOE
Rabbi Mordechai Richler 530.314.7677

SUNNYVALE
Rabbi Yisroel Hecht 408.720.0553

TEMECULA
Rabbi Yonason Abrams 951.234.4196

THOUSAND OAKS
Rabbi Chaim Bryski 805.370.5770

TUSTIN
Rabbi Yehoshua Eliezrie 714.508.2150

UNIVERSITY CITY
Rabbi Yechiel Cagen 832.691.1825

VENTURA
Rabbi Yakov Latowicz 805.658.7441

WEST HILLS
Rabbi Avi Rabin 818.337.4544

WEST HOLLYWOOD
Rabbi Mordechai Kirschenbaum 310.275.1215

WEST LOS ANGELES
Rabbi Mordechai Zaetz 424.652.8742

YORBA LINDA
Rabbi Dovid Eliezrie 714.693.0770

COLORADO

ASPEN
Rabbi Mendel Mintz 970.544.3770

AURORA
Rabbi David Araiev 720.388.2704

DENVER
Rabbi Mendel Popack 720.515.4337
Rabbi Yossi Serebryanski 303.744.9699

FORT COLLINS
Rabbi Yerachmiel Gorelik 970.407.1613

HIGHLANDS RANCH
Rabbi Avraham Mintz 303.694.9119

LONGMONT
Rabbi Yakov Borenstein 303.678.7595

VAIL
Rabbi Dovid Mintz 970.476.7887

WESTMINSTER
Rabbi Benjy Brackman 303.429.5177

CONNECTICUT

FAIRFIELD
Rabbi Shlame Landa 203.373.7551

GLASTONBURY
Rabbi Yosef Wolvovsky 860.659.2422

GREENWICH
Rabbi Yossi Deren
Rabbi Menachem Feldman 203.629.9059

MILFORD
Rabbi Schneur Wilhelm 203.887.7603

NEW HAVEN
Rabbi Mendy Hecht 203.589.5375

NEW LONDON
Rabbi Avrohom Sternberg 860.437.8000

STAMFORD
Rabbi Yisrael Deren
Rabbi Levi Mendelow 203.3.CHABAD

WEST HARTFORD
Rabbi Shaya Gopin 860.232.1116

WESTPORT
Rabbi Yehuda L. Kantor 203.226.8584

DELAWARE

WILMINGTON
Rabbi Chuni Vogel 302.529.9900

DISTRICT OF COLUMBIA

WASHINGTON
Rabbi Levi Shemtov
Rabbi Yitzy Ceitlin 202.332.5600

FLORIDA

ALTAMONTE SPRINGS
Rabbi Mendy Bronstein 407.280.0535

BAL HARBOUR
Rabbi Dov Schochet 305.868.1411

BOCA RATON
Rabbi Zalman Bukiet
Rabbi Arele Gopin 561.994.6257
Rabbi Moishe Denburg 561.526.5760
Rabbi Ruvi New 561.394.9770

BONITA SPRINGS
Rabbi Mendy Greenberg 239.949.6900

BOYNTON BEACH
Rabbi Yosef Yitzchok Raichik 561.732.4633

BRADENTON
Rabbi Menachem Bukiet 941.388.9656

CAPE CORAL
Rabbi Yossi Labkowski 239.963.4770

CORAL GABLES
Rabbi Avrohom Stolik 305.490.7572

CORAL SPRINGS
Rabbi Yankie Denburg 954.471.8646

CUTLER BAY
Rabbi Yossi Wolff 305.975.6680

DAVIE
Rabbi Aryeh Schwartz 954.376.9973

DELRAY BEACH
Rabbi Sholom Ber Korf 561.496.6228

FISHER ISLAND
Rabbi Efraim Brody 347.325.1913

FLEMING ISLAND
Rabbi Shmuly Feldman 904.290.1017

FORT LAUDERDALE
Rabbi Yitzchok Naparstek 954.568.1190

FORT MYERS
Rabbi Yitzchok Minkowicz
Mrs. Nechama Minkowicz 239.433.7708

HALLANDALE BEACH
Rabbi Mordy Feiner 954.458.1877

HOLLYWOOD
Rabbi Leizer Barash 954.965.9933
Rabbi Leibel Kudan 954.801.3367

KENDALL
Rabbi Yossi Harlig 305.234.5654

KEY WEST
Rabbi Yaakov Zucker 305.304.7713

LAKELAND
Rabbi Moshe Lazaros 863.510.5968

LONGWOOD
Rabbi Yanky Majesky 407.636.5994

MAITLAND
Rabbi Sholom Dubov
Rabbi Levik Dubov 470.644.2500

MIAMI
Rabbi Mendy Cheruty 305.219.3353
Rabbi Yakov Fellig 305.445.5444

MIAMI BEACH
Rabbi Yisroel Frankforter 305.534.3895

N. MIAMI BEACH
Rabbi Eli Laufer 305.770.4412

OCALA
Rabbi Yossi Hecht 352.330.4466

ORLANDO
Rabbi Yosef Konikov 407.354.3660

ORMOND BEACH
Rabbi Asher Farkash 386.672.9300

PALM BEACH
Rabbi Zalman Levitin 561.659.3884

PALM BEACH GARDENS
Rabbi Dovid Vigler 561.624.2223

PALM CITY
Rabbi Shlomo Uminer 772.288.0606

PALM HARBOR
Rabbi Pinchas Adler 727.789.0408

PALMETTO BAY
Rabbi Zalman Gansburg 786.282.0413

PARKLAND
Rabbi Mendy Gutnick 954.796.7330

PEMBROKE PINES
Rabbi Mordechai Andrusier 954.874.2280

PLANTATION
Rabbi Pinchas Taylor 954.644.9177

PONTE VEDRA BEACH
Rabbi Nochum Kurinsky 904.543.9301

S. AUGUSTINE
Rabbi Levi Vogel 904.521.8664

S. PETERSBURG
Rabbi Alter Korf 727.344.4900

SARASOTA
Rabbi Chaim Shaul Steinmetz 941.925.0770

SATELLITE BEACH
Rabbi Zvi Konikov 321.777.2770

SOUTH PALM BEACH
Rabbi Leibel Stolik 561.889.3499

SOUTH TAMPA
Rabbi Mendy Dubrowski 813.922.1723

SOUTHWEST BROWARD COUNTY
Rabbi Aryeh Schwartz 954.252.1770

SUNNY ISLES BEACH
Rabbi Alexander Kaller 305.803.5315

VENICE
Rabbi Sholom Ber Schmerling 941.493.2770

WELLINGTON
Rabbi Mendy Muskal 561.386.3090

WESLEY CHAPEL
Rabbi Mendy Yarmush
Rabbi Mendel Friedman 813.731.2977

WEST PALM BEACH
Rabbi Yoel Gancz 561.659.7770

WESTON
Rabbi Yisroel Spalter 954.349.6565

GEORGIA

ALPHARETTA
Rabbi Hirshy Minkowicz 770.410.9000

ATLANTA
Rabbi Yossi New
Rabbi Isser New 404.843.2464
Rabbi Alexander Piekarski 678.267.6418

ATLANTA: INTOWN
Rabbi Eliyahu Schusterman
Rabbi Ari Sollish 404.898.0434

CUMMING
Rabbi Levi Mentz 310.666.2218

GWINNETT
Rabbi Yossi Lerman 678.595.0196

MARIETTA
Rabbi Ephraim Silverman 770.565.4412

HAWAII

KAPA'A
Rabbi Michoel Goldman 808.647.4293

IDAHO

BOISE
Rabbi Mendel Lifshitz 208.853.9200

ILLINOIS

CHAMPAIGN
Rabbi Dovid Tiechtel 217.355.8672

CHICAGO
Rabbi Mendy Benhiyoun 312.498.7704
Rabbi Meir Hecht 312.714.4655
Rabbi Dovid Kotlarsky 773.495.7127
Rabbi Yosef Moscowitz 773.772.3770
Rabbi Levi Notik 773.274.5123

DES PLAINES
Rabbi Lazer Hershkovich 224.392.4442

ELGIN
Rabbi Mendel Shemtov 847.440.4486

GLENVIEW
Rabbi Yishaya Benjaminson 847.910.1738

GRAYSLAKE
Rabbi Sholom Tenenbaum 847.782.1800

HIGHLAND PARK
Mrs. Michla Schanowitz 847.266.0770

NAPERVILLE
Rabbi Mendy Goldstein 630.778.9770

NORTHBROOK
Rabbi Meir Moscowitz 847.564.8770

OAK PARK
Rabbi Yitzchok Bergstein 708.524.1530

PEORIA
Rabbi Eli Langsam 309.692.2250

SKOKIE
Rabbi Yochanan Posner 847.677.1770

VERNON HILLS
Rabbi Shimmy Susskind 847.984.2919

WILMETTE
Rabbi Dovid Flinkenstein 847.251.7707

INDIANA

INDIANAPOLIS
Rabbi Avraham Grossbaum
Rabbi Dr. Shmuel Klatzkin 317.251.5573

IOWA

BETTENDORF
Rabbi Shneur Cadaner 563.355.1065

KANSAS

OVERLAND PARK
Rabbi Mendy Wineberg 913.649.4852

KENTUCKY

LOUISVILLE
Rabbi Avrohom Litvin 502.459.1770

LOUISIANA

BATON ROUGE
Rabbi Peretz Kazen 225.267.7047

METAIRIE
Rabbi Yossie Nemes
Rabbi Mendel Ceitlin 504.454.2910

NEW ORLEANS
Rabbi Mendel Rivkin 504.302.1830

MAINE

PORTLAND
Rabbi Levi Wilansky 207.650.1783

MARYLAND

BALTIMORE
Rabbi Velvel Belinsky 410.764.5000
Classes in Russian

BEL AIR
Rabbi Kushi Schusterman 443.353.9718

BETHESDA
Rabbi Sender Geisinsky 301.913.9777

CHEVY CHASE
Rabbi Zalman Minkowitz 301.260.5000

COLUMBIA
Rabbi Hillel Baron
Rabbi Yosef Chaim Sufrin 410.740.2424

FREDERICK
Rabbi Boruch Labkowski 301.996.3659

GAITHERSBURG
Rabbi Sholom Raichik 301.926.3632

OLNEY
Rabbi Bentzy Stolik 301.660.6770

OWINGS MILLS
Rabbi Nochum H. Katsenelenbogen 410.356.5156

POTOMAC
Rabbi Mendel Bluming 301.983.4200
Rabbi Mendel Kaplan 301.983.1485

ROCKVILLE
Rabbi Shlomo Beitsh 646.773.2675
Rabbi Moishe Kavka 301.836.1242
Rabbi Levi Raskin 240.444.3345

MASSACHUSETTS

ANDOVER
Rabbi Asher Bronstein 978.470.2288

BOSTON
Rabbi Yosef Zaklos 617.297.7282

BRIGHTON
Rabbi Dan Rodkin 617.787.2200

CAPE COD
Rabbi Yekusiel Alperowitz 508.775.2324

HINGHAM
Rabbi Levi Lezell 617.862.2770

LONGMEADOW
Rabbi Yakov Wolff 413.567.8665

NEWTON
Rabbi Shalom Ber Prus 617.244.1200

SUDBURY
Rabbi Yisroel Freeman 978.443.0110

SWAMPSCOTT
Rabbi Yossi Lipsker 781.581.3833

MICHIGAN

ANN ARBOR
Rabbi Aharon Goldstein 734.995.3276

BLOOMFIELD HILLS
Rabbi Levi Dubov 248.949.6210

GRAND RAPIDS
Rabbi Mordechai Haller 616.957.0770

WEST BLOOMFIELD
Rabbi Elimelech Silberberg 248.855.6170

MINNESOTA

MINNETONKA
Rabbi Mordechai Grossbaum
Rabbi Shmuel Silberstein 952.929.9922

S. PAUL
Rabbi Shneur Zalman Bendet 651.998.9298

MISSOURI

S. LOUIS
Rabbi Yosef Landa 314.725.0400

NEVADA

LAS VEGAS
Rabbi Yosef Rivkin 702.217.2170

SUMMERLIN
Rabbi Yisroel Schanowitz
Rabbi Tzvi Bronchtain 702.855.0770

NEW JERSEY

BASKING RIDGE
Rabbi Mendy Herson
Rabbi Mendel Shemtov 908.604.8844

CHERRY HILL
Rabbi Mendel Mangel 856.874.1500

CLINTON
Rabbi Eli Kornfeld 908.623.7000

FAIR LAWN
Rabbi Avrohom Bergstein 201.362.2712

FORT LEE
Rabbi Meir Konikov 201.886.1238

FRANKLIN LAKES
Rabbi Chanoch Kaplan 201.848.0449

GREATER MERCER COUNTY
Rabbi Dovid Dubov
Rabbi Yaakov Chaiton 609.213.4136

HASKELL
Rabbi Mendy Gurkov 201.696.7609

HOLMDEL
Rabbi Shmaya Galperin 732.772.1998

MADISON
Rabbi Shalom Lubin 973.377.0707

MANALAPAN
Rabbi Boruch Chazanow
Rabbi Levi Wolosow 732.972.3687

MEDFORD
Rabbi Yitzchok Kahan 609.451.3522

MOUNTAIN LAKES
Rabbi Levi Dubinsky 973.551.1898

MULLICA HILL
Rabbi Avrohom Richler 856.733.0770

OLD TAPPAN
Rabbi Mendy Lewis 201.767.4008

RED BANK
Rabbi Dovid Harrison 718.915.8748

ROCKAWAY
Rabbi Asher Herson
Rabbi Mordechai Baumgarten 973.625.1525

RUTHERFORD
Rabbi Yitzchok Lerman 347.834.7500

SCOTCH PLAINS
Rabbi Avrohom Blesofsky 908.790.0008

SHORT HILLS
Rabbi Mendel Solomon
Rabbi Avrohom Levin 973.725.7008

SOUTH BRUNSWICK
Rabbi Levi Azimov 732.398.9492

TEANECK
Rabbi Ephraim Simon 201.907.0686

TENAFLY
Rabbi Mordechai Shain 201.871.1152

TOMS RIVER
Rabbi Moshe Gourarie 732.349.4199

VENTNOR
Rabbi Avrohom Rapoport 609.822.8500

WAYNE
Rabbi Michel Gurkov 973.694.6274

WEST ORANGE
Rabbi Mendy Kasowitz 973.325.6311

WOODCLIFF LAKE
Rabbi Dov Drizin 201.476.0157

NEW MEXICO

LAS CRUCES
Rabbi Bery Schmukler 575.524.1330

S. FE
Rabbi Berel Levertov 505.983.2000

NEW YORK

BAY SHORE
Rabbi Shimon Stillerman 631.913.8770

BEDFORD
Rabbi Arik Wolf 914.666.6065

BINGHAMTON
Mrs. Rivkah Slonim 607.797.0015

BRIGHTON BEACH
Rabbi Moshe Winner 718.946.9833

BRONXVILLE
Rabbi Sruli Deitsch 917.755.0078

BROOKLYN
Rabbi Nissi Eber 347.677.2276
Rabbi Dovid Okonov 917.754.6942

BROOKVILLE
Rabbi Mendy Heber 516.626.0600

CEDARHURST
Rabbi Zalman Wolowik 516.295.2478

COMMACK
Rabbi Mendel Teldon 631.543.3343

DIX HILLS
Rabbi Yaakov Saacks 631.351.8672

DOBBS FERRY
Rabbi Benjy Silverman 914.693.6100

EAST HAMPTON
Rabbi Leibel Baumgarten
Rabbi Mendy Goldberg 631.329.5800

ELLENVILLE
Rabbi Shlomie Deren 845.647.4450

FOREST HILLS
Rabbi Yossi Mendelson 917.861.9726

GREAT NECK
Rabbi Yoseph Geisinsky 516.487.4554

KINGSTON
Rabbi Yitzchok Hecht 845.334.9044

LARCHMONT
Rabbi Mendel Silberstein 914.834.4321

LITTLE NECK
Rabbi Eli Shifrin 718.423.1235

LONG BEACH
Rabbi Eli Goodman 516.897.2473

MONTEBELLO
Rabbi Shmuel Gancz 845.746.1927

NYACK
Rabbi Chaim Zvi Ehrenreich 845.356.6686

NYC KEHILATH JESHURUN
Rabbi Elie Weinstock 212.774.5636

NYC TRIBECA
Rabbi Zalman Paris 212.566.6764

NYC UPPER EAST SIDE
Rabbi Uriel Vigler 212.369.7310

NYC UPPER WEST SIDE
Rabbi Shlomo Kugel 212.864.5010

OCEANSIDE
Rabbi Levi Gurkow 516.764.7385

OSSINING
Rabbi Dovid Labkowski 914.923.2522

OYSTER BAY
Rabbi Shmuel Lipszyc
Rabbi Shalom Lipszyc 347.853.9992

PARK SLOPE
Rabbi Menashe Wolf 347.957.1291

PORT WASHINGTON
Rabbi Shalom Paltiel 516.767.8672

PROSPECT HEIGHTS
Rabbi Mendy Hecht 347.622.3599

ROCHESTER
Rabbi Nechemia Vogel 585.271.0330

ROSLYN
Rabbi Yaakov Reiter 516.484.8185

SEA GATE
Rabbi Chaim Brikman 917.975.2792

SOUTHAMPTON
Rabbi Chaim Pape 917.627.4865

STATEN ISLAND
Rabbi Mendy Katzman 718.370.8953

STONY BROOK
Rabbi Shalom Ber Cohen 631.585.0521

SUFFERN
Rabbi Shmuel Gancz 845.368.1889

YORKTOWN HEIGHTS
Rabbi Yehuda Heber 914.962.1111

NORTH CAROLINA

ASHEVILLE
Rabbi Shaya Susskind 828.505.0746

CARY
Rabbi Yisroel Cotlar 919.651.9710

CHARLOTTE
Rabbi Yossi Groner
Rabbi Shlomo Cohen 704.366.3984

GREENSBORO
Rabbi Yosef Plotkin 336.617.8120

RALEIGH
Rabbi Pinchas Herman
Rabbi Lev Cotlar 919.637.6950

OHIO

BEACHWOOD
Rabbi Shmuli Friedman 216.282.0112

CINCINNATI
Rabbi Yisroel Mangel 513.793.5200

COLUMBUS
Rabbi Yitzi Kaltmann 614.294.3296

DAYTON
Rabbi Nochum Mangel
Rabbi Shmuel Klatzkin 937.643.0770

OKLAHOMA

OKLAHOMA CITY
Rabbi Ovadia Goldman 405.524.4800

TULSA
Rabbi Yehuda Weg 918.492.4499

OREGON

PORTLAND
Rabbi Chaim Wilhelm 503.309.4490
Rabbi Mordechai Wilhelm 503.977.9947

SALEM
Rabbi Avrohom Yitzchok Perlstein 503.383.9569

PENNSYLVANIA

AMBLER
Rabbi Shaya Deitsch 215.591.9310

BALA CYNWYD
Rabbi Shraga Sherman 610.660.9192

DOYLESTOWN
Rabbi Mendel Prus 215.340.1303

LAFAYETTE HILL
Rabbi Yisroel Kotlarsky 484.533.7009

LANCASTER
Rabbi Elazar Green 717.368.6565

MONROEVILLE
Rabbi Mendy Schapiro 412.372.1000

NEWTOWN
Rabbi Aryeh Weinstein 215.497.9925

PHILADELPHIA: CENTER CITY
Rabbi Yochonon Goldman 215.238.2100

PITTSBURGH
Rabbi Yisroel Altein .... 412.422.7300 EXT. 269

PITTSBURGH: SOUTH HILLS
Rabbi Mendy Rosenblum 412.278.3693

READING
Rabbi Yosef Lipsker 610.921.1522

RYDAL
Rabbi Zushe Gurevitz 267.536.5757

WYNNEWOOD
Rabbi Moishe Brennan 610.529.9011

PUERTO RICO

CAROLINA
Rabbi Mendel Zarchi 787.253.0894

RHODE ISLAND

LINCOLN
Rabbi Aryeh Laufer 401.499.2574

WARWICK
Rabbi Yossi Laufer 401.884.7888

SOUTH CAROLINA

COLUMBIA
Rabbi Hesh Epstein
Rabbi Levi Marrus 803.782.1831

GREENVILLE
Rabbi Leibel Kesselman 864.256.1770

MYRTLE BEACH
Rabbi Doron Aizenman 843.385.2240

TENNESSEE

CHATTANOOGA
Rabbi Shaul Perlstein 423.490.1106

KNOXVILLE
Rabbi Yossi Wilhelm 865.588.8584

MEMPHIS
Rabbi Levi Klein 901.754.0404

TEXAS

AUSTIN
Rabbi Mendy Levertov 512.905.2778

BELLAIRE
Rabbi Yossi Zaklikofsky 713.839.8887

DALLAS
Rabbi Mendel Dubrawsky
Rabbi Moshe Naparstek 972.818.0770

FORT WORTH
Rabbi Dov Mandel 817.263.7701

FRISCO
Rabbi Mendy Kesselman 214.460.7773

HOUSTON
Rabbi Dovid Goldstein
Rabbi Zally Lazarus 281.589.7188
Rabbi Moishe Traxler 713.774.0300

HOUSTON: RICE UNIVERSITY AREA
Rabbi Eliezer Lazaroff 713.522.2004

LEAGUE CITY
Rabbi Yitzchok Schmukler 281.724.1554

MISSOURI CITY
Rabbi Mendel Feigenson 832.758.0685

PLANO
Rabbi Mendel Block
Rabbi Yehudah Horowitz 972.596.8270

S. ANTONIO
Rabbi Chaim Block
Rabbi Levi Teldon 210.492.1085
Rabbi Tal Shaul 210.877.4218

SOUTHLAKE
Rabbi Levi Gurevitch 817.451.1171

THE WOODLANDS
Rabbi Mendel Blecher 281.719.5213

UTAH

SALT LAKE CITY
Rabbi Benny Zippel 801.467.7777

VERMONT

BURLINGTON
Rabbi Yitzchok Raskin 802.658.5770

VIRGINIA

ALEXANDRIA/ARLINGTON
Rabbi Mordechai Newman 703.370.2774

FAIRFAX
Rabbi Leibel Fajnland 703.426.1980

GAINESVILLE
Rabbi Shmuel Perlstein 571.445.0342

LOUDOUN COUNTY
Rabbi Chaim Cohen 248.298.9279

NORFOLK
Rabbi Aaron Margolin
Rabbi Levi Brashevitzky 757.616.0770

RICHMOND
Rabbi Shlomo Pereira 804.740.2000

TYSONS CORNER
Rabbi Chezzy Deitsch 703.829.5770
Chapter founded by Rabbi Levi Deitsch, OBM

WASHINGTON

BELLINGHAM
Rabbi Yosef Truxton 360.224.9919

MERCER ISLAND
Rabbi Elazar Bogomilsky 206.527.1411
Rabbi Nissan Kornfeld 206.851.2324

OLYMPIA
Rabbi Yosef Schtroks 360.867.8804

SPOKANE COUNTY
Rabbi Yisroel Hahn 509.443.0770

WISCONSIN

BAYSIDE
Rabbi Cheski Edelman 414.439.5041

KENOSHA
Rabbi Tzali Wilschanski 262.359.0770

MADISON
Rabbi Avremel Matusof 608.231.3450

MEQUON
Rabbi Menachem Rapoport 262.242.2235

MILWAUKEE
Rabbi Levi Emmer 414.277.8839
Rabbi Mendel Shmotkin 414.961.6100

WAUKESHA
Rabbi Levi Brook 925.708.4203

ARGENTINA

BUENOS AIRES
Mrs. Chani Gorowitz 54.11.4865.0445
Rabbi Menachem M. Grunblatt 54.911.3574.0037
Rabbi Mendi Mizrahi 54.11.4963.1221
Rabbi Mendy Gurevitch 55.11.4545.7771
Rabbi Pinhas Sudry 54.1.4822.2285
Rabbi Shloimi Setton 54.11.4982.8637
Rabbi Shiele Plotka 54.11.4634.3111
Rabbi Yosef Levy 54.11.4504.1908

CORDOBA
Rabbi Menajem Turk 54.351.233.8250

SALTA
Rabbi Rafael Tawil 54.387.421.4947

S. MIGUEL DE TUCUMÁN
Rabbi Ariel Levy 54.381.473.6944

AUSTRALIA

NEW SOUTH WALES

DOUBLE BAY
Rabbi Yanky Berger 612.9327.1644

DOVER HEIGHTS
Rabbi Motti Feldman 614.0400.8572

NORTH SHORE
Rabbi Nochum Schapiro
Rebbetzin Fruma Schapiro 612.9488.9548

QUEENSLAND

BRISBANE
Rabbi Levi Jaffe 617.3843.6770

VICTORIA

CAULFIELD
Rabbi Mendel Groner 613.9532.7299

MOORABBIN
Rabbi Elisha Greenbaum 614.0349.0434

WESTERN AUSTRALIA

PERTH
Rabbi Shalom White 618.9275.2106

AZERBAIJAN

BAKU
Mrs. Chavi Segal 994.12.597.91.90

BELARUS

BOBRUISK
Mrs. Mina Hababo 375.29.104.3230

MINSK
Rabbi Shneur Deitsch
Mrs. Bassie Deitsch 375.29.330.6675

BELGIUM

BRUSSELS
Rabbi Shmuel Pinson 375.29.330.6675

BRAZIL

CURITIBA
Rabbi Mendy Labkowski 55.41.3079.1338

S. PAULO
Rabbi Avraham Steinmetz 55.11.3081.3081

CANADA

ALBERTA

CALGARY
Rabbi Mordechai Groner 403.281.3770

EDMONTON
Rabbi Ari Drelich
Rabbi Mendy Blachman 780.200.5770

BRITISH COLUMBIA

KELOWNA
Rabbi Shmuly Hecht 250.575.5384

RICHMOND
Rabbi Yechiel Baitelman 604.277.6427

VANCOUVER
Rabbi Dovid Rosenfeld 604.266.1313

VICTORIA
Rabbi Meir Kaplan 250.595.7656

MANITOBA

WINNIPEG
Rabbi Shmuel Altein 204.339.8737

ONTARIO

LAWRENCE/EGLINTON
Rabbi Menachem Gansburg 416.546.8770

MAPLE
Rabbi Yechezkel Deren 647.883.6372

MISSISSAUGA
Rabbi Yitzchok Slavin 905.820.4432

NIAGARA FALLS
Rabbi Zalman Zaltzman 905.356.7200

OTTAWA
Rabbi Menachem M. Blum 613.843.7770

RICHMOND HILL
Rabbi Mendel Bernstein 905.770.7700

THORNHILL
Rabbi Yisroel Landa 416.897.3338
Rabbi Moishe Schurder 647.770.9351

THORNHILL WOODS
Rabbi Chaim Hildeshaim 905.881.1919

TORONTO AREA
Rabbi Sholom Lezell 416.809.1365

GREATER TORONTO REGIONAL OFFICE & THORNHILL
Rabbi Yossi Gansburg 905.731.7000

WATERLOO
Rabbi Moshe Goldman 226.338.7770

YORK MILLS
Rabbi Levi Gansburg 416.551.9391

QUEBEC

CÔTE S.-LUC
Rabbi Levi Naparstek 438.409.6770

HAMPSTEAD
Rabbi Moshe New
Rabbi Berel Bell 514.739.0770

MONTREAL
Rabbi Ronnie Fine
Pesach Nussbaum 514.738.3434

OLD MONTREAL/GRIFFINTOWN
Rabbi Nissan Gansbourg
Rabbi Berel Bell 514.800.6966

S. LAZARE
Rabbi Nochum Labkowski 514.436.7426

TOWN OF MOUNT ROYAL
Rabbi Moshe Krasnanski
Rabbi Shneur Zalman Rader 514.342.1770

WESTMOUNT
Rabbi Yossi Shanowitz
Mrs. Devorah Leah Shanowitz 514.937.4772

SASKATCHEWAN

SASKATOON
Rabbi Raphael Kats 306.384.4370

CAYMAN ISLANDS

GRAND CAYMAN
Rabbi Berel Pewzner 717.798.1040

COLOMBIA

BOGOTA
Rabbi Chanoch Piekarski 57.1.635.8251

COSTA RICA

S. JOSÉ
Rabbi Hershel Spalter
Rabbi Moshe Bitton 506.4010.1515

CROATIA

ZAGREB
Rabbi Pinchas Zaklas 385.1.4812227

DENMARK

COPENHAGEN
Rabbi Yitzchok Loewenthal 45.3316.1850

DOMINICAN REPUBLIC

S. DOMINGO
Rabbi Shimon Pelman 829.341.2770

ESTONIA

TALLINN
Rabbi Shmuel Kot 372.662.30.50

FRANCE

BOULOGNE
Rabbi Michael Sojcher 33.1.46.99.87.85

DIJON
Rabbi Chaim Slonim 33.6.52.05.26.65

LA VARENNE-S.-HILAIRE
Rabbi Mena'hem Mendel Benelbaz 33.6.17.81.57.47

MARSEILLE
Rabbi Eliahou Altabe 33.6.11.60.03.05
Rabbi Mena'hem Mendel Assouline 33.6.64.88.25.04
Rabbi Emmanuel Taubenblatt 33.4.88.00.94.85

PARIS
Rabbi Yona Hasky 33.1.53.75.36.01
Rabbi Acher Marciano 33.6.15.15.01.02
Rabbi Avraham Barou'h Pevzner 33.6.99.64.07.70

PONTAULT-COMBAULT
Rabbi Yossi Amar 33.6.61.36.07.70

SEINE-ET-MARNE
Rabbi Yossi Amar 33.1.60.29.50.17

VILLIERS-SUR-MARNE
Rabbi Mena'hem Mendel Mergui 33.1.49.30.89.66

GEORGIA

TBILISI
Rabbi Meir Kozlovsky 995.32.2429770

GERMANY

BERLIN
Rabbi Yehuda Tiechtel 49.30.2128.0830

DUSSELDORF
Rabbi Chaim Barkahn 49.173.2871.770

HAMBURG
Rabbi Shlomo Bistritzky 49.40.4142.4190

HANNOVER
Rabbi Binyamin Wolff 49.511.811.2822

GREECE

ATHENS
Rabbi Mendel Hendel 30.210.323.3825

GUATEMALA

GUATEMALA CITY
Rabbi Shalom Pelman 502.2485.0770

ISRAEL

ASHKELON
Rabbi Shneor Lieberman 054.977.0512

BALFURYA
Rabbi Noam Bar-Tov 054.580.4770

CAESAREA
Rabbi Chaim Meir Lieberman 054.621.2586

EVEN YEHUDA
Rabbi Menachem Noyman 054.777.0707

GANEI TIKVA
Rabbi Gershon Shnur 054.524.2358

GIV'ATAYIM
Rabbi Pinchus Bitton 052.643.8770

JERUSALEM
Rabbi Levi Diamond 055.665.7702
Rabbi Avraham Hendel 054.830.5799

KARMIEL
Rabbi Mendy Elishevitz 054.521.3073

KFAR SABA
Rabbi Yossi Baitch 054.445.5020

KIRYAT BIALIK
Rabbi Pinny Marton 050.661.1768

KIRYAT MOTZKIN
Rabbi Shimon Eizenbach 050.902.0770

KOCHAV YAIR
Rabbi Dovi Greenberg 054.332.6244

MACCABIM-RE'UT
Rabbi Yosef Yitzchak Noiman 054.977.0549

NES ZIYONA
Rabbi Menachem Feldman 054.497.7092

NETANYA
Rabbi Schneur Brod 054.579.7572

RAMAT GAN-KRINITZI
Rabbi Yisroel Gurevitz 052.743.2814

RAMAT GAN-MAROM NAVE
Rabbi Binyamin Meir Kali 050.476.0770

RAMAT YISHAI
Rabbi Shneor Zalman Wolosow 052.324.5475

RISHON LEZION
Rabbi Uri Keshet 050.722.4593

ROSH PINA
Rabbi Sholom Ber Hertzel 052.458.7600

TEL AVIV
Rabbi Shneur Piekarski 054.971.5568

JAPAN

TOKYO
Rabbi Mendi Sudakevich 81.3.5789.2846

KAZAKHSTAN

ALMATY
Rabbi Shevach Zlatopolsky 7.7272.77.59.49

KYRGYZSTAN

BISHKEK
Rabbi Arye Raichman 996.312.68.19.66

LATVIA

RIGA
Rabbi Shneur Zalman Kot
Mrs. Rivka Glazman 371.6720.40.22

LITHUANIA

VILNIUS
Rabb Sholom Ber Krinsky 370.6817.1367

LUXEMBOURG

LUXEMBOURG
Rabbi Mendel Edelman 352.2877.7079

MEXICO

S. MIGUEL DE ALLENDE
Rabbi Daniel Huebner 347.559.1304

NETHERLANDS

ALMERE
Rabbi Moshe Stiefel 31.36.744.0509

AMSTERDAM
Rabbi Yanki Jacobs 31.644.988.627
Rabbi Jaacov Zwi Spiero 31.652.328.065

EINDHOVEN
Rabbi Simcha Steinberg 31.63.635.7593

HAGUE
Rabbi Shmuel Katzman 31.70.347.0222

HEEMSTEDE-HAARLEM
Rabbi Shmuel Spiero 31.23.532.0707

MAASTRICHT
Rabbi Avrohom Cohen 32.48.549.6766

NIJMEGEN
Rabbi Menachem Mendel Levine 31.621.586.575

ROTTERDAM
Rabbi Yehuda Vorst 31.10.265.5530

PANAMA

PANAMA CITY
Rabbi Ari Laine
Rabbi Gabriel Benayon 507.223.3383

RUSSIA

ASTRAKHAN
Rabbi Yisroel Melamed 7.851.239.28.24

BRYANSK
Rabbi Menachem Mendel Zaklas 7.483.264.55.15

CHELYABINSK
Rabbi Meir Kirsh 7.351.263.24.68

MOSCOW
Rabbi Aizik Rosenfeld 7.906.762.88.81
Rabbi Mordechai Weisberg 7.495.645.50.00

NIZHNY NOVGOROD
Rabbi Shimon Bergman 7.920.253.47.70

NOVOSIBIRSK
Rabbi Shneur Zalmen Zaklos 7.903.900.43.22

OMSK
Rabbi Osher Krichevsky 7.381.231.33.07

PERM
Rabbi Zalman Deutch 7.342.212.47.32

ROSTOV
Rabbi Chaim Danzinger 7.8632.99.02.68

S. PETERSBURG
Rabbi Shalom Pewzner 7.911.726.21.19
Rabbi Zvi Pinsky 7.812.713.62.09

SAMARA
Rabbi Shlomo Deutch 7.846.333.40.64

SARATOV
Rabbi Yaakov Kubitshek 7.8452.21.58.00

TOGLIATTI
Rabbi Meier Fischer 7.848.273.02.84

UFA
Rabbi Dan Krichevsky 7.347.244.55.33

VORONEZH
Rabbi Levi Stiefel 7.473.252.96.99

SINGAPORE

SINGAPORE
Rabbi Mordechai Abergel 656.337.2189
Rabbi Netanel Rivni 656.336.2127
Classes in Hebrew

SOUTH AFRICA

CAPE TOWN
Rabbi Levi Popack 27.21.434.3740

JOHANNESBURG
Rabbi Dovid Masinter
Rabbi Ari Kievman 27.11.440.6600

SWITZERLAND

BASEL
Rabbi Zalmen Wishedski 41.77.958.8418

LUZERN
Rabbi Chaim Drukman 41.41.361.1770

THAILAND

BANGKOK
Rabbi Yosef C. Kantor 6681.837.7618

UKRAINE

BERDITCHEV
Mrs. Chana Thaler 380.637.70.37.70

DNEPROPETROVSK
Rabbi Dan Makagon 380.504.51.13.18

NIKOLAYEV
Rabbi Sholom Gotlieb 380.512.37.37.71

ODESSA
Rabbi Avraham Wolf
Rabbi Yaakov Neiman .... 38.048.728.0770 EXT. 280

ZAPOROZHYE
Mrs. Nechama Dina Ehrentreu 380.957.19.96.08

ZHITOMIR
Rabbi Shlomo Wilhelm 380.504.63.01.32

UNITED KINGDOM

BOURNEMOUTH
Rabbi Bentzion Alperowitz 44.749.456.7177

CHEADLE
Rabbi Peretz Chein 44.161.428.1818

LEEDS
Rabbi Eli Pink 44.113.266.3311

LONDON
Rabbi Mendel Cohen 44.777.261.2661
Rabbi Shneor Glitzenstein 44.792.585.7050
Rabbi Chaim Hoch 44.753.879.9524
Rabbi Dovid Katz 44.207.624.2770
Rabbi Yisroel Lew 44.207.060.9770
Rabbi Gershon Overlander 44.208.202.1600
Rabbi Hillel Gruber 44.208.202.1600
Rabbi Shlomo Odze 44.791.757.3558
Rabbi Yossi Simon 44.208.458.0416
Rabbi Bentzi Sudak 44.207.078.7469

MANCHESTER
Rabbi Levi Cohen 44.161.792.6335
Rabbi Shmuli Jaffe 44.161.766.1812

URUGUAY

MONTEVIDEO
Rabbi Mendy Shemtov 598.2628.6770

The Jewish Learning Multiplex

Brought to you by the Rohr Jewish Learning Institute

In fulfillment of the mandate of the Lubavitcher Rebbe, of blessed memory, whose leadership guides every step of our work, the mission of the Rohr Jewish Learning Institute is to transform Jewish life and the greater community through the study of Torah, connecting each Jew to our shared heritage of Jewish learning.

While our flagship program remains the cornerstone of our organization, JLI is proud to feature additional divisions catering to specific populations, in order to meet a wide array of educational needs.

The Rohr **JEWISH LEARNING INSTITUTE**

a subsidiary of Merkos L'Inyonei Chinuch,
the adult educational arm of the Chabad-Lubavitch movement

TORAH STUDIES

Torah Studies provides a rich and nuanced encounter with the weekly Torah reading.

MYSHIUR
TALMUD LEARNING INITIATIVE

MyShiur courses are designed to assist students in developing the skills needed to study Talmud independently.

SINAI SCHOLARS SOCIETY

This rigorous fellowship program invites select college students to explore the fundamentals of Judaism.

JLI TEENS
IN PARTNERSHIP WITH CTEEN: CHABAD TEEN NETWORK

Jewish teens forge their identity as they engage in Torah study, social interaction, and serious fun.

ROSH CHODESH society

The Rosh Chodesh Society gathers Jewish women together once a month for intensive textual study.

TORAHCafé™

TorahCafe.com provides an exclusive selection of top-rated Jewish educational videos.

BRILLIANT LEARNING NATURALLY
NATIONAL JEWISH RETREAT

This yearly event rejuvenates mind, body, and spirit with a powerful synthesis of Jewish learning and community.

THE LAND & THE SPIRIT
JLI ISRAEL EXPERIENCE

Participants delve into our nation's past while exploring the Holy Land's relevance and meaning today.

PEDAGOGY • CURRICULUM • MARKETING
JLI ACADEMY

Select affiliates are invited to partner with peers and noted professionals, as leaders of innovation and excellence.

מכון שמואל
THE SAMI ROHR RESEARCH INSTITUTE

Machon Shmuel is an institute providing Torah research in the service of educators worldwide.